For those who believe that covenanted members of the chu the issue of children's participa a difficult one. If they may be admitted to one ordinance, why not to the other? This timely and useful book not only answers that question definitively and persuasively, it also explores much more besides: the relationship between Passover and Lord's Supper, the theological, confessional and liturgical implications of the sacraments, and the place of children in the covenant of grace. This is a careful guide around a difficult subject, full of pastoral insight and biblical teaching.

Iain D. Campbell,
Minister, Point Free Church of Scotland, Isle of Lewis

Like an unending case of the "terrible two's," infant communion advocacy stubbornly persists in many Reformed churches. *Finally* we have a single resource to counter the scope of exegetical, biblico-theological, historical, systematic, and practical arguments proffered by paedocommunion proponents. Honest, persuasive, yet irenic, this compilation of essays puts to bed infant communion's errant theologizing and exposes the ecclesiologically hazardous results of its practice. But the authors have done much more than polemicize. They have served a positively edifying and nourishing meal for the Church on the theology and practice of the Lord's Table. I heartily recommend partaking in *Children and the Lord's Supper.*

David B. Garner,
Associate Professor of Systematic Theology,
Westminster Theological Seminary, Philadelphia, Pennsylvania

Pastors and elders are shepherds of the hearts and souls of their people. Parents are shepherds of the hearts and souls of their children. All shepherds have a significant stake in this consideration of whether covenant children should participate in the Lord's Supper prior to making their own public profession of faith. Are shepherds hurting the children by keeping them from coming to Christ if they keep them from participating in the Supper or are they helping and protecting the children by pointing them to Christ before they participate in the Supper? I believe the latter and I am grateful for this careful Biblical consideration of the issue.

Robert C. (Ric) Cannada, Jr.,
Chancellor and CEO, Reformed Theological Seminary

The present and persistent debate within the Reformed community over paedocommunion, as the editors of this volume note, presents both challenge and opportunity. It is a challenge because long held convictions are called into question, and the bases for making this challenge are fundamentally exegetical and theological. It is an opportunity because we are called back to the foundations of our confessions and traditions, to examine the Scriptures afresh, to insure that we handle accurately the word of truth, and shepherd the flock of the Lord as we should. These essays meet the challenge at the high level it demands and deserves, so that those who dig into this debate will find themselves renewed in both faith and practice.

Mark E. Ross,
Associate Dean and Associate Professor of Systematic Theology,
Columbia campus of Erskine Theological Seminary,
Director of the Institute for Reformed Worship

Children and the Lord's Supper

Let a man examine himself

edited by
Guy Waters and Ligon Duncan

MENTOR

Contents

Introduction
Guy Prentiss Waters and Ligon Duncan 11

1. *Passover and the Lord's Supper: Continuity or Discontinuity?*
Bryan D. Estelle 31

2. *Christ Our Passover*
Iain M. Duguid 59

3. *1 Corinthians 11:17-34: The Lord's Supper: Abuses, Words of Institution and Warnings and the Inferences and Deductions with respect to Paedocommunion*
George W. Knight III 75

4. *'Not a Particle of Sound Brain' – a theological response to Paedocommunion*
Derek W. H. Thomas 97

5. *Paedocommunion and the Reformation Confessions*
Cornelis Venema 119

6. *Children at the Lord's Table in the Patristic Era*
Nick Needham 145

7. *'Only for His Believers': Paedocommunion and the Witness of the Reformed Liturgies*
Joel R. Beeke 163

8. *Where Do We Go From Here? Some Pastoral Reflections on the Covenant of Grace, the Children of the Church, and the Lord's Supper*
Guy Prentiss Waters and Ligon Duncan 181

Contributors

Dr. Joel R. Beeke
Dr. Joel R. Beeke is president and professor of systematic theology and homiletics at Puritan Reformed Theological Seminary, a pastor of the Heritage Netherlands Reformed Congregation in Grand Rapids, Michigan, editor of Banner of Sovereign Grace Truth, editorial director of Reformation Heritage Books, president of Inheritance Publishers, and vice-president of the Dutch Reformed Translation Society. He has written, co-authored, or edited sixty books (most recently, *Living for the Glory of God: An Introduction to Calvinism, Meet the Puritans, Contagious Christian Living, Calvin for Today, Developing a Healthy Prayer Life,* and *Taking Hold of God*), and contributed fifteen hundred articles to Reformed books, journals, periodicals, and encyclopedias. His Ph.D. is in Reformation and Post-Reformation theology from Westminster Theological Seminary. He is frequently called upon to lecture at seminaries and to speak at Reformed conferences around the world. He and his wife Mary have been blessed with three children: Calvin, Esther, and Lydia.

Dr. Iain Duguid

Dr. Iain Duguid studied at Edinburgh University and Westminster Theological Seminary, before receiving his Ph.D. in Old Testament from Cambridge University. He is professor of Old Testament and Hebrew at Grove City College and pastor of Christ Presbyterian Church, an ARP church plant. He is the author of numerous books and articles on the Old Testament, including *Ezekiel* in the NIV Application Commentary series, *Ether and Ruth*, and *Daniel* in the Reformed Expository Commentary Series.

Dr. Ligon Duncan

Ligon is Senior pastor of the Historic First Presbyterian Church of Jackson and Distinguished Visiting Professor of Systematic and Historical Theology at Reformed Theological Seminary. He received his Ph.D. from Edinburgh University. Dr. Duncan is the President of the Alliance of Confessing Evangelicals as well as the author of numerous books and articles including *Fear Not!, Does Grace Grow Best in Winter?* and *Gospel clarity: challenging the new perspective on Paul.* Dr. Duncan has two children, Sarah Kennedy and Jennings, and is married to Anne.

Dr. Bryan Estelle

Dr. Estelle is the author of *Salvation through Judgment and Mercy: The Gospel According to Jonah* (P & R) and contributor and co-editor of *The Law is not of Faith: Essays on Works and Grace in the Mosaic Covenant* (P & R). He has also contributed articles and reviews to other books and journals. He is a minister in the Orthodox Presbyterian Church. Prior to taking his position at Westminster Seminary in California, he was a pastor in an Orthodox Presbyterian congregation in Maryland and was involved in planting a church in Oregon for the Presbyterian Church in America. He lectured in Hebrew at The Catholic University of America between 1997 and 2000, where he also received his Ph.D.

Dr. George W. Knight III

A ministerial member of the Orthodox Presbyterian Church who pastored in West Collingswood, New Jersey and Naples, Florida, and as Teacher at Redeemer Presbyterian Church (OPC), Charlotte, North Carolina. He served as Professor of New Testament at Covenant Theological Seminary, Knox Theological Seminary (also Administrator and Dean), and now as Adjunct Professor and Chairman of the Board at Greenville Presbyterian Theological Seminary. He is a Past Moderator of the General Assembly of the Orthodox Presbyterian Church and is Chairman of its Committee on Ecumenicity.

Dr. Knight has published the following books and booklets: *The Faithful Sayings in the Pastoral Letters, Role Relationship of Men and Women, Abortion: How Does God's Word Regard the Unborn Child? Prophesy in the New Testament*, A Commentary on the Pastoral Epistles (NIGTC), and many other journal articles.

Dr. Nick Needham

Nick Needham is a Londoner by birth and upbringing. He studied theology at New College, Edinburgh University, where he specialized in Church History. He also taught a course at New College on the life and works of the Swiss Reformer Ulrich Zwingli, at the same time completing his PhD thesis on the nineteenth-century Scottish theologian Thomas Erskine of Linlathen. He then taught Systematic Theology at the Scottish Baptist College in Glasgow for several years before spending a semester at the Samuel Bill Theological College, where he taught Church History. After a period as assistant pastor in a church in north London, he moved to the Highland Theological College, Dingwall, where he teaches Church History. He recently accepted a call to a pastorate in Inverness.

Dr. Derek W. H. Thomas

Dr. Derek Thomas is Minister of Teaching and Preaching at the First Presbyterian Church of Columbia, South Carolina as well as Distinguished Visiting Professor of Systematic and

Historical Theology at Reformed Theological Seminary. He is the Editorial Director for the Alliance of Confessing Evangelicals and author of numerous books including commentaries on Acts (P&R 2011), Revelation (Banner of Truth, 2003), and Isaiah (Evangelical Press, 2003).

Dr. Cornelis P. Venema

President and Professor of Doctrinal Studies, Mid-America Reformed Seminary, Dyer, Indiana, co-editor of the *Mid-America Journal of Theology* and contributing editor of a column on doctrine for the monthly periodical, *The Outlook.* Author of two studies of the creeds and confessions: *But for the Grace of God: An Exposition of the Canons of Dort* and *What We Believe: An Exposition of the Apostle's Creed.* Author of the following books: *The Promise of the Future* (Banner of Truth, 2000); *Heinrich Bullinger's Doctrine of Predestination* (Baker Book House, 2002); *Getting the Gospel Right* (Banner of Truth, 2005); *The Gospel of Free Acceptance in Christ* (Banner of Truth, 2006); *Accepted and Renewed in Christ: The "Twofold Grace of God" and the Interpretation of Calvin's Theology* (Vandenhoeck & Ruprecht, 2007); *Christ and the Future* (Banner of Truth, 2008); and *Children at the Lord's Table? Assessing the Case for Paedocommunion* (Reformation Heritage Books, 2009). Previously served as the pastor of the Ontario Christian Reformed Church in Ontario, California, and presently an associate pastor of the Redeemer United Reformed Church of Dyer, Indiana. He is married to Nancy and they have four children.

Dr. Guy Prentiss Waters

Guy Prentiss Waters is Associate Professor of New Testament, Reformed Theological Seminary, Jackson, Mississippi, USA; and a Teaching Elder in the Presbyterian Church in America (PCA). He is the author or editor of seven books, including *A Christian's Pocket Guide to Justification: Being Made Right With God?* (CFP), and *How Jesus Runs the Church* (P&R). He and his wife, Sarah, have three children.

Introduction

Guy Prentiss Waters and
J. Ligon Duncan III

The chapters in this book address the doctrine of 'paedo-com-munion'. The word 'paedocommunion', or 'child communion', admits of various definitions.[1] We define 'paedocommunion' as the admittance of a covenant child to the Lord's Supper on the basis of his descent from at least one professing Christian parent.[2] Paedocommunion, then, maintains that a child's mem-bership in the visible church is sufficient to admit him to the Table.

Although it remains a minority position, paedocommunion has had vocal support within the conservative Reformed com-munity. A century ago, few, if any, North American Reformed and Presbyterian pastors or teachers openly advocated the prac-tice. Today, paedocommunion is finding advocates not only among individual ministers and congregations,[3] but also within

---

1. See the definitional discussion at Cornelis Venema, *Children at the Lord's Table? Assessing the Case for Paedocommunion* (Grand Rapids: Reformation Heritage, 2009), 2-4.

2. What Venema has termed 'strict' paedocommunion in distinction from a 'soft' form of paedocommunion wherein 'younger covenant members who have made a simple but credible profession of the Christian faith' are entitled to the Lord's Supper, *Paedocommunion*, 3.

3. To say nothing of websites and blogs that promote the practice, two recent books that have vigorously advocated paedocommunion within the Reformed church are Gregg Strawbridge, ed. *The Case for Covenant Communion* (Monroe, La.: Athanasius Press, 2006),

historically Presbyterian and Reformed denominations.[4] Denominations that have recently acted to permit paedocommunion include the Presbyterian Church (USA) and the Reformed Church in America. Although it presently does not officially approve paedocommunion, the Christian Reformed Church has been earnestly discussing the possibility of allowing paedocommunion since at least 1984.

Other ecclesiastical bodies have declined to embrace paedocommunion. In 2004, the United Reformed Church in North America upheld its constitutional standards' prohibition of paedocommunion. Both the Presbyterian Church in America and the Orthodox Presbyterian Church have received study reports concerning paedocommunion. In each case, a majority and a minority report were submitted.[5] In both cases, the confessional standards of each body, the Westminster Standards, were left unamended.

In surveying recent discussion concerning paedocommunion, one question that arises is 'why paedocommunion, and why now?' Why is a position that is a minority report within Protestantism generally, and within the Reformed tradition particularly, now receiving so much attention in conservative Reformed circles?[6] Why is it that recent literature on the

and Tim Gallant, *Feed My Lambs: Why the Lord's Table Should Be Restored to Covenant Children* (Grande Prairie, Alberta, Canada: Pactum Reformanda Publishing, 2002).

4. We are grateful to Ryan F. Biese whose research yielded the following denominational information.

5. In the PCA, the majority report was critical of paedocommunion, while the minority report was supportive of paedocommunion. In the OPC, the majority report was supportive of paedocommunion, while the minority report was critical of paedocommunion. The PCA reports may be found at the website of the PCA Historical Center (www.pcahistory.org). The OPC reports may be found at the OPC's denominational website (www.opc.org).

6. This judgment is true whether we take into consideration individual theologians or confessional statements. Four and a half centuries of Reformed confessions univocally reject paedocommunion. Virtually every recognized Reformed theologian before the mid-twentieth century denied that a child's church membership was sufficient to warrant his admittance to the Table. In his chapter in this volume, Derek Thomas observes that 'the only notable exception in Reformed theology [to its rejection of paedocommunion] came from Wolfgang Musculus (1497–1563) in his *Loci communes theologiae sacrae* (Basel: Heruagiana, 1567), 471-73, cited by Herman Bavinck, *Reformed Dogmatics*, 4 vols. Ed. John Bolt, trans. John Vriend (Grand Rapids, MI: Baker Academic, 2008), 4:583. Richard Muller describes Musculus as one of the 'important second-generation codifiers of the Reformed faith,' alongside Calvin, Vermigli, and Hyperius. *Post-Reformation Reformed Dogmatics*, 4 vols. (Grand Rapids, MI: Baker Academic, 2003), 1:31.

Lord's Supper by Reformed writers and for Reformed audiences must now assume the burden of addressing the question of paedocommunion?[7]

A comprehensive answer to these questions is beyond the scope of this essay. Any such answer, however, must surely reckon with the overtly and unashamedly theological character of arguments for paedocommunion. Supporters within Reformed and Presbyterian bodies frequently claim that paedocommunion is a practice that belongs organically within Reformed theology, if not the historical Reformed tradition. Paedocommunion, it is argued, is not a practice that is unnaturally grafted upon the tree of Reformed theology. If one grasps Reformed covenant theology properly, it is said, then one is bound to conclude that paedocommunion is an authentically Reformed practice. This conclusion is maintained even though most Reformed theologians and all Reformed confessions have concluded the contrary. This historical state of affairs, paedocommunionists sometimes argue, reflects the failure of earlier generations of Reformed thinkers to grasp the full implications of Reformed covenant theology.

Seen in this light, paedocommunion reflects an effort on the part of self-identified Reformed students of the Scripture to think exegetically and theologically on the covenants of Scripture, the doctrine of the church, the nature of church membership, the nature of the Lord's Supper, and the role of the Supper in the Christian life. To acknowledge this point is not to approve or lend credence to the results of such efforts. It is to say that the debate falls along lines that are overtly and predominantly theological – not sentimental or sociological.[8]

Paedocommunion, then, gives the Reformed church both a challenge and an opportunity. Paedocommunion challenges the Reformed church to uphold her confessional standards as faithful

---

7. See, for instance, Robert Letham, *The Lord's Supper: Eternal Word in Broken Bread* (Phillipsburg, N.J.: P&R, 2001); and Malcolm Maclean, *The Lord's Supper* (Fearn, Ross-shire, Scotland: Christian Focus Publications, 2009).

8. This is not to deny that either of these latter two factors may play some role in these discussions. It is to say that, on paedocommunionists' own terms, the case for paedocommunion is predominantly theological.

expositions of the teaching of Holy Scripture. Paedocommunion offers the church the opportunity to reflect anew upon a number of lines of biblical teaching. Through fresh examination of the Scripture, she has the opportunity to reconfirm the exegetical and theological soundness of the findings of her ancestors in the faith. How could the church fail to benefit from a clearer grasp of the Scripture's teaching on the covenants, the church, and the Lord's Supper? How could God's people fail to profit from pastors and elders committed afresh to a biblical understanding of the Christian life, and of the means that God has appointed to grow believers in the grace and in the knowledge of our Lord and Savior Jesus Christ?

The contributions to this volume address paedocommunion from several angles. The first set of essays examines paedocommunion in light of the teaching of the Old Testament and of the New Testament. They conclude that paedocommunion does not have the exegetical foundation that its proponents claim for it. The second set of essays examines paedocommunion in light of Reformed theology generally, and of the Reformed Confessions specifically. These essays conclude that paedocommunion is a stranger to the Reformed theology both articulated and confessed by our forebears and, most importantly, maintained by the Scripture itself. The third set of essays addresses paedocommunion from the perspective of church history. Does paedocommunion have precedent in church history? For Protestants, this question is not determinative of whether a practice may or may not be introduced into the worship of the church. Scripture alone settles such a matter. Neither is this question, however, irrelevant to our consideration. If paedocommunion has strong and considered support from church history, then that fact merits the attention of Reformed Christians. It is such support, these essays reason, that patristic-era and Reformation-era church history does not afford.

The final essay steps back from paedocommunion in order to ask and answer certain pastoral questions broached by this teaching. What precisely is the relationship of the children of believers to the church? What are their privileges and responsibilities? How do parents and elders know that a child is prepared to receive the Lord's Supper? How can pastors and elders encourage congregations not only to understand but also to value the Lord's Supper as a means of grace that Christ has appointed for the edification of his people? Concluding this volume with such reflections is one way that we, as the Reformed church, may seize upon the above-mentioned opportunities that the paedocommunion question affords to the church.

The remainder of this introduction has two objectives. First, we wish to offer a brief statement of the case against paedocommunion. This statement will try to survey in short compass what the contributors have gone to greater lengths to accomplish. Consider this portion of the book an appetizer before the main course.

Second, we wish to underscore some of the pastoral implications of paedocommunion. As Richard Weaver long ago noted, 'ideas have consequences,' and paedocommunion is no exception to the rule. Seen in this light, we want to consider whether paedocommunion is an eccentric but harmless addition to the contemporary choir of Reformed theological voices, or whether paedocommunion has the potential to call into question doctrines and practices that Reformed theology has long upheld from the Scripture.

The Case Against Paedocommunion

What is the case against paedocommunion? We may ask the question another way. What are some of the leading arguments *for* paedocommunion, and how may we respond briefly and charitably to them? We may propose at least four such arguments.[9]

Argument 1: The Argument from Passover

Paedocommunionists frequently argue that the children of Old Testament believers were admitted to the annual Passover meal. In support of this position, they appeal particularly to Exodus 12, which apparently assumes the presence of children at

---

9. The following arguments are identified as four leading arguments for paedocommunion by Venema at *Paedocommunion,* 4-8. Our sequencing and treatment of these arguments, however, are independent of his analysis in those pages.

the family Passover observance (see Exodus 12:26-27), and may plausibly be read to say that children ate of the Passover Lamb at that feast. Since the New Testament draws a parallel between the Passover and the death of Christ (John 1:29, 1 Cor. 5:7), and since the Lord's Supper represents the death of Christ for believers (Luke 22:14-23), the Passover and the Lord's Supper are thus analogous ordinances: both point to the death of Christ for sin. Since children were admitted to the old covenant feast anticipating the death of the Christ yet to come, it is argued, therefore children under the new covenant ought to partake of the feast celebrating the finished death of Christ. There is no basis, paedocommunionists claim, for denying children under the new covenant a privilege that was extended to their counterparts under the old covenant. If the children of believers were permitted to eat of the Passover meal, on what grounds do we deny them access to the corresponding new covenant meal, the Lord's Supper?

We may reply to this argument along several lines. First, it is not altogether clear that children under the old covenant ate of the Passover meal. This is true whether we are considering the household observance instituted and commanded at Exodus 12, or the observance at Jerusalem instituted and commanded at Deuteronomy 16. Independently of the paedocommunion question, interpreters are divided with respect to whether old covenant children were authorized to partake of the Passover meal.

Second, we recognize that the Passover is analogous to the Lord's Supper. To affirm this point, however, says nothing determinative of how the Lord's Supper is to be observed under the New Covenant. To put it another way, simply because old covenant children may have been admitted to the Passover feast does not necessarily mean that new covenant children are now to be admitted to the Lord's Supper.

It is important, therefore, to recognize that while there is an analogy between the two ordinances, it is just that – an analogy. To argue, as paedocommunists do, that we may 'determine the practice of the new covenant community of faith by a simple, direct appeal to the practice of the old covenant' suggests a much stronger relationship between the ordinances of Passover and the Lord's Supper than the Scripture warrants.[10] In light of the progressive character of redemptive history, for example, we expect certain dissimilarities between these two ordinances. As Bryan Estelle has noted in this volume, the Supper 'is symbolizing fulfillment but it is also symbolizing something inceptive. That is to say that there is something significantly new: "the meal Jesus partakes of with his disciples assumes a prefigurative character.... The relation between Eucharist and eating and drinking in the coming kingdom of God is not merely that between symbol and reality, but that between commencement and fulfillment."'[11] Passover and the Lord's Supper are not, therefore, two synonymous or interchangeable ordinances. The Supper has unique eschatological significance, pointing the people of God forward to the consummation of the Kingdom of God already inaugurated in the accomplished, redemptive work of Christ. In light of that redemptive-historical significance, should we be surprised to learn of disparity with respect to the parties qualified to participate in each ordinance? More to the point, should the terms of participation in the old covenant feast – whatever they may be – necessarily determine the terms of participation in the new covenant feast? The progressive character of redemptive history prompts us to answer the latter question decidedly in the negative.

It is precisely this disparity of terms of participation that we encounter in another pairing of analogous ordinances in the old and new covenants: circumcision and baptism. All paedobaptist Reformed interpreters grant that circumcision and baptism are analogous – they serve as the initiatory sign and seal in the old and new covenants, respectively.[12] All recognize, furthermore, that whereas circumcision was administered only to males under

---

10. The quoted words are Venema's, *Paedocommunion,* 60.

11. Bryan Estelle, "Passover and the Lord's Supper: Continuity or Discontinuity". Estelle is quoting Herman Ridderbos, *The Coming of the Kingdom* (trans. R. Zorn; Phillipsburg: N. J.: P&R, 1962), 412.

12. In this light, see Westminster Confession of Faith 27.5, 'the sacraments of the old testament, in regard of the spiritual things thereby signified and exhibited, were, for substance, the same with those of the new.'

the old covenant, baptism is to be administered to both sexes under the new covenant. In light of this alteration, therefore, one cannot simply transfer the terms of participation in one old covenant ordinance to an analogous new covenant ordinance.

It may be objected that, if the scope of the recipients of the initiatory sign and seal of the old covenant was thus expanded under the new covenant, then surely the scope of the recipients of the Passover could not have been contracted under the new covenant. This objection assumes, of course, that the children of believers were admitted to the Passover feast under the old covenant. Let us, for the sake of argument, grant this point. It still would not follow that God could not restrict or limit the scope of the recipients of the analogous ordinance of the Lord's Supper. The Passover set forth the Christ who was to come. It did so as type and shadow. The Lord's Supper, however, is administered 'in remembrance' of the Christ who has already come, and will return in glory. The Lord's Supper commemorates the accomplished death of Christ for sinners, and it is this death that believers 'proclaim' as often as they partake (1 Cor. 11:26). Because the Lord's Supper is tied to the accomplished redemptive death of Christ, Paul stresses that to partake of the elements 'in an unworthy manner' is to render oneself 'guilty of profaning the body and blood of the Lord' (1 Cor. 11:27). In other words, what has transpired in the progress of redemptive history from the Passover to the Lord's Supper has lent a poignancy and significance to the Supper that heightens the sin of careless or heedless partaking. Given this state of affairs, should we be surprised if the New Testament sets particularly firm and strict parameters on who may approach the Lord's Supper?

Argument 2: The Argument from 1 Corinthians 11
Paedocommunionists recognize that 1 Corinthians 11:17-34 is a critical passage relating to the administration and observance of the Lord's Supper. They claim that Paul's prevailing concern in this passage is the unity of the body of Christ. Paul is admonishing the Corinthian believers for fracturing the unity

of the church by the way in which they are observing the Lord's Supper. Paul's prescriptions are said to concern the Lord's Supper as an ordinance that primarily upholds the unity of the body of believers. For this reason, it is argued, Paul is not excluding the children of believers from the Table. Were he to do so, he would be cutting the nerve of his pastoral response to the problem of Corinthian disunity.

Paedocommunionists observe that Paul introduces his discussion of the Lord's Supper with a denunciation of the 'divisions' that exist at Corinth (1 Cor. 11:18). This discussion of division at Corinth sets the stage for the apostle's discussion of the Lord's Supper, and the way in which factions within the church have corrupted the church's observance of the sacrament (1 Cor. 11:20-22). Paul, furthermore, warns the church about partaking of the Supper 'in an unworthy manner' (1 Cor. 11:27). In context, it is argued, 'unworthiness' must refer to fostering divisions and promoting factions. A person must therefore 'examine himself,' that is, ensure that he is living in such a way as to promote the unity and fellowship of the body (1 Cor. 11:28), before he comes to the Table. He must particularly 'discern the body', that is the unity of the body of believers, before he would partake (1 Cor. 11:29). Since all members of the church – young and old alike – are capable of meeting such qualifications, therefore all members of the church may be invited to come to the Table. Far from overturning paedocommunion, Paul's argument in 1 Corinthians 11 is said to uphold the practice.

In reply, we may certainly note that the divisions and factions within the Corinthian church occasioned Paul's discussion of the Lord's Supper. We may furthermore recognize that this Corinthian problem had spilled over into the church's observance of this sacrament, and that Paul is writing to redress this problem. The difficulty with paedocommunionist readings of this passage is that Paul's words in 1 Corinthians 11:23-26 are attenuated, if not altogether neglected. In these verses, Paul stresses that the sacrament fundamentally sets forth the death of Jesus Christ for the sins of his people. This death, Paul stresses elsewhere in this letter, benefits believers who are united to Jesus in his death (1 Cor. 1:30). United to Jesus, believers also have fellowship with one another as members of one body (1 Cor. 12:12-13, 27). The Lord's Supper is a visible and pointed expression not only of our union with Christ in his death and life (1 Cor. 10:16), but also of our corresponding bond with fellow believers as the body of Christ (1 Cor. 10:17). These two realities may be distinguished but they may never be separated. The Corinthians, Paul reasons in 1 Corinthians 11, are making a mockery of the sacrament by behaviors inconsistent with the fellowship that the sacrament is intended to manifest. Such a cavalier approach to the Supper necessarily reflects poorly on their preparedness to commune with Christ in the sacrament. Because the Corinthians have manifestly not taken this primary meaning of the sacrament to heart, he turns from his discussion of factions and divisions within the church (1 Cor. 11:17-22) to the primary meaning of the Lord's Supper: the believer's communing with Jesus Christ crucified, and receiving the benefits of his death (1 Cor. 11:23-26).

It is in this light that we are to observe Paul's exhortations in 1 Corinthians 11:27-29.[13] Paul's statements in 1 Corinthians 11:23-26 are determinative of his exhortations in 1 Corinthians 11:27-29. If the Lord's Supper is a 'remembrance of [Jesus],' then surely this 'remembrance' character of the sacrament defines what it means for the recipient to be qualified to approach the Table. To 'discern the body', to 'examine oneself,' and to eat and drink in a 'worthy manner', in context, must refer to a participation in the Lord's Supper that acknowledges and upholds what Christ has instituted the Supper to be. If the Lord's Supper is an occasion for the believer's communion with Christ, how could the believer possibly commune with Christ apart from an informed understanding and an enlivened faith in relation to what the Supper sets forth – the death of Christ for sinners? This state of affairs helps to explain why the believer, before approaching the Table, should undergo a period of self-

---

13. In 1 Corinthians 11:30-34, Paul returns to the problem of division at the Corinthian church and, in light of his preceding argument, makes specific and positive application of the principles earlier enumerated to the Corinthians' circumstances.

examination concerning his sins, his knowledge, and his faith, repentance, and other Christian graces.[14]

Because Paul is setting forth here the true and abiding nature of the Lord's Supper, and the requirements that it lays upon those who would worthily participate in it, his discussion has applicability beyond the first-century Corinthian church. Paul's discussion of the Supper is occasioned by the divisions and factions within the Corinthian church. His principles, however, are not determined by those divisions and factions. In other words, the principles of 1 Corinthians 11:23-29 have wider applicability than simply the church in Corinth, and simply the problem of church division. They apply to the church in every age, 'until [Jesus] comes' (1 Cor. 11:26).

First Corinthians 11, then, sets forth clear criteria for participation in the Lord's Supper. The Supper is not for all church members. It is for church members who meet the intellectual and spiritual qualifications set forth by the apostle. When a young church member demonstrates to the satisfaction of the elders of church that he has met these qualifications, then the church, acting through her elders, may admit this young person to the Lord's Table. To uphold these qualifications is to uphold what both Jesus and his apostle, Paul, teach to be the leading signification of the sacrament – the body of Christ given, and the blood of Christ shed for his people.

Argument 3: The Argument from Church Membership
Paedocommunionists and non-paedocommunionists alike agree that the child of at least one professing believer is a member of the visible church. This membership, Presbyterians have historically argued, is the birthright of the covenant child. This birthright explains why covenant children are granted the privilege of the sacrament of baptism.

The difference between paedocommunionists and the Reformed confessions concerns whether partaking of the Lord's

---

14. Compare here 2 Corinthians 13:5, 'examine yourselves, to see whether you are in the faith. Test yourselves. Or do you not realize this about yourselves, that Jesus Christ is in you? – unless indeed you fail to meet the test.' See also Westminster Larger Catechism Q&A 171 for a helpful summary of the Scripture's teaching concerning what is involved in this self-examination.

Supper is a privilege that all church members may exercise, or whether it is a privilege that only some church members may exercise. Paedocommunionists frequently charge that their non-paedocommunionist brethren are compromising the membership of the children of the church. One proponent provocatively titled his work advocating paedocommunion, *Daddy, Why Was I Excommunicated?*[15] This title insinuates that children of the church are deprived, without process, of a privilege that they are entitled to exercise.[16] If, it is argued, we admit without examination the children of the church to one covenant ordinance to which their membership entitles them, namely baptism, then why should we not so admit them to another covenant ordinance, the Lord's Supper, that Christ has given his people?

The paedocommunionist argument from church membership frequently appears in the form of a classical logical fallacy, *petitio principii,* or 'begging the question'. That is to say, the argument assumes in its premises what it sets out to prove. Paedocommunionist literature often assumes, with little or no argument, that admission to the Lord's Table is the right of every covenant child by virtue of his church membership.

We may respond to this position in a couple of ways. First, a critical distinction is in order. It is one thing to possess a privilege. It is another to exercise that privilege. While we may affirm that admission to the Lord's Supper is a privilege in the possession of covenant children, this privilege is not theirs to exercise until they meet the requisite intellectual and spiritual qualifications of 1 Corinthians 11. One responsibility attending the church membership of the children of professing believers is that they make profession of faith, and so voluntarily claim all the privileges that attend their membership.

In this respect, the position of the covenant child is analogous to the position of a minor in the commonwealth.[17]

---

15. Peter J. Leithart, *Daddy, Why Was I Excommunicated?: An Examination of Leonard J. Coppes'* Daddy, May I Take Communion? (Niceville, Fla.: Transfiguration Press, 1992). As the subtitle indicates, Leithart's title is a response to the title of Coppes' critical examination of paedocommunion, Leonard J. Coppes, *Daddy, May I take Communion: Paedocommunion vs. the Bible* (Thornton, Colo., 1988).

16. Compare the subtitle of Tim Gallant's work, *Feed My Lambs: Why the Lord's Table Should be Restored to Covenant Communion,* so Venema, *Paedocommunion,* p.6 n.4.

17. We will develop this point in our concluding chapter.

A minor is a recognized citizen of the state. He has privileges and responsibilities attending his citizenship. He must reach maturation, however, before he may exercise such privileges as voting, serving in public office, and serving in the armed forces. His exclusion from exercising those privileges in no way calls into question the legitimacy of his membership in that society.

Or, consider an individual who is a member of a church and has come under the discipline of the church. One means of discipline can be the suspension of that person from the sacrament of the Lord's Supper. This particular exercise of discipline does not nullify his membership. It does, however, limit the disciplined person's exercise of one privilege attending church membership. This specific case illustrates the principle that we above observed – church membership by itself does not entitle one to the exercise of all the privileges attending church membership.

Second, we do well to remember why it is that Christ has called younger members of the church to make profession of faith before they approach the Table. It is because the Lord's Supper 'represents and exhibits Christ as spiritual nourishment to the soul, and confirms our continuance and growth in him.'[18] The Lord's Supper does not *create* spiritual life in a person. The Lord's Supper nourishes the spiritual life of the believer. Unless that life is already present in the believer, the Lord's Supper will not profit him spiritually. Unless a person has made a public and credible profession of faith, the church has no biblical warrant to admit him to an ordinance designed to nurture faith.

When the church honors the scriptural qualifications for admission to the Lord's Table, then, she is giving no slight to her younger members who have not yet made profession of faith. The regular administration of the Lord's Supper, rather, is a reminder to these younger members of the responsibility that they have, upon maturation, to make profession of faith and so to enter into the exercise of this privilege of membership.

---

18. Westminster Larger Catechism, Q & A 177.

Once they are ready and willing to profess faith in the Lord and Savior, Jesus Christ, then they may and ought to come to the Table that their faith may be nourished and strengthened. In this way, the Lord's Supper serves to honor and uphold the membership of believers' children who have not yet made profession of faith.

Argument 4: The Argument from Church History

Advocates of paedocommunion believe that church history is on their side. They urge that the practice of requiring a credible profession of faith before admitting a young member of the church to the Lord's Table is a 'Johnny come lately' of Christian practice. If we consider patristic and medieval practice, and if we look at the practice of the church both East and West, paedocommunionists argue, then we will conclude that paedocommunion is an ancient and longstanding Christian practice worthy of the contemporary church's consideration.

In response, three observations are in order. First, paedo-communionists would surely agree with all Protestants that Scripture alone regulates the worship of the church. In the words of *the Westminster Confession of Faith*, 'the acceptable way of worshipping the true God is instituted by Himself, and so limited by His own revealed will, that He may not be worshipped according to the imaginations and devices of men, or the suggestions of Satan, under any visible representation, or any other way not prescribed in the Holy Scripture.'[19] Furthermore, the *Larger Catechism's* exposition of the second commandment warns the church to take heed of adding to the worship of God, 'whether invented and taken up of ourselves, or received by tradition from others, though under the title of antiquity, custom, devotion, good intent, or any other pretence whatsoever.'[20] We raise this point simply to underscore a matter upon which all Protestants, whether paedocommunionist or not, agree. As helpful as church history is to the modern church, it is the Scripture that has the final word.

---

19. Westminster Confession of Faith 21.1.

20. Westminster Larger Catechism Q&A 109.

Second, with rare exception, paedocommunion has no historical precedent within the Reformed tradition. As Joel Beeke argues in this volume, the sixteenth century Reformers and their heirs were well aware of the practice of paedocommunion and decidedly rejected it on biblical grounds. No historical Reformed confession espouses paedocommunion, and many Reformed confessions expressly preclude the practice. That paedocommunion is a 'new kid on the block' within the Reformed community does not, of course, make the practice wrong. It does, however, lay the burden on advocates of paedocommunion to show precisely what it is that centuries of Reformed reflection have missed in its nearly univocal rejection of the practice.

Third, with respect to the patristic and medieval evidence, it is fair to say that much more historical homework needs to be done in order to render any definitive judgments concerning the practice of the church in those eras. Venema has observed that 'in the writings of advocates of paedocommunion, this story is often told in an unduly simplistic manner.'[21] Nick Needham's contribution to this book is an example of a nuanced and balanced consideration of the evidence. He concludes that it is premature to conclude that paedocommunion has any rightful claim to being the 'majority report' of the church's practice in the first four centuries of her history. The evidence, rather, points to a 'diversity of practice' in this period.[22] Such a conclusion underscores the limitations of appealing to church history in support of a particular church practice. It furthermore helps us to appreciate the fact that it is the Scripture alone that regulates the faith and the worship of the church.[23]

Some Initial Thoughts on the Pastoral Implications of Paedocommunion

Like any other doctrine, paedocommunion carries with it certain consequences for the faith and life of the church. In this section, we will reflect on some of the implications that

---

21. Venema, *Paedocommunion,* 20.

22. 'Diversity of practice would not, I think, be an intolerable conclusion…,' Nick Needham, 'Children at the Lord's Table' (chapter seven of this work).

23. As, rightly, Needham concludes, *ibid.*

paedocommunion may carry for the church. We are not saying that what follows is an accurate or full description of what every advocate of paedocommunion espouses. Nor are we saying that what follows necessarily depicts the life of congregations where paedocommunion is a permitted practice. We are saying, however, that the doctrine of paedocommunion raises some significant pastoral questions and concerns. These questions fall along at least three broad lines. The first concerns the church and membership in the church. The second concerns the nature and purpose of the Lord's Supper. The third concerns the doctrines of regeneration and conversion.

The Church and Membership in the Church

Paedocommunion raises certain questions with respect to the doctrine of the church and, particularly, the nature of membership within the church. Reformed Christians have historically acknowledged that the children of at least one professing believer are, by birthright, members of the church. They have also acknowledged that these children must first make a credible, or believable, profession of faith in order to be admitted to the Lord's Table. Presbyterians have often expressed this biblical distinction with the terminology of 'non-communing' and 'communing' membership in the church. Consider how the Presbyterian Church in America articulates this distinction of membership.

> The children of believers are, through the covenant and by right of birth, non-communing members of the church. Hence they are entitled to Baptism, and to the pastoral oversight, instruction and government of the church, with a view to their embracing Christ and thus possessing personally all benefits of the covenant.

> Communing members are those who have made a profession of faith in Christ, have been baptized, and have been admitted by the Session to the Lord's Table… [These only] are entitled to all the rights and privileges of the church.[24]

---

24. *BCO* 6-1, 6-2, 6-4.

In this way, we may honor the Scripture's teaching that the children of believers are members of the church by birthright, but also recognize that there are certain privileges that they may not lawfully exercise until maturation. Paedocommunionists urge that the privilege of partaking of the Lord's Supper belongs to all church members *as church members.* This position raises the question whether there are any privileges that a paedocommunionist believes the Scripture to forbid a child member from exercising. In other words, paedocommunion calls into question the integrity of the communing/non-communing member distinction, and may even call into question the distinction itself. A whole host of pastoral questions surface. Is a six or seven year old member of the church entitled to vote in congregational elections? To stand for church office, if the congregation so desires? What about church discipline? In the Presbyterian Church in America, there are special procedures for the discipline of non-communing members.[25] Would a paedocommunionist understand young members of the church to be subject to the same formal judicial process to which communing members are subject?

The Nature and Purpose of the Lord's Supper
Paedocommunionists often argue from 1 Corinthians 11 that the Lord's Supper is a meal that celebrates the Christian unity of the church. The leading criterion of participation concerns whether one is promoting or hindering the united fellowship of believers. On this reading, the Lord's Supper is an ordinance in which even the youngest of church members may legitimately participate.

To approach the Lord's Supper in this fashion is imbalanced at best. The apostle Paul, following Jesus, stresses in 1 Corinthians 11 that participants in the Lord's Supper 'remember' the Lord Jesus Christ, crucified for sinners. In this fashion, they 'proclaim his death until he comes' (1 Cor 11:26). The Lord's Supper is a powerful and public testimony to the church's commitment to the gospel of grace. The Lord's Supper is a powerful

---

25. See *BCO* 28.

confirmation to the sin-conscious believer of the sufficiency of God's pardoning grace in Christ. When the Lord's Supper is understood primarily in terms of a community meal, we may fairly ask of our paedocommunionist brethren how and in what ways their administration of the Lord's Supper will communicate these precious gospel truths.

We may mention one further concern. According to an historical Reformed understanding of the Lord's Supper, paedocommunionists are permitting unqualified persons to approach the Lord's Table. They do so from the best of motives and from a desire to uphold in the church what they understand to be the teaching of the Scripture. It is, however, important to remember that the Scripture has somber words concerning the admission of unqualified persons to the Lord's Table. The person who 'eats the bread or drinks the cup of the Lord in an unworthy manner will be guilty of profaning the body and blood of the Lord' (1 Cor. 11:27, cf. 1 Cor. 11:29). These words remind us that there are high stakes in this question. This question is not an academic exercise independent of spiritual consequences for Christians and for the church. If paedocommunionists are mistaken, then they are placing young persons in the church in a position that Scripture has warned the church not to place them.

Regeneration and Conversion

If paedocommunionists follow Reformed theology in understanding the sacrament of the Lord's Supper to be a means of nourishing the recipient spiritually, and if paedocommunionists allow children from a very young age to partake of the Supper, then do they believe that these covenant children, as a class, have in them genuine spiritual life?

If the answer to this question is 'no', then this answer raises such further questions as, 'What, then, is the Lord's Supper?' 'What purpose does the Supper serve in the church?' We have already broached this set of questions in our preceding discussion concerning the nature and purpose of the Lord's Supper. If, however, the answer to these questions is 'yes', then we must ask, 'On what basis do we affirm or presume that these young people have in them genuine spiritual life?'

There is no particularly attractive answer to this question. If we affirm or presume their regeneration of covenant children as a class, then we are left searching for some biblical support for this position. There is, however, no such biblical support. On the contrary, the Scripture tells us of individuals, born into covenant families, who were never savingly renewed by the sovereign grace of God.

We must further account for the fact that many young people in the church turn away from the faith of their parents never, apparently, to return. Sadly, this is no hypothetical scenario, but one that has tragically played itself out in many Christian homes. Surely, as biblical Christians, we do not want to say that a truly regenerate Christian has become totally and finally apostate. But how do we avoid such a conclusion if we maintain that covenant children, as a class, have in them genuine spiritual life?

Furthermore, we must ask whether paedocommunion will foster the regular pressing of the doctrines of regeneration and conversion upon the covenant children of God. To put it another way, how would a paedocommunionist bring the gospel to covenant children? In a context where the youngest of covenant children partake of the Lord's Supper, it seems incongruous that these same children would be told that they are, by nature, children of wrath; that they must be born again to gain entrance into the kingdom of God; and that they must be brought out of the domain of darkness into the kingdom of God's beloved Son.

One may legitimately express concern that children in such settings will be tempted to believe that they are already renewed, whether by virtue of their church membership or of their baptism; and that they will not be exhorted to flee to Christ. And if so, does not paedocommunion, then, court the very formalism that both testaments of the Scripture so frequently condemn?

The chapters that follow will assist you in thinking through the biblical, theological, historical, and practical questions raised by paedocommunion. As we hope that you have already seen, paedocommunion is not a teaching that sits at a distance from the life of the Christian or the life of the church. It is our hope and prayer that this book will not only help you to appreciate the pastoral challenges and problems that paedocommunion brings to the church, but also to prize the Lord's Supper for what Christ meant it to be – a means for the spiritual strengthening and nourishment of his people.

1

Passover and the Lord's Supper: Continuity or Discontinuity?[1]

Bryan D. Estelle

Introduction

She was about six. Her brothers' recent admission to the Lord's Supper upon becoming communicant members became a topic of slight concern and momentary disorientation to her. Her confidence in what she had always been taught, that she too was a member of Christ's church, was shaken. After some brief instruction from her father, she once again gained the confidence that 'withholding the Lord's Supper from the children does not deprive them of any benefit of the covenant of grace'.[2] When her grandfather, also a Presbyterian minister like her own father, was visiting a couple of weeks later, she exclaimed at the dinner table with all the exuberance of a six year old, 'Grandpa, did you hear that my brothers became communicant members a few weeks ago!' Grandpa replied, 'Yes, I did, isn't that wonderful!' Then, my daughter quickly and confidently added, 'I'm a member too, I'm

---

1. I want to thank John Fesko for reading a draft of this article and for his many helpful comments especially with regards to the comments about Exodus 24 in footnote 54 and the eschatological nature of the Lord's Supper as represented in footnote 58. I am indebted to my New Testament colleague, Steve Baugh, for nudging me to strengthen the point in this paper about Christ being the fulfillment of the whole sacrificial system as represented in footnote 94.

2. Herman Bavinck, *Reformed Dogmatics*, Vol. 4, *Holy Spirit, Church, and New Creation* (trans. John Vriend; ed. John Bolt; Grand Rapids, Michigan: Baker, 2008), 584.

just not a drinking member yet.' This, as you can imagine, brought thunderous laughter to the dinner table from Grandpa and the rest of the gallery as well.

Too often the Passover and the Lord's Supper (i.e., the supper at which the Lord presides as host) are connected in one way or another without qualification, clarification or discernment. The fact of the matter is that our Lord instituted the perpetual ordinance of his parting meal, the Lord's Supper, on the occasion of the Passover. Even so, to suggest that the Lord's Supper 'fulfilled' Passover needs qualification. In what sense? Answering this question will inform how we respond to some of the arguments of those proposing paedocommunion practices. How are we to relate the Jewish paschal meal to the Lord's Supper, according to the Scriptural record? If the Passover is the 'background' for the Lord's Supper, in what sense is it? Indeed, such a simple question can impoverish the true sense of the relation between the two. Therefore, we must strive to be precise in our formulations.

This chapter will argue that the Lord's Supper did occur on the occasion of the paschal meal; however, that occasion should not be construed as *merely* the fulfillment of the paschal service. Such a notion does not adequately explain the relationship between the two. Rather, the Lord's Supper is not to be identified with the Passover meal.[3] Assuming a facile relationship can lead to such fallacious nomenclature calling the Lord's Supper a 'greater Passover of the church'.[4]

Ironically, by focusing too much on the details of the Passover, we may actually miss the point of Jesus being alluded to as our Passover. The purpose of the Gospel presentation is not to give a detailed account of a paschal meal. The purpose of the Gospels is to tell us about the special things that Jesus said and did. Although the paschal meal should be seen as a background within which

---

3. I will not be arguing that there is no parallel between the Passover and the Lord's Supper nor will I be arguing that the Lord's Supper destroyed the old rite and established a completely new unprecedented rite with no connection to the old. For that position, see Balthasar Hübmaier, *Dialogue with Zwingli's Baptism Book* (eds. and trans., H. Wayne Pipkin and John H. Yoder; Scottdale: Herald Press, 1989), 188. However, I will be arguing about what is new in the Lord's Supper, as evidenced by the words of institution which were spoken by our Lord on the occasion of the Passover.

4. James Jordan, 'Children and the Religious Meals of the Old Creation,' in *The Case for Covenant Communion* (ed. by Gregg Strawbridge; Monroe, Louisiana: Athanasius Press, 2006), 67.

the Lord's Supper is interpreted, it is not the only rubric through which the Lord's Supper should be viewed. Indeed, what I shall demonstrate is that the Lord's Supper, far from merely fulfilling the Passover meal, actually fulfills the *entire* sacrificial system. Jesus fulfills the whole sacrificial order, not just the Passover.

I will proceed in this chapter to introduce the Passover. Next, I will explore Passover as the occasion of the institution of the Lord's Supper. Building on the exegetical work of Herman Ridderbos, I will then talk about the relationship between Passover and the Lord's Supper as instituted by our Lord. Finally, I will discuss theoretical considerations on the subject of biblical allusions since this shall influence our understanding of some biblical statements such as, 'Christ our Passover.'

A Brief Introduction to the Passover

Passover plays a central and important part in the Bible's teaching. It is described in many key Old Testament texts (e.g., Exod. 12; 13; 34:25; Lev. 23:5-8; Num. 9:1-14; 28:16-25; 2 Chr. 30:1-9) and referenced or alluded to in many others. Passover was the meal celebrated by those Hebrew families that were delivered from the Angel of Death after they had marked the doorposts of their houses with blood taken from a sacrificed lamb. The remaining meat was roasted and eaten. Julius Wellhausen, who is often considered the father of the modern method of biblical literary criticism, felicitously stated, 'Because Pharaoh refuses to allow the Hebrews to offer to their God the firstlings of cattle that are His due, Jehovah seizes from him the first-born of men.'[5] Arrogant Pharaoh, debased and God-smitten, finally released the Hebrews from enslavement. Indeed, the Egyptians urged them to depart in haste lest they all die (Exod. 12:33).

When Moses gave the Hebrews instructions about the Passover (Exod. 12:21-27), he gave them specific instructions for the urgency of the moment. He also gave instructions in commemorating the Passover in the future, alluding to children asking for explanations of the ritual. Strangely, in this section of Scripture (Exod. 12:21-27),

---

5. Julius Wellhausen, *Prolegomena to the History of Ancient Israel* (Gloucester, Mass.: Peter Smith, 1973; A Meridian Books Library Edition first published August 1957), 88; repr. of *Prolegomena to the History of Israel* (trans. J. Sutherland Black and Allan Enzias, with preface by W. Robertson Smith; Edinburgh: Adam & Charles Black, 1885: trans. of *Prolegomena zur Geschichte Israels* 2d ed.; Berlin: G. Reimer, 1883).

he says nothing of the practice of eating unleavened bread for seven days (the Feast of Unleavened Bread), which was to become part of the regular custom of the festival as it was practiced later. This has been a perplexing problem for many scholars.

In the biblical books, the Passover tradition experienced a long evolution and development.[6] For example, when did the commemorative celebration of the Passover become a pilgrimage festival such as we see in the New Testament? There are numerous studies in the secondary literature that describe all kinds of developments from various perspectives. Wellhausen thought that the biblical Passover derived not from the historical occasion described in Exodus, but he and others following him thought that the Passover derived from a nomadic practice of sacrifice of firstlings. Additionally, he thought that alleged discrepancies in the biblical accounts, particularly the combining of later commemorative feasts, are best explained by positing various literary sources in the Bible.[7]

The tensions which Wellhausen ingeniously demonstrated, and have been subsequently developed by so many others in one way or another,[8] are largely put to rest if we recognize something significant about the Pentateuch at various places: it is descriptive for the moment, but it engages in polity-making for the future. In other words, if we view the prescriptions for Passover given by Moses in Exodus 12 and 13 as giving instructions for the urgency of the moment (i.e., to leave Egypt in haste), but also as commemorative directions given for the future, then the Wellhausian problems largely fade away.

This chapter will assume that the institution of the Passover is best understood if one takes a confident view of the history

---

6. For a survey of some possible developments (some of which are informed by higher critical presuppositions), see Anthony J. Saldarini, *Jesus and Passover* (New York: Paulist Press, 1984), 5-40. Also see for an up-to-date summary of various recent proposals for theories about the Passover, Tamara Prosic, *The Development and Symbolism of Passover until 70 CE* (JSOTSup 414; London: T & T Clark International, 2004), 19-32.

7. Wellhausen, *Prolegomena*, 89.

8. See J.B. Segal, *The Hebrew Passover: From the Earliest Times to A.D. 70* (London Oriental Series 12; London and New York: Oxford, 1963), 42-70. Segal's book, a vast reference, may not be neglected for all who wish to do serious work on the Passover. Some of his assertions may be overstated, however, such as minors not being admitted to the Passover until after A.D. 70. See Roger T. Beckwith, 'The Age of Admission to the Lord's Supper,' *WTJ* 38/2 (Winter, 1976): 123-51; Also see, T.D. Alexander, 'The Passover Sacrifice' in *Sacrifice in the Bible* (ed. Roger T. Beckwith and Martin J. Selman; Grand Rapids: Baker, 1995), 2-4.

portrayed in Exodus 12 and 13: instructions for the Passover sacrifice were given by Moses for the urgency of the moment as the Hebrews escaped from the iron furnace of the Egyptians, and for future generations that would commemorate the Passover as one of the primary festal events of the Israelites.[9]

Many others followed in a similar but variously nuanced vein of source criticism (e.g., most significantly S.R. Driver). More recently, those following the methods of 'historical minimalism' have written from a vantage-point that clearly does not trust the historical veracity of the biblical text.[10] For those working in the minimalist camp, the Hebrew Bible is a product of the late Persian-Hellenistic period and is merely a literary or social construct not containing a reliable historical record.

How the Passover was celebrated by the first generation of Israelites fleeing out of Egypt is different from how it was practiced in Jesus' day with the preparation of the sacrifice made at the Temple, which in turn is different from how the Passover was celebrated by Jews outside of Jerusalem after the destruction of the Temple in A.D. 70 when there is an absence of the sacrificial animal, which is different from how the Passover is presently practiced by contemporary Jews.

There is no extant record of the order of the Passover described from Jesus' time, either the *seder* (order of things eaten) or the *haggadah* (narrative associated with the feast).[11] It is not until the Mishnah (tractate Pesahim, in particular, encoded sometime between A.D. 175–200, but probably reflecting some of the practice of the previous century) that we have any kind of detailed record regarding the practice of the Passover Meal.[12] During the celebration of Passover in Jesus' time it is estimated that somewhere between 85,000 and 125,000 pilgrims made the journey to

---

9. See T.D. Alexander, 'The Passover Sacrifice,' 1-24. Alexander demonstrates that all the Pentateuchal sources, apart from Exodus 12:1–13:16 and Leviticus 23:5-6 link the Passover with the Exodus event (Exod. 23:15; 34:18; Num. 9:1; 33:3; Deut. 16:1, 3, 6).

10. Prosic, *Development and Symbolism of Passover*, 76-79.

11. Ashkenazic Jews continue to call the Passover by the name *seder* after the order and Sephardic Jews call it the *haggadah* after the story.

12. Philo also refers to the Passover throughout his writings, but discussing this would take us beyond the purpose of this chapter. For another interpretation of the form in which Passover may have taken place during the time of Jesus, see Robin Routledge, 'Passover and Last Supper,' *TynBul* 53.2 (2002): 203-21.

Jerusalem for the festival.[13] A summary of the Passover service would run something like this:[14]

1. The first cup of wine was mixed with spices and water and the head of the Seder meal would recite a benediction over the wine.

2. Unleavened bread, lettuce, *haroseth* (finely ground fruit, nuts, and spices mixed with wine and vinegar – possibly in order to mitigate the bitterness of other elements), and the roasted lamb itself (during the days of the Jerusalem temple) were then brought to the table but not eaten yet.

3. A second cup of wine was mixed (but not yet drunk) and at that time the son asked his father certain questions about the meaning of the night and the meal.

4. Then the father instructed the child according to the Passover *haggadah* (in Aramaic), the core of which was based upon Deuteronomy 26.

5. Psalms 113 and possibly 114 (the beginning of the so-called *Hallel)* were recited (in Hebrew), depending on which rabbinical tradition one followed.[15]

6. The meal was then eaten.

7. The third cup of wine was mixed and grace recited.

8. The fourth cup of wine was mixed and the remainder of the *Hallel* (Psalms 114–118) was recited.

9. Participants could not depart for revelry (*afikoman*) after the meal. The Talmud (Pesahim 109a, b) did reinterpret

---

13. Joachim Jeremias, *The Eucharistic Words of Jesus* (New York: Charles Scribner's Sons, 1966), 42.

14. The author is indebted to the fine paraphrase given by Feeley-Harnik, *The Lord's Table: Eucharist and Passover in Early Christianity* (Philadelphia: University of Pennsylvania Press, 1981), 121-27. This book is an anthropological study. The main thesis is that food is language and both meals – Passover and the Lord's Supper – consist of foods that must be 'translated' when they are eaten. Her book has some useful insights but lacks the rigor of biblical scholarship that incorporates serious language work, both ancient and modern. The order proposed by Joachim Jeremias is slightly different, *Eucharistic Words*, 85-86, but certain comments from Jeremias' work are incorporated in the summary above.

15. The Schools of Hillel and Shammai differed as to whether the first part of the recitation of the Hallel (Psalms 113–118) included Psalm 114 or not. For details and bibliography on the debate, see Andrew C. Brunson, *Psalm 118 in the Gospel of John* (WUNT 158; Tübingen: Mohr Siebeck, 2003), 73-77.

this *afikoman* later to be a piece of unleavened bread that was kept for the end of the meal primarily for the sake of the children and served as a stimulus to keep the children attentive throughout the long ritual.[16]

This is probably a fair description of the ritual as it took place in Jesus' time, according to the German scholar, Joachim Jeremias.[17] Feeley-Harnik states that this piece of unleavened bread 'served as a symbolic reminder of the paschal lamb that had been eaten at the end so its taste would remain in the mouth.'[18] The important point I wish to make here however, and develop throughout this chapter, is the fact that most of the 'critical ingredients of the Passover service are conspicuously absent from the Last Supper [as described in the Bible].'[19]

Leithart's Illegitimate Children for the Supper Argument

At first glance this may sound too provocative: bastard children participating at the Lord's Supper? That is not why I chose the heading. I chose the adjective *illegitimate* for several reasons that will become clear in the discussion below. There are arguments afoot today that seek to change the practice of confessional Reformed churches by allowing very young children to participate in the Lord's Supper. This is a practice eschewed in most confessionally Reformed churches since the expectation is that children should be catechized and pass through membership classes before becoming communicants so that they may participate intelligently.

Before we begin discussing the Lord's Supper occurring on the occasion of the Passover meal, I will briefly discuss Peter Leithart's argument.[20] His treatment is potentially significant since it discusses the hermeneutics (interpretive method and principles) of

---

16. The *afikoman* was a kind of after-supper dessert. See Routledge, 'Passover and the Lord's Supper,' 205.

17. Jeremias, *Eucharistic Words*, 86.

18. Feeley-Harnik, *The Lord's Table*, 124.

19. Feeley-Harnik, *The Lord's Table*, 126.

20. Peter J. Leithart, 'Sacramental Hermeneutics and the Ceremonies of Israel,' in *The Case for Covenant Communion* (ed. Gregg Strawbridge; Monroe, Louisiana: Athanasius Press, 2006), 111-31.

paedocommunion advocates, including underlying hermeneutical practices and assumptions. In a chapter representing his recently-published work, Leithart says, 'this chapter is an effort to justify the assumed but often unstated hermeneutical assumptions embedded in the paedoarguments.'[21]

In fairness to Leithart, he does not argue for total continuity between the institutions of the old and new covenants. However, he is keenly interested in certain features of the new covenant that show aspects of continuity with the old covenant.[22] For Leithart, his starting point is Augustine of Hippo, 'my guide, the fountainhead of Western sacramental theology.'[23] Building on Augustine's principle of the Old Testament typological principle of *totus Christus* – the whole Christ, Leithart proposes that there are Old Testament ceremony to New Testament ceremony typologies.[24] He argues that we shouldn't think in terms of the Old Testament types being fulfilled merely in Christ; rather, they are fulfilled in Christ *and* his church, both head and body. 'Near the heart of the paedocommunion argument is at least an implicit affirmation of the Augustinian principle of the *totus Christus*. According to this principle, the entire Old Testament is fulfilled in Jesus, but it is equally fulfilled in the Christian Church,' asserts Leithart.[25] Space

---

21. Leithart, 'Sacramental Hermeneutics,' 117.

22. Leithart, 'Sacramental Hermeneutics,' 113. His explanation in his dissertation, *The Priesthood of the Plebs: A Theology of Baptism* (Eugene, Oregon: Wipf and Stock Publishers, 2003), is helpful to understand his view. Building on a musical metaphor of Augustine, Leithart wants to reinforce the principle of continuity: 'Moreover, just as a conjugation is not a transition from language to not-language but a transformation from one linguistic form to another, so also the transition from Old to New remains within the economy of linguistic and cultural signs. The New is a radically fresh and surprising variation on the themes of the preceding movement but it is not a wholly new musical departure. New Covenant rites and signs are thus not grudging concessions to the weakness of the flesh but are necessary to develop redemptive themes in the symphony of universal history' (37-38).

23. Peter J. Leithart, *The Priesthood of the Plebs*, 33.

24. With regards to how the Reformed Faith should appeal to the *Totus Christus* principle, especially in light of many other trends in modern theology, see Michael S. Horton, *People and Place: A Covenant Ecclesiology* (Louisville: Westminster John Knox Press, 2008), 155-89.

25. Leithart, 'Sacramental Hermeneutics,' 117. Leithart's commitments are more fully discussed in his reworked dissertation, *Priesthood of the Plebs*, where he says: 'Appealing to Jesus' statement that He came to fulfill not to destroy the Law (Matt. 5:17), Augustine's alternative paradigm is not so much a "spiritualization" as a "humanization" of the Old Covenant order. Preeminently, Christ, the God-Man, fulfills the rites and institutions of Israel, but for Augustine Christ and His body are inseparable. Regarding the Eucharist, Augustine claims that the Christ who is the *res* of the sacraments is the *totus Christus* comprising Head and body', 39.

restrictions do not allow me to engage his entire argument, but I think that one serious error needs to be addressed at this point.

As mentioned previously, I did not choose the language of 'illegitimate children' merely to be provocative. I use the term in the sense of 'unlawful' or 'illegal', that is, 'unauthorized.' As other essays in our book make clear, a credible profession of faith is what is required in order to become a communicant according to the Westminster Standard (e.g., *Larger Catechism* 177). We should ask if those requirements of our secondary standards are justified by our primary standard of the Bible. I think that the essays in this book will make that case. Here, however, I just insert one overarching criticism of Leithart's proposal. I find Leithart's treatment on typology unsatisfying and faulty.

Biblical typological exegesis has fallen on hard times recently even though it has a very distinguished pedigree in Reformed exegesis. Friedbert Ninow provides one of the most helpful surveys through the centuries of the use and study of typology as a way of understanding the Scriptures.[26] Although frequently practiced in the early church it often did not have careful constraints and the practice of typological interpretation frequently slid into allegory.

In the eighteenth and nineteenth centuries, rationalism – especially that of Johann S. Semler and Johann D. Michaels – introduced a skepticism to the notion of the unity of the Old and New Testaments. This move introduced troubled waters for typology which had assumed a unity of the Old and New Testaments. Indeed, for many in the church prior to this point, the Old was somehow incomplete and unfinished. Prior to the rise of serious biblical criticism, the Scriptures were assumed to be one organic whole. With the advent of biblical criticism, the focus shifted to the distinct and individual contribution of various books of the Bible and the assumed homogeneity of the inspired Scriptures was questioned. Source criticism, trying to identify the various strands and traditions within the biblical corpus, consumed the energies of talented and well-trained biblical scholars. Whether it was the classic Wellhausian late-dating desire to identify parsimoniously redactors who brought the pieces (or schools) together, or whether it was the Von Radian tendency to identify *Sagas* and their tradents,

---

26. Ninow, *Indicators of Typology Within the Old Testament: The Exodus Motif* (Frankfurt: Peter Lang, 2001), 15-97.

schools of tradition growing simultaneously yet separately before coming together in a ostensibly complete whole, it all produced one grand effect: an erosion of confidence in how the Scriptures fit together and what the story actually means. Even the common response of systematic theologians and well-meaning conservatives about 'unity within diversity' became the quick and somewhat easy answer; however, deep challenges and issues remained. Therefore, almost any argument that appeals to revivifying typology among evangelicals may have a certain appeal. Hence, the importance of identifying specious arguments.

Leithart's typological hermeneutic with respect to Old Testament ceremony to New Testament ceremony fails on what I call an *illegitimate totality transfer*. This is an awkward phrase used in lexical semantics which basically says, 'any one instance of a word will not bear all the meanings possible for that word.'[27] The danger here is to import the total meaning of a given word with a possible wide semantic range without due consideration of the context in which the word occurs. A fisherman in a story, for example, could be described as being 'green'. One had better make sure whether the context is describing him as inexperienced or actually somewhat green in color based on his seasickness. He could be both, of course, but the context would indicate that.

I am saying that Leithart commits something like this fallacy – illegitimate totality transfer – on the level of hermeneutics. What was legitimate for the ritual ceremony in the Old Testament may not be legitimate in the New. Leithart commits an illegitimate totality transfer, not necessarily on the semantic level, but definitely on the hermeneutical and exegetical level. Consequently, I find much of his exegesis of individual texts wanting and something that space constraints do not allow me to engage at this time. Even so, do we really want to make such a statement about Old Testament typology run through a *totus Christus* grid? I think not. Even some slight reflection on this level with respect to other Old Testament types will yield some rather silly and absurd notions. Moreover, to draw a focus too narrowly between the Passover and its regulations compared with the Lord's Supper and the newness

---

27. Moisés Silva, *Biblical Words and Their Meaning: An Introduction to Lexical Semantics* (Academie Books; Grand Rapids, Michigan: Zondervan, 1983), 25. Also see, D.A. Carson, *Exegetical Fallacies* (Grand Rapids, MI: Baker, 1996), 53 and 60-61.

communicated there, especially as evidenced in the words of institution, is to diminish the comprehensiveness and profundity of the Lord's Supper. Jesus' expiatory death, as expressed in the words of institution at the Lord's Supper, demonstrates the fulfillment of the entire sacrificial system, not just the paschal offering. More will be discussed on this below. But now I turn to the subject of the relationship that does exist between Passover and the Lord's Supper.

The Passover Connection: The Occasion of the Last Supper

What was the relationship of the Lord's Supper of the New Covenant to the Passover celebration? My position is that the Lord's Supper is not to be identified with the Passover of the old covenant and its regulations. Even though the Passover may have provided *the occasion* for the institution of the perpetual ordinance of the New Covenant, it is not to be identified with it. Many will say simply that the Lord's Supper *is* a Passover meal. 'Jesus' death during the Passover season has linked the traditions inextricably,' says Saldarini.[28] True enough, but how? Or put more poignantly: Is the Last Supper represented in Holy Scripture as a Passover Seder?[29] To state the question is to introduce complexity because the synoptic Gospels do seem to represent it that way (Matt. 26:2, 17-30; Mark 14:1, 12-26; Luke 22:1, 7-23); however, John does not (John 13:1-30, cf., 6:52-58)![30] John seems to indicate that the Passover took place after the crucifixion. I cannot address in any detail why the synoptics present a 'simpler' view of the relationship between the Lord's Supper and Passover. Even so, before I delve into the real rub of the argument of this chapter, this preliminary question, whether or not the Lord's Supper is a *seder*, obviously needs to be addressed. Although this discussion concerning chronology and the Passover is complex, for the purposes of this chapter, I will attempt a brief introduction to some of the issues since it is integrally related to the topic of this essay.[31]

---

28. Saldarini, *Jesus and Passover* (New York: Paulist Press, 1984), 51.

29. *Seder* merely means order and has to do with the order of prayers and events that make up the Passover.

30. Routledge, 'Passover and Last Supper,' 206-07, states that more recent trends are to favor John's chronology over the Synoptics which are allegedly later additions by the Early Church, whereas the traditional view was that Synoptic Gospels presented the more accurate picture.

31. Readers are invited to turn to Appendix II: 'Dating the Crucifixion' in Raymond Brown, *The Death of the Messiah: From Gethsemane to the Grave* (2 vols.; New York:

First, it should be noted that some of the most important ingredients from the Jewish Passover meal seem to be missing from the Gospel accounts: there is only one cup of wine mentioned (with the exception of Luke if the longer textual version is adopted), only Mark and Luke end the meal with a hymn (which may have been from the *Hallel*, i.e., Psalms 114–118), there are no references to bitter herbs or haroseth, there is no narrative describing the Passover, and most importantly, the paschal lamb itself is absent [so to speak].

What about the bread? It is probably true that the unleavened bread 'bears a symbolic weight which it did not have when the Temple was still standing and participants sat with the Passover lamb roasted on the table.' Indeed, it is possible that after the Temple and the Passover lamb were gone, 'the unleavened bread came more and more to replace the Passover lamb symbolically.'[32] But may the same be said about the Last Supper on the night in which our Lord offered up his body symbolized in the bread? I doubt so.

In my judgment, the differences of opinion with regards to the significance of the relation between Passover and the Lord's Supper have to do with the function of the Lord's Supper at this period in Redemptive History. The Supper is a commensal (eating at the same table) meal. It is symbolizing fulfillment but it is also symbolizing something inceptive. That is to say that there is something significantly new: 'the meal Jesus partakes of with his disciples assumes a prefigurative character.... The relation between the Eucharist and eating and drinking in the coming kingdom of God is not merely that between symbol and reality, but that between commencement and fulfillment,' says Ridderbos.[33]

When Christ institutes the ordinance of the Supper, He is doing something *new* and radically different vis-à-vis the Passover. Schilder eloquently expresses this when he says:

> In this *unique hour* the Holy Spirit broods over the room of the Passover and moves the soul of the man Christ, who Himself is also active to that end, to give the Holy Supper to the church.

Doubleday, 1993), 1350-73 for more details and bibliography. Although I do not agree with all of Brown's analysis or conclusions, the bibliography and outline of the issues at stake in this discussion are conveniently catalogued in the pages referenced above.

32. Saldarini, *Jesus and Passover*, 44.

33. Herman Ridderbos, *The Coming of the Kingdom* (Phillipsburg, New Jersey: P & R, 1962), 412.

He takes bread; bread is that which has no blood in it. And He takes wine; wine, too, has no blood in it. He takes bread and wine, bloodless symbols both, as His signs. The agonizing bleat of the dying lamb will never rend the atmosphere again; every pain will be subdued by the one cry of the dying Lamb of God: it is finished! By this single shedding of blood every other stream will be effectually stopped.[34]

In short, all this is to say that I recognize that the institution of the Lord's Supper happened on the occasion of the Passover. Some modern scholars who attempt to rectify some of the difficulties discussed above, especially as they relate to the date of Jesus' death, have made such suggestions as the occasion of Jesus' death was *prior* to the Passover.[35] Or, they suggest that this was a *kiddush* or *chabura* meal, or something which was like what they practiced at Qumran, not the Passover.[36] But this will not satisfy. The Passover was indeed the *occasion* of the new Lord's Supper. Notice that Mark 14:22 and Matthew 26:26 say 'while they were eating', probably a reference to the fact that Jesus' institution of this perpetual ordinance occurred during the Passover.

The Apostle Luke, for example, clearly depicts the institution of the Lord's Supper as occurring on the occasion, 'this Passover' (Luke 22:15).[37] Luke mentions two cups that were passed, which may reflect the custom of celebrating Passover as mentioned above in this chapter. In Luke 22:18, our Lord says, 'For I tell you I will not drink again of the fruit of the vine until the kingdom of God comes.' The phrase 'fruit of the vine' was standard parlance of the day for Jewish Paschal rites.[38] This much may be conceded, therefore: the occasion of the institution of the Lord's Supper was the Passover meal. Even so, that is not the focal point of the biblical narratives.

The real focal point is the *new* material. And the new material, as Matthew and Mark would have us understand (Mark 14:25 and Matthew 26:29), is that the Last Supper must be understood with

---

34. K. Schilder, *Christ in His Suffering* (trans. Henry Zylstra; Grand Rapids, Michigan: 1938), 242 [emphasis original].

35. See Raymond Brown's appendix, referred to in footnote 31.

36. For details about this suggestion, see the secondary works, especially Jeremias, *Eucharistic Words*, 26-36.

37. See Ridderbos, *Coming*, 418.

38. Ridderbos, *Coming*, 411.

respect to Jesus' teaching about the Kingdom of God, especially his preaching about the coming of the Kingdom of God. Luke makes a similar point about the *newness* in the language of fulfillment: 'For I tell you, I will not eat it again until it finds fulfillment in the kingdom of God.' So what is most important here is not the old but the new, and the new is best comprehended in the inauguration of the coming of the Kingdom. Here is a Lord that is concerned with the past and the future, and with the new which has come and will come.

The Dominant Motifs of the Lord's Supper

In the last section, I stated that the New Testament Lord's Supper is not to be identified directly with the Passover and its regulations. At this point in the argument, I will demonstrate why from certain texts of Scripture. As mentioned previously, Herman Ridderbos is concerned to describe the institution of the Lord's Supper from the standpoint of the preaching of the coming of the Kingdom of God (Matt. 26:26-29; Mark 14:22-25; Luke 22:15-20) versus a methodology informed merely by dogmatic (that is systematic) theology.[39] He is concerned to make apparent the redemptive-historical meaning of the Lord's Supper.[40]

He has argued persuasively in my opinion that there are two dominant motifs associated with the institution of the Lord's Supper: the eschatological motif and the expiatory death motif. Both of these motifs must be recognized, and one motif should not prevail over the other. Indeed, intimately related to the presence of these two motifs is the question of their relationship to one another.[41] Additionally, the secret of what Jesus proclaimed is integral to recognizing the basis of his death as part and parcel of the meaning of the Lord's Supper.[42]

This revelation of Jesus Christ in the Lord's Supper was essentially an eschatological one as Ridderbos has pointed out. By this I do not mean that it was merely focussed on the future; rather, it was

---

39. Ridderbos, *Coming*, 398. See also, David Wenham, 'How Jesus understood the Last Supper: a parable in action,' *Them* Vol. 20/2 (January, 1995):11-16. Wenham says in regard to the background and context of the Last Supper, 'The first thing to say is that the Last Supper story must be seen in the context of Jesus' proclamation of the kingdom of God, because it was so central to his ministry', 12.

40. Ridderbos, *Coming*, 406 and following.

41. Ridderbos, *Coming*, 397-443.

42. Ridderbos, *Coming*, 412-13.

an intrusion of the heavenly into the mundane, earthly sphere. The king had come. His kingdom was not of this world. *All* sacrificial types now found their fulfillment in him: not only the Passover, but all.[43] What is central and governing in the Scriptures is the way all things in scripture point to Christ, 'a hermeneutical principle that Jesus himself authorizes.'[44]

Just as Moses had given instructions about the Passover which included the urgency of the moment as well as directions for the commemoration of the event in the future, so Christ breaks bread with his disciples in and for the reality of the moment but at the same time sets polity for future commemorations of the breaking of bread and the drinking of wine in commemoration of his great sacrifice.

Although the eschatological aspect is one of two important motifs in the institution of the supper, it is the *new* feature that is revealed by our Lord at the institution of this perpetual ordinance that becomes absolutely essential to its understanding. In comparison to the eating and drinking of Passover, it is not the eating and drinking of the Lord's Supper that is the *new* element, nor, as Ridderbos points out, is the *new* element the messianic meal, nor the institution of a communal meal, per se.[45] *The new feature is that 'from henceforth Jesus' body will be the food and his blood the drink of his disciples.'*[46]

So we have both a fulfillment aspect and a provisional aspect.[47] In the future, there yet awaits a more glorious participation of eating and drinking in the Kingdom of God. In the present fulfillment, the disciples sup with their Lord in solemn celebration of all that he has accomplished in his redemption. As Ridderbos elegantly points out, not only is there anticipation of the distant future but there is an eating and drinking of his body for the pilgrim way in the

---

43. Consider circumcision, for example (Col. 2:11-12). Baptism does not replace circumcision; rather, Christ replaces circumcision. More precisely, Christ fulfills circumcision and then inaugurates a new sacrament. There is a correspondence but Christ is at the center between the two. I am indebted to John Fesko for this comment. This applies to Jesus' sacrifice generally.

44. Michael S. Horton, *Covenant and Eschatology: The Divine Drama* (Louisville: Westminster John Knox, 2002), 18.

45. Ridderbos, *Coming*, 416-17.

46. Ridderbos, *Coming*, 417 [emphasis original].

47. Ridderbos, *Coming*, 417.

near future.[48] Over and against those that would emphasize the eschatological only, the expiatory motif imparts the proper valence and meaning to the Supper. 'All their eating and drinking is done only *in anticipation* of the new earth and of the new wine, i.e., of the fullness of joy.'[49]

This is the liability of those who would draw too close an identity between the Passover and the institution of the Lord's Supper miss the communicative intention of the synoptic Gospels' main point: the objective is not to describe the Passover or its participants in detail; rather, the goal is to 'tell us about the special things that Jesus said and did'.[50] The Passover stands as a backdrop, one may even say the foundation, for the Lord's Supper; however, that is not the communicative focus. Noticing carefully what Jesus said and did on this occasion is the crucial point that can illustrate the communicative focus of the text.

Notice the words of institution: 'Take, eat; this is my body, which is *given* for you; this do in remembrance of me.'[51] And again, probably an echo to Exodus 24:6-8, Jesus says, 'This cup is the new covenant in my blood, which is *shed* for many for the remission of sins; drink ye all of it.' Notice that both *given* and *shed* clearly refer to 'Jesus' impending death'.[52] It does not follow that Jesus is directly connecting himself in these words of institution with the paschal lamb (e.g., notice Jesus' connection with bread, not the lamb). Nor is the wine to be directly connected with the thought of the blood of the paschal lamb, thus communicating at this point that Jesus is the true Paschal lamb.[53] This reinforces that the Lord's Supper draws on much more than the Passover, especially because of the clear allusion to Exodus 24.[54]

---

48. Ridderbos, *Coming*, 417.

49. Ridderbos, *Coming*, 417.

50. Ridderbos, *Coming*, 419.

51. See the biblical references cited at the beginning of this subsection.

52. Ridderbos, *Coming*, 424.

53. Ridderbos, *Coming*, 425-26.

54. See Exodus 24:6-8, where the sprinkling of the blood on the people is about covenant ratification. The ratification occurs in the context of sacrifice and a communion meal on the mountain (cf. Exodus 24:1, 9-11). Noteworthy is the context and the significance for the new covenant, the Lord's Supper, and the final eschatological banquet of the redeemed people of God. Cf. also Wenham, 'How Jesus understood the Last Supper' (48); and Meredith G. Kline, *God, Heaven and Har Magedon: A Covenantal Tale of Cosmos and Telos* (Eugene, Oregon: Wipf & Stock, 2006), 122-24.

It is true that our Lord indicates in other places throughout the New Testament that he is the true Paschal lamb (1 Cor. 5:7; John 19:36, also John 1:29, 36; 1 Pet. 1:19; Rev. 5:6; 12:11). More on this will be discussed in the section below. But that is not the exact point here at the words of institution. To say so would be to impoverish the words of institution. For the words of institution set Jesus' expiatory death in a much wider, broader, and more profound horizon: the expiatory death of Jesus must be viewed as fulfilling the *entire* Old Testament sacrificial system, not just Passover.[55]

Although one might say that 'the meaning of the Supper is entirely determined by the character of the paschal meal,' one must continue to clarify by saying, 'That which held for it now holds for the "fulfilled" meaning of the Lord's Supper; it is a sacrificial repast [archaic for "meal"], the sacrificial repast in a pre-eminent sense, viz., that of the new covenant.'[56]

Thus, as a side note, there are no grounds whatsoever for the Roman Catholic inclination to connect these words of institution with the sacrifice itself; rather, the words talk of Jesus' impending death and sacrifice. Thus, even the words of institution associated with the wine should not be construed to think of his blood being poured out on our behalf, symbolically illustrating his sacrifice; rather, what is symbolized is not 'Christ's self-surrender, but its fruits in the life of his followers' as Ridderbos asserts.[57] In other words, it is *not the altar but the table* of the commensal, corporate meal that characterizes our Lord's Supper, and this table ultimately anticipates the marriage supper of the Lamb.[58] The Lord's Supper is not the sacrifice itself; the sacrifice is the presupposition of the meal at which the eating and drinking take place.[59] Beyond this, I will not enter into further discussion about the centuries-old debate between the meaning of the Lord's body and the bread nor between

---

55. Ridderbos, *Coming*, 426.

56. Ridderbos, *Coming*, 426-27.

57. Ridderbos, *Coming*, 430.

58. See G.K. Beale, 'The New Testament and New Creation,' in *Biblical Theology: Retrospect and Prospect* (ed. Scott J. Hafemann, Downer's Grove, Illinois: InterVarsity Press, 2002). Beale says after commenting on 1 Corinthians 11:21-34, 'Hence the Supper contains in itself a beginning form of the last judgment, which will be consummated at the end of time', 170.

59. Ridderbos, *Coming*, 430.

the meaning of the wine and his blood with reference to symbol and reality and the much disputed meaning of the copula 'is'.

In the next section of my argument, I will discuss the nature of certain allusions to Jesus and the Passover, with special reference to 1 Corinthians 5:7 and following.

The Nature of Allusion and its Application to the Passover/ Lord's Supper

An allusion is usually defined as a tacit or indirect reference to another's work. Most would maintain the intentional aspects of allusion. 'An allusion is an intentional echo of an earlier text: it not only reminds us; it means to remind us.'[60] However, most people who read and interpret literature, including biblical scholars, have been merely operating with received assumptions and practices about how an allusion works. Many literary authorities in the last fifty years are aware that something more is required: a rigorous analysis of how allusions work and function. This need for a theory of literary allusion was picked up and addressed in the 1960s and following. Interestingly, the center for work in this area has emerged in Israel.[61] Ziva Ben-Porath has provided some of the most extensive analysis of how one may identify allusions and how they work.[62] According to her, a theory of allusion is a desideratum in literary theory and the same could be said about biblical studies.[63]

A full theoretical discussion of the nature of allusion is beyond the space restrictions of this brief article.[64] Even so, an introduction to the subject is germane here and would seem to help in

---

60. Chandler, 'Romantic Allusiveness,' *Critical Inquiry* 8 (1982): 461-87, especially 463.

61. Chana Kronfeld, *On the Margins of Modernism: Decentering Literary Dynamics*, Contraversions: Critical Studies in Jewish Literature, Culture, and Society Series (Berkeley: University of California Press, 1996), 114-42.

62. Ziva Ben-Porath, 'The Poetics of Allusion' (Ph.D. diss., University of California Berkley, 1967); also see Ziva Ben-Porath, 'The Poetics of Literary Allusion,' *PTL: A Journal for Descriptive Poetics and Theory of Literature* 1 (1976): 105-28.

63. Ben-Porath, *Poetics of Allusion*, 19-20. She states: 'The problem is not one of a plethora of contradictory theories. On the contrary, there are in fact scarcely any theories dealing with allusion, and there is a lack of studies on allusion *qua* allusion. Allusion has either been treated as a very vague term, covering so many structures that it could not be discussed phenomenologically, or it has been taken for granted as a very common feature of the language. Similarly the reader has been assumed to exist in order to decode a set of signs. The passivity of his role has been taken for granted.'

64. For more detail, see my forthcoming work on the Exodus motif in Scripture.

understanding the nature of certain Scriptural statements about Jesus being our Passover. Ben-Porath takes pains to understand the nature of literary allusions in a way that goes beyond traditional dictionary definitions. According to her, the traditional views allow almost everything to come under the cover of allusion, making all literature 'a massive tissue of allusion'.[65]

First, she asserts that the language of literature is opaque, 'drawing attention to itself as well as its referents.'[66] Secondly, tipping the hat to Northrop Frye, she further states that every reader is aware of certain conventions, that is to say, that every allusion is made within the bounds of a certain set of conventions that constitute a genre. This point opens the way for the third point: the role of the reader. The nature of literature, according to Ben-Porath, is that 'everything represented in a literature text is always presented only partially and with varying degrees of distortion.'[67] It is then the reader's responsibility to provide the links to infer a pattern. Indeed, she is especially interested to bring the role of the reader into the process of understanding allusions, something which has been strangely absent from traditional definitions and theories of allusion and conservative approaches to biblical literature.[68]

In this process of 'actualization', according to Ben-Porath, a reader goes through several different stages. First, there is the recognition of a marker of allusion and an identification of the source. Next, there is the realization of the marked literary component together with its own contextual elements joined by the linking of marker and marked components in each of their respective literary contexts.

For Ben-Porath, the reader indeed takes an active role and not a passive role in the interpretation of an allusion. In fact, one can say that for Ben-Porath, the pattern by which the marked components in an allusion become active in a complex relationship is 'created' by the reader of a text. This may sound risky and dangerous to readers of this book, especially those who are hesitant to locate any meaning outside the determination of the objective text as is so common in many literary theories today. Even so, Ben-Porath's

---

65. Ben-Porath, *Poetics of Allusion*, 24.

66. Ben-Porath, *Poetics of Allusion*, 25.

67. Ben-Porath, *Poetics of Allusion*, 25.

68. Ben-Porath, *Poetics of Allusion*, 29.

point is to say that the reader plays a crucial and complex role in the development of a pattern that does actually recognize and moreover create a pattern in which all elements of an allusion come into play and partner in the actualization of a meaningful allusion.

What must the reader do in such a circumstance of allusion? 'The reader must distinguish between a so-called "allusion" to a word, which is actually a form of punning, and a literary allusion introduced by means of a word, which is a true allusion in the sense in which the term is used in this study,' says Ben-Porath.[69] In a true *allusion*, vis-à-vis *borrowing*, as she is using the terms, a reader implicitly agrees to invoke contextual meanings from the original context of the text alluded to, thus incorporating something of the evoked text.[70]

How does this work out in practice? If I am preaching on John 12:12-19 and I note that John quotes not only Psalm 118 but also Zechariah 9, then it is incumbent upon me to note elements from those original contextual fields, in their immediate context as well as their canonical context. In the case of Psalm 118, that means that John is concerned to evoke the whole Psalm when he alludes to verses 25-26.[71] In the case of the Zechariah 9 allusion, I would suggest that the Messianic and second Exodus overtones of that immediate passage (especially in the light of Zechariah 10 and 14) need to be brought into play. Moreover, the testament of Jacob (Gen. 49:8-12) is undoubtedly in the background as well, and consequently, it too should be part of the pattern that a reader will create as she moves towards a thicker and deeper understanding of the text.

Now we are ready to explain Paul's statement: 'Clean out the old leaven so that you may be a new lump, just as you are unleavened. For Christ *our Passover* also has been sacrificed' (1 Cor. 5:7), which Jeremias calls 'an abrupt introduction of the comparison between Jesus and the Passover lamb'.[72] As is evident from the discussion

---

69. Ben-Porath, *Poetics of Allusion*, 40.

70. Ben-Porath, *Poetics of Allusion*, 92-93. She comments: 'In a borrowing the reader agrees to disregard recognition of other texts within the text and not to activate the original context. The *only* criterion for allusion is the validity of the activation of elements from the summoned text.'

71. See Andrew C. Brunson, *Psalm 118 in the Gospel of John* (WUNT 158: Tübingen, Mohr Siebeck, 2003), 186.

72. Jeremias, *Eucharistic Words of Jesus*, 60.

above, the role of the reader in recognizing and even creating a pattern to understand such an allusion is crucial. 'All allusions should be regarded as symbols or metaphors or both,' according to Roland Bartel.[73] What would such an oblique reference as we notice activate for the audience? To answer that question we need to do a little more theoretical work: this time with regards to metaphor and how it works in an allusion.

The Nature of Metaphor and its Application to Passover/Lord's Supper

Metaphor suggests that 'the creative potential of language is unlimited'.[74] Some scholars would suggest subtle differences between metaphor and symbols.[75] Paul D. Duke, for example, quoting Norman Friedman, in Duke's own stimulating book on the use of irony in the fourth Gospel would say, 'Metaphor is a device which speaks of one thing (tenor) in terms which are appropriate to another (vehicles), with the vehicle serving as the source of traits to be transferred to the tenor.'[76]

Symbol is a little different. By nature it is 'more stable and repeatable, characteristics not necessarily held by a metaphor, and symbol need not reveal to the reader the precise tenor to which it refers, as metaphor usually does.'[77] Some metaphors recur frequently enough that they can develop stability and expanding suggestiveness that would qualify them as symbols.[78] This seems to be the case in Scripture with references made to Jesus as the lamb or Passover of God (1 Cor. 5:7; John 1:29, 36; 19:36; 1 Pet. 1:19; Rev. 5:6; 12:11). Consequently, I interpret Paul's oblique reference in 1 Corinthians 5:7 as a metaphor and a symbol since Paul invites comparison between Christ and the Passover. The following discussion will be focused on the use of metaphor in 1 Corinthians 5:7 as an example of how we are to think about Christ and the Passover.

---

73. Roland Bartel, *Metaphors and Symbols: Forays into Language* (Urbana, Illinois: National Council of Teachers of English, 1983), 63.

74. Bartel, *Metaphors and Symbols*, 75.

75. On the similarities and differences between metaphors and symbols, see Bartel, *Metaphors and Symbols*, 61-74.

76. Paul D. Duke, *Irony in the Fourth Gospel* (Atlanta: John Knox Press, 1985), 143.

77. Duke, *Irony*, 143.

78. Duke, *Irony*, 143.

Theoretical discussions of metaphor have been receiving much attention lately in the writings of linguists, philosophers and biblical scholars.[79] Readers eager to learn more about this area of study should consult Bonnie Howe's recent book.[80] A cognitive theory of metaphor, gaining in recognition and importance, can be attributed to the ground-breaking works of Lakoff and Johnson.[81] They especially took pains to demonstrate that metaphors are not simply the adornment of ornate and poetic language; rather, metaphors are the stuff of everyday life and make up the very fabric of our mental imaging and conceptual world.[82] The Conceptual Metaphor theory is not without its critics, however.[83]

Let's apply this to the biblical passage at hand. It may be helpful for the reader to remember that Paul is dealing with a congregation that has egregious sin in their midst. In verses 1-5, Paul observes that there is an incestuous member present in the church. In verses 6-13, the apostle commands the church to maintain purity by means of faithful discipline.

Now we turn to understanding the allusion. When Paul says, 'Christ our Passover' in verse 5, this enriches our understanding of Christ in a particular way. Many cognitive linguists would identify 'Passover' in the above comparison to be a conceptual metaphor. In

---

79. For a good, simple overview, see Alec Basson, *Divine Metaphors in Selected Hebrew Psalms of Lamentation* (Tübingen: Mohr Siebeck, 2006), 41-62; Ian Paul, 'Metaphor and Exegesis,' in *After Pentecost: Language and Biblical Interpretation* (ed. Craig Bartholomew, Colin Greene, and Karl Möller; vol. 2 of *Scripture and Hermeneutic Series*; Grand Rapids: Zonderevan, 2001), 2.387–402. Ian Paul is a good introduction to the importance of Ricoeur's theory of metaphor.

80. Bonnie Howe, *Because You Bear This Name: Conceptual Metaphor and the Moral Meaning of 1 Peter* (Leiden: Brill, 2006). For a helpful and thorough overview, note Part A, 'Historical and Contemporary Metaphor Theories: Implications for Biblical Hermeneutics and Ethics' (pages 11-158).

81. See, for example, George Lakoff and Mark Johnson, *Metaphors We Live By* (Chicago: University of Chicago Press, 1980; Afterword, 2003).

82. They are saying we need and use metaphor in order to speak about abstract matters. They are not claiming that everything in thought is metaphor-based.

83. See, for example, Rosa E. Vega Moreno, *Creativity and Convention: The pragmatics of everyday figurative speech* (Pragmatics and Beyond New Series 156; Philadelphia: John Benjamins Publishing Company, 2007). Moreno argues for a relevance-theoretic approach to metaphor. Relevance theory is an important new theory that works on the assumption that communication is largely inferential and that human cognition is relevance-oriented. For more detail on this debate and its importance for interpreting metaphor in Scripture, see my forthcoming work on the Exodus motif. I am especially grateful to my colleague, Josh VanEe, for drawing Moreno's work to my attention.

other words, the knowledge the reader has of 'Passover' helps the reader understand the abstract categories of what Passover does and accomplishes.[84] Even if one rejects Conceptual Metaphor Theory, there is still much worth retaining from that theory and it is applicable here, since people are capable of 'making analogical mappings between distinct domains'.[85] In other words, human beings do have the ability to 'exploit resemblances and draw analogies'.[86]

The hearers of 1 Corinthians are indeed familiar with the Passover and will begin to think in terms of the events and meanings of the things that Passover signified: deliverance from enemies, blood sprinkled upon the lintel of doorposts that turned away the wrath of God mediated through the avenging Angel of Death, etc…(see Deuteronomy 26, which made up the source of regular instruction).

Therefore, when Paul says that Christ is our Passover, it is not merely the literal and ritual practices of Passover that would have been brought to mind, but the events, and the things which Passover symbolized which would have and should come to mind. Furthermore, little words, including the use of certain pronouns, can be huge conveyors of meaning.[87] Since this is the case, it is very significant that Paul says that Christ is *our* Passover. Thus, the reference to 'Passover' applied to Christ enriches our understanding of the expiatory and eschatological aspects of Christ's work in this oblique reference.

In 1 Corinthians 5:7 leaven is used figuratively to symbolize sin.[88] It reads, 'clean out the old leaven so that you may be a new lump, just as you are unleavened,' and should remind the reader of the role of unleavened bread in the Exodus as well (Exod. 12). When we turn to the New Testament letters of Paul, we see that it

---

84. See Howe, *Because You Bear This Name*, 66-84, for a discussion of how cognitive linguistic theory would interpret metaphors according to mental spaces and cognitive domains.

85. Moreno, *Creativity and Convention*, 137.

86. Moreno, *Creativity and Convention*, 137.

87. See Roger Brown and Albert Gilman, 'The Pronouns of Power and Solidarity,' in *Style in Language* (ed. Thomas Sebeok: Cambridge, Mass.: MIT Press; New York: John Wiley and Sons, 1960), 252-76; Peter Mühlhäusler and Rom Harré, *Pronouns and People: The Linguistic Construction of Social and Personal Identity* (Oxford: Basil Blackwell, 1990); B.F. Head, 'Respect Degrees in pronominal reference,' *Universals of Human Language* (ed. J.H. Greenberg: vol. 3 *Word Structure*, Stanford: Stanford University Press, 1978), 151-211.

88. See the exposition of Charles Hodge, *An Exposition of the First Epistle to the Corinthians* (Grand Rapids, Michigan: Eerdmans, reproduction of the revised 1886 edition), 86.

was a reference to purgation.[89] Then, we need to ask the question with reference to the correspondence between Christ as our Passover and the original Passover, which had been memorialized in the minds and hearts of countless generations which regularly practiced and participated in the festival.

The point of the allusion actualized is to say that Christ is *our* Passover. Why and how? Just as the blood of the first lamb sprinkled upon the lintels of their houses turned away the Angel of Death and God's wrath from the Israelites, the blood of this Passover lamb turns away the wrath of God in the propitiating act of the Son.[90] When the Passover lamb was sacrificed, the Hebrews of old were to purge their houses. Paul's argument is similar: now that *the* Passover lamb has come and has been sacrificed, it is incumbent upon them to purge themselves from sin.[91] The Corinthians are not exhorted to celebrate literally 'the Christian feast that corresponds to Israel's feast of Passover-Unleavened Bread,' as Leithart suggests.[92] This exegesis misses the essential thrust of Paul's exhortation.[93] Christ is the fulfillment of the whole sacrificial system, not just the Passover feast. Space constraints don't allow me to comment at length on 1 Corinthians 10:16-18, but that seems to be an implication of the apostle's comments there as well. [94]

---

89. Hodge, *First Epistle to the Corinthians*, 86-87. Hodge comments, 'When the paschal lamb was slain, the Hebrews were required to purge out all leaven from their houses, Exod. 12; 15. The death of Christ imposes a similar obligation on us to purge out the leaven of sin.'

90. Hodge, *First Epistle to the Corinthians*, 87. Ridderbos, *Coming*, 431, says this is the purpose he wanted to achieve: 'He pointed out to his disciples his propitiatory death as the cause and the foundation of the salvation he had proclaimed to them as the gospel of the kingdom which consisted in the realization of the new covenant promised by the prophets.'

91. See Hodge, *First Epistle to the Corinthians*, 87-88.

92. Leithart, 'Sacramental Hermeneutics,' 120-22.

93. Routledge, 'Passover and Last Supper,' 204 states it well when he comments: 'The writers of the Synoptic Gospels do present the Last Supper as a Passover meal; but they emphasise only the bread and wine, and do not refer to other traditional elements such as the lamb and bitter herbs. Paul emphasises the theological significance of Christ as the Passover lamb, but he does not link this with his instructions about the Lord's Supper. *This suggests that the Passover setting is important historically and theologically, but not liturgically'* [emphasis mine].

94. Related to the exegesis of this section is Paul's explanation in 1 Corinthians 10:16-18 of the 'cup of blessing' and Israel after the flesh partaking in the altar. Paul in these verses is concerned to demonstrate that participation is what is noteworthy in these religious acts, whether it is Christian communion, pagan festivals, or Israel partaking of the altar by eating of the sacrifices. He is not arguing that the Lord's Supper is a new sacrifice replacing the old. But notice that he asks in verse 18: 'are not they which eat of the sacrifices partakers of the

Rather, 'since our passover Christ is slain, let us keep the feast,' means, comments Hodge:

> This is not an exhortation to keep the Jewish passover – because the whole context is figurative, and because the death of Christ is no reason why the Corinthians should keep the Jewish passover. Christians are nowhere exhorted to observe the festivals of the old dispensation. Neither is the feast referred to the Lord's Supper. There is nothing in the connection to suggest a reference to that ordinance.[95]

Hodge is right and very lucid here. The feast has to do with the consecration of a certain amount of time.[96] To keep the feast as a sacred festival means consecrate your whole lives to God. Paul is concerned to exhort them to overall purity in this passage – on the basis of Christ's final sacrifice.

Such an understanding of the typology of Passover is not satisfactory for proponents of paedocommunion. Leithart wants to see the typology of the Passover as not merely applying to Christ but to Eucharistic practices as well. For example, as mentioned above, Leithart argues that the 'Old Testament is typological not of Jesus simply but of the *totus Christus*, the whole Christ, both head and body. Circumcision points not only to the "cutting of Jesus'" flesh on the cross but to the baptismal rite of passage; Passover points not merely to the cross but the Eucharist.' But in what way, one may ask? He goes on to ask, 'Does the New Testament justify this form of typology?'[97] The answer should now be clear: No, not in the manner Leithart suggests for the Lord's Supper.

In response, I say that the essence of Paul's allusion is the continuities with the old covenant, even though the *new* elements would transcend the old. But notice the discontinuities as well!

altar?' Participation is the point. In other words, it is not just Passover alone that the apostle points to, but he says that Israel in the flesh (i.e., the Jews as a nation) were participating in the whole sacrificial system when they ate the sacrifices. Consequently, Christ having come, has now done away with the whole sacrificial system. Participating in the new cup of blessing becomes communion in the blood of Christ and the bread that we break becomes communion of the body of Christ (spiritually speaking, not in the Lutheran or Roman Catholic manner from which we should demur). In short, Christ is the fulfillment of the whole sacrificial system. See Hodge, *First Epistle to the Corinthians*, 185-91.

95. Hodge, *First Epistle to the Corinthians*, 87.

96. Hodge, *First Epistle to the Corinthians*, 87.

97. Leithart, 'Sacramental Hermeneutics,' 112-13.

Stonehouse said it well in his discussion of the longer textual version in Luke 22:19:

> Luke, in common with the other New Testament records which report the institution of the Lord's Supper, reports the teaching of Jesus that through the sacrifice of His body and the shedding of His blood there would be inaugurated a divine covenant transcending the covenant of Sinai, which was also ratified by a sacrifice in which blood was shed.[98]

We are now ready to ask what the preceding treatment teaches us.

Conclusion

The Westminster Larger Catechism, in response to the question, *Wherein do the sacraments of baptism and the Lord's Supper differ?* (Q & A, 177) clearly identifies that baptism is 'even to infants' whereas the Lord's Supper is 'only to such as are of years and ability to examine themselves'. Some scholars, such as Leithart, imply that the Westminster Divines were incorrect and that we should reform our practice based on further hermeneutical reflection on the Bible and its exegesis.[99] With regards to those notions that are currently afoot in some churches and popular among some authors, we may say what Geerhardus Vos said years ago in another context: 'Having now the proposed exegesis before us, we perceive at a glance that it seems to commend itself by that most popular of credentials, surface simplicity. But, as is frequently the case, the difficulties lie beneath the surface.'[100]

After considering some of the scholarly discussion about the relationship between Passover and the Lord's Supper, I then described Leithart's argument, which I considered as a faulty

---

98. Ned B. Stonehouse, *The Witness of the Synoptic Gospels to Christ: One Volume combining The Witness of Matthew and Mark to Christ and The Witness of Luke to Christ* (Grand Rapids, MI: Baker, 1979), 138.

99. Although Leithart's article, 'Sacramental Hermeneutics,' was cited most frequently in this article, his hermeneutical principles are set forth in greater detail in *Priesthood of the Plebs*, 1-47. His concern for what he calls 'practical Marcionism' and 'Marcionite Sacramentology' (i.e., a diminishing of Old Testament influence in Sacramental theology) is evident throughout. For his logic applied to the Lord's Supper and paedocommunion, see 142-54.

100. Geerhardus Vos, *The Pauline Eschatology* (Phillipsburg, New Jersey: Presbyterian and Reformed Publishing Co., 1986), 238.

method based upon a kind of illegitimate totality transfer at the hermeneutical level. Next, I argued that there is a connection between the Lord's Supper and Passover, but the Lord's Supper of the new covenant as instituted by our Lord Jesus is not to be understood merely as a Passover meal nor are the Passover regulations and practices to govern the new covenant ordinance. Even so, since the Passover provided the occasion for the institution of the Lord's Supper, understanding the custom of the Passover can help us understand the Lord's Supper, especially the allusions associated with the former feast and its practice. Next, I discussed the two dominant motifs of the Lord's Supper and tried to mediate much of the helpful exegesis of H. Ridderbos' fine treatment of the Supper in light of the Passover, giving time to similarities and differences and especially discussing the *newness* stressed in the institution of the Lord's Supper. Finally, this chapter spent time discussing the nature of allusions and metaphors so that the reader could make some sense of the important biblical references to Christ as our Passover lamb that takes away sin.

If the above explanations are true, then the question of whether children were present or participated in religious meals that the Hebrew Scriptures describe and whether that was important for regulations practiced in the New Covenant meal of the Lord's Supper are really moot points. The Passover is not to be identified with the Lord's Supper in some facile manner even though it was the occasion on which the Lord's Supper was instituted. The Passover was a meal of covenant communion. So too is the Lord's Supper. But one may not determine the age level of participants within the framework of simplistic exegesis.

Aside from considerations of the source and cause of these recent errors, what may be said in the meantime with respect to covenant youth in the church that are not yet 'of years and ability to examine themselves'? We may tell them and teach them, and moreover, they may proclaim with utter confidence, 'I'm a member too, I'm just not a drinking member yet.'

2

Christ Our Passover

Iain M. Duguid

The exact relationship between the Lord's Supper and Passover is of importance to the question of who may rightly participate in the sacrament. In what ways is the Lord's Supper a new covenant re-enactment of the old covenant Passover, and in what ways is it something entirely new? On the face of it, the connection between Lord's Supper and Passover is obvious: both are meals in which the covenant community gathers to celebrate its deliverance through a miraculous intervention of God on their behalf. Yet there are also differences between them: Passover was an annual event, in which the central feature was the slaughter of a lamb, while the Lord's Supper is generally celebrated more frequently and involves the use of bread and wine.[1] In this chapter, we shall seek to trace out the continuities and discontinuities between the Old Testament feast and its New Testament fulfillment and to consider how precisely the Old Testament Passover points us forward to the

---

1. In his book, *Daddy, May I Take Communion? Paedocommunion vs. the Bible* (p.p., 1988), Leonard Coppes highlights a number of significant differences between Passover and Lord's Supper, which leads him to the conclusion that Passover is merely one among many antecedents of the Lord's Supper. As we shall see, this probably overstates the discontinuity between them.

coming of Christ and directs our practice in celebrating the Lord's Supper today.

Background: The Old Testament Feast

The Passover was the first of the three great annual festivals in the Old Testament, occurring at the time of the barley harvest in early spring; it was followed about seven weeks later by the Feast of Weeks or Pentecost at the time of the wheat harvest, while the Festival of Ingathering or Tabernacles took place along with the fruit and olive harvest in the early fall. All three festivals have parallels in Canaanite religion (not surprisingly, since the agricultural processes of development were common to both ancient Near Eastern cultures). Yet in the Bible each festival is assigned a redemptive-historical motivation, tying these general celebrations of God's providence together to his great acts in redemptive history.

In this regard, it is notable that the calendar in use in Israel is different from the Canaanite version, which began and ended in the fall, with the Festival of Ingathering.[2] Israel's calendar began with the month of Abib in the spring, as a memorial of God's great work of salvation in the Passover (Exod. 12:2). Thus at the outset, a redemptive-historical view of the world was imposed on the festival year simply by starting the year with the celebration of God's great work of redemption in the exodus. The Feast of Weeks came to be associated with the giving of the Law on Mount Sinai,[3] which took place three months after the exodus from Egypt, and the Feast of Tabernacles looked forward to the time when Israel would enter the Promised Land. This redemptive historical ordering of the annual calendar immediately suggests comparison with the fundamental structure of the week, which in the Old Testament period ends in the Sabbath, looking forward to the rest that is not yet accomplished. After the resurrection, the Sabbath moves to the first day of the week, to mark the accomplishment of our rest in God's great work of redemption in Christ.

---

2. As is clear from the Gezer Calendar, which dates from around 1000 BC.

3. This connection was certainly being made by the time of the New Testament, though whether it had this association already during the Old Testament period is less clear.

The Passover was strictly speaking a double festival, the Feast of Passover followed immediately by the Feast of Unleavened Bread. There is a redemptive-historical logic to the connection of the two festivals, for the historical Passover-Exodus event was followed by the provision of bread from heaven, the manna in the wilderness. This connection also underlies John 6, where Jesus, having announced himself as the true bread of heaven, the fulfillment of the old covenant manna, invites his hearers to 'eat the flesh of the Son of Man and drink his blood' (John 6:53). Given the programmatic statement at the outset of the feeding of the five thousand that 'the Jewish Passover feast was near' (John 6:4), Jesus is clearly evoking the imagery of the Passover lamb and adapting it in a way that foreshadows the Lord's Supper as its new covenant antitype.[4]

The Passover took place on the full moon of the first month of the year. On the tenth day of the month, each family was to select a one-year old male lamb or goat, without defect (Exod. 12:5). They were to take care of it until twilight on the 14th, when they were to slaughter it, daubing some of the blood on the doorpost and lintels of the doorway. That same night they were to consume the meat, along with unleavened bread and bitter herbs – all of it was to be eaten, with none left until morning. None of the sacrificial animal's bones were to be broken (Num. 9:12). The family unit, along with neighbors if necessary, were to eat it dressed for travel, as if packed up and ready to go on a trip. Then, for the next seven days they were to eat only unleavened bread, observing the first and seventh as days of rest and sacred assembly (Exod. 12:1-20). Deuteronomy, looking forward to the time when the Israelites would be settled and dispersed throughout the land, adds the requirement that this festival should no longer be celebrated at home but as a national festival in the 'place of God's choosing' (Deut. 16:5-7). It was thus one of the three times a year when all adult male Israelites were required to present themselves before their covenant overlord at the central sanctuary.

---

4. C. John Collins rather surprisingly brackets this passage out of his discussion completely, saying 'It remains to be seen whether and how it applies to the Eucharist' ('The Eucharist as Christian Sacrifice: How Patristic Authors Can Help Us Read the Bible,' *WTJ* 66 [2004], 2 n.3).

The Chronicler records such celebrations of the Passover under Hezekiah (2 Chr. 30) and Josiah (2 Chr. 35), though prior to Hezekiah's reign the practice of national assembly seems to have been in abeyance (2 Chr. 30:5).

The meaning of the Passover and Feast of Unleavened Bread is explained in the Old Testament in terms of Israel's historical deliverance from Egypt. In response to the natural questions, the Israelite parents were supposed to instruct their children that 'this is the Passover sacrifice to the Lord, who passed over the houses of the Israelites in Egypt and spared our homes when he struck down the Egyptians' (Exod. 12:27). It was not simply a memorial sign of that event, in the way that Joshua's pillar of stones was to be a memorial of crossing the River Jordan (Josh. 4:6), though it contained that memorial aspect as an element. Nor was the feast simply an acted out drama, the gospel made visible and tangible. Rather, it was a sacrament in the full sense of the word, conveying the blessing that it depicted. Each time the Passover was celebrated, the participants joined together in a sacred meal before the Lord. In it, through the death of the sacrificial lamb, the participants experienced renewed fellowship with God, who protected them from his own judgment curse that fell on their enemies and promised them a glorious inheritance. They reminded themselves that they were strangers and aliens in this world, living between deliverance and consummation. Passover was also a community-defining event, for those who failed to 'keep the Passover' and were found eating bread with yeast during the seven days of the festival were required to be cut off from the covenant community (Exod. 12:15). Even those who were unable to partake for the reason of ceremonial uncleanness were in danger of being cut off, which provided the rationale for the 'second-chance' Passover, introduced in Numbers 9. This practice allowed those with valid grounds for missing the Passover, such as having come into contact with a dead body or being on a journey, to celebrate the Passover in the second month rather than the first.

The passage in Exodus also specifically links the Passover with the tenth plague in Egypt, the death of the firstborn. Every firstborn in Egypt, man or beast, from the highest to the lowest, was slain by the Lord in the tenth plague. Israel's firstborn, however, were protected as long as they remained under the blood of the sacrifice. This safety lay not in any magic quality inherent in the blood, but specifically in the divine response to the sign of the blood: it is not the blood itself that prevented the destroying angel from entering into the homes of the Israelites, but the Lord (Exod. 12:23). In view of this protection, every firstborn male in Israel was to be dedicated to the Lord (Exod. 13:2). In the case of animals, the firstborn males were to be sacrificed if they were clean animals or killed if they were unclean, while in the case of sons, they were to be redeemed (Exod. 13:15). The first generation of firstborn Israelite sons were not simply redeemed with money, however. The Levites as a tribe became their substitutes, taking their place in the service of God (Num. 3:12).

The centralization of the Festival at the national sanctuary, envisaged in Deuteronomy 16 and carried out during the period of the monarchy (2 Chr. 30 and 35), necessitated some changes in the Passover ritual. Since many of the people were now a long way from their homes, the blood could no longer be applied to the doorposts; instead it was apparently sprinkled on the altar, as it was for other sacrifices.[5] With the destruction of the Temple in 586 BC, further changes must have occurred in the ritual since there was now no holy place where the lambs could be slaughtered. It was perhaps at this stage that the cup was introduced into the Passover ritual; according to the Mishnah, the wine was mixed with hot water (*Pesachim* 7:13), which must have increased the symbolism of the liquid as representing the blood of the lamb. This was not part of the original ritual, but became part of the ceremony as it was observed by Jesus.

The Symbolism of the Feast

In all of this Old Testament ritual, there is a rich blend of symbolism pointing forward to the Lord Jesus, whom Paul calls

---

5. See 2 Chronicles 30:16, 35:11, though as other sacrifices were apparently being offered at the same time, it is not absolutely conclusive that the blood was that of the Passover sacrifices. However, in the absence of any other scheme for disposing of the blood, it would seem the natural thing to do.

'our Passover lamb' (1 Cor. 5:7). Jesus Christ is the one through whose blood, shed on the cross, peace is made between us and God, and we are reconciled to him (Col. 1:20). Jesus is the pure and righteous one, who substitutes his own holiness for that required from God's people, just as the Levites were required to be holy substitutes for the firstborn sons of that first Passover generation. He is 'the Firstborn over all creation' (Col. 1:15), the only begotten of God, the firstborn Son whom God did *not* redeem but instead gave up to death out of his great love for the world (John 3:16). That is why on the cross, Christ's legs were not broken, as were those of the two criminals crucified alongside him (John 19:33), so that the symbolism of the Passover lamb, with its unbroken limbs, could be fulfilled. As Passover lamb, Christ took the judgment curse of God in our place, while as substitute firstborn he fulfilled the law's righteous demands as the dedicated servant of God. Now we may boldly stand before God, sheltered by his blood, which is our only defense against the wrath of the destroying angel.

Foreshadowing the Lord's Table

There is little debate over whether the Passover points forward to Jesus' suffering and death in our place, however. The point at issue is whether the Passover specifically prefigures the Lord's Supper, in the same way that circumcision foreshadows baptism, or whether it is merely part of a much larger Old Testament background. C. John Collins, for example, insists that the proper background of the Lord's Supper is not to be found in the Passover but rather in the peace offerings (*shelamim*) of the Old Testament.[6]

Yet there are a number of particularly striking parallels between Passover and the Lord's Supper meal, which are not present in other peace offering meals. Seeing Jesus as our Passover lamb brings out more clearly the significance of Jesus' statement in the institution of the Lord's Supper: 'Take and eat; this is my body' (Matt. 26:26). In the normal peace offering meal, part of the animal was burnt on the altar while the participants feasted

---

6. C. John Collins, 'Eucharist as Christian Sacrifice.'

on the remaining body of the sacrifice, which could be an ox, a sheep or a goat. There was no particular focus on the death of the animal as an atonement in this sacrifice, or as a protection against the deity's wrath.[7] Indeed, since peace offerings could be made for a variety of reasons, the requirements for them were significantly diminished, including the possibility of offering animals that would not be acceptable for other sacrifices (Lev. 22:23). In the Passover, however, the object of feasting was specifically a perfect lamb, whose death protected them from the wrath of God as well as establishing communion amongst the family unit, and between them and God. In the Lord's Supper, Jesus invites his disciples to recognize him as the Passover lamb of the new covenant, the one whose death atoned for the sins of the covenant people of God and protected them from his wrath, establishing their communion with one another and with God.

Likewise, there is no particular place in the peace offering meals for the cup. Yet by the time of Jesus, the role of several cups of wine mixed with hot water, symbolizing the blood of the lamb was well-established. Thus when Jesus said, 'This cup is the new covenant in my blood' (1 Cor. 11:25), his disciples would have understood the connection to the blood of the Passover lamb symbolized by the wine at that meal. Yet by calling it the cup of the new covenant, Jesus also pointed them on to the new and definitive exodus that God was going to accomplish at the cross, where he would deliver his people from their bondage to sin and death. A central feature of the new covenant was the Lord's definitive action to give his people new hearts of love for God and obedience to his law so that their relationship with him might be a blessing, not a curse (Jer. 31:31-34). This new heart is something that Christ purchased for us through his death on the cross and which the Spirit creates in us through the means of grace, including the Lord's Supper.

Eating the bread and drinking the cup of the new covenant is also a defining ordinance for the new covenant community. As Jesus himself said, 'Truly, truly, I say to you, unless you eat the flesh of the Son of Man and drink his blood, you have

---

7. See J. Milgrom, *Leviticus 1-16* (AB: New York: Doubleday, 1991) 221-2.

no life in you. Whoever feeds on my flesh and drinks my blood has eternal life, and I will raise him up on the last day' (John 6:53-54). Here too, the Lord's Supper is more like the Passover than the other peace offering meals. Since those who participated were symbolically entering the community of those under the protection of the blood of the lamb, the Passover regulations regularly state that all of the participants must be circumcised (Exod. 12:44, 48; compare also the connection between circumcision and Passover in Joshua 5). Yet the same requirement of circumcision does not seem anywhere to be attached to partaking in the peace offerings.

Finally, there was no necessary emphasis on remembering in a peace offering meal. Certainly, if it were a peace offering for thanksgiving, there would likely be reflection on the event that occasioned the offering, but this is incidental rather than central to the peace offering. A freewill offering need not have any specific occasion or cause other than general thankfulness to the Lord. The Passover meal, on the other hand, was designed as an annually occurring pilgrimage, a regular reminder to look back and to look forwards. Every year, as they celebrated the Passover, they would look back on the exodus that God had accomplished when he brought them out of Egypt. Every year, as they ate unleavened bread for seven days, they were reminded of the demands of God's holiness and also of their wilderness wanderings and the manna that God provided for them there. In this way, every Passover celebration prodded them to recognize that this world was not their home and that they were still living a kind of wilderness existence. They were still looking forward to the fullness of what God had promised them.

So too, as Paul reminds us, whenever we eat this bread and drink this cup at the Lord's Supper, we look backwards and forwards: we look back and proclaim the Lord's death on the cross for our sins and we look forwards 'until he comes' (1 Cor. 11:26). Every Lord's Supper is thus both a reminder of God's past faithfulness to us in Christ and also a foreshadowing of the ultimate feast, the marriage supper of the Lamb. In the meantime, as pilgrims living out of a suitcase on a journey, it is perhaps fitting that our present 'feast' consists of a mere scrap of bread and sip of wine. It is the hors d'oeuvre, not the main course; it is a foretaste of the fellowship that lies in front of us, not the banquet itself. This is a feast that we leave hungry, longing for the fullness of the final banquet that still lies ahead of us.

Continuity and Discontinuity: The Lord's Table and Passover

It seems certain, then, that the Passover meal forms the type under the Old Testament scheme that most strongly foreshadows the Lord's Supper. Yet the differences are also striking. Few modern Christians view the Lord's Supper as an annual festival that requires a pilgrimage to a special location,[8] nor do we dress as pilgrims and eat the same Passover foods. Learning lessons from the Old Testament for our contemporary worship practices is always challenging because it requires refracting the original practices through the lens of fulfillment in Christ. The result will rarely be a 'proof text' that definitively establishes one position or outlaws another, and yet there are still indicators that may and should guide our actions. As Jeremiah Burroughs, one of the framers of the Westminster Confession, put it:

> In matters of worship we must have warrant from the Word, but it does not follow that we must have a direct, expressed warrant in everything. As it is many times in some kind of picture, the great art is in the cast of the looks. You cannot say it's in the drawing of this line or the other line, but altogether. It is the cast of the looks that causes the beauty of the picture. So in the Scripture you cannot say that this one line or the other line proves it, but let them all be laid together and there will be a kind of aspect of God's mind. We may see that this is the mind of God rather than the other and we are bound to go that way.[9]

What are the practical implications of these biblical-theological connections between Passover and Lord's Supper?

---

8. Historically, the pattern of communion in Scotland came close to this, with annual celebrations in each parish. In practice, however, many people could have communed more than once a year by attending communion seasons in neighboring parishes.

9. *Gospel Worship* (Ligonier, PA: Soli Deo Gloria, 1990 reprint of 1648 edition), 23.

First, now that the final Passover lamb has been slain at the cross, the figure under which the communion is celebrated shifts from an unblemished lamb to the associated image of unleavened bread. Almost all of the Old Testament sacrifices were required to be leaven-free, for leaven symbolizes change and decay.[10] In contrast, the image of unleavened bread symbolizes the purity that must be ours as Christians, the sanctification which must accompany our justification. Thus Paul, having called Christ 'our Passover lamb', goes on to say, 'Therefore let us keep the Festival, not with the old yeast, the yeast of malice and wickedness, but with bread without yeast, the bread of sincerity and truth' (1 Cor. 5:8). Using unleavened bread is a means to remind us that participating in the Lord's Supper entails not simply a matter of remembering Christ's death in our place. It is also a commitment on our part to a life of renewed holiness and purity, as individuals and as a community. As the *Westminster Confession of Faith* puts it, for believers the Lord's Supper is, among other things, 'their further engagement in and to all duties that they owe unto him' (29.1). It is interesting that this discussion of 'keeping the feast purely' with unleavened bread occurs in the context of a case that required church discipline. The Corinthians are instructed not even to eat with a man who does not maintain appropriate holiness of lifestyle (1 Cor. 5:11), which clearly precludes his attendance at the Lord's Supper. The application of cleansing of the leaven of sin from the community in terms of participation in the Lord's Supper provides a further link between Passover and Lord's Supper, and anticipates Paul's later discussion of worthy participation in the Lord's Supper at 1 Corinthians 11.

Second, there is the question of the frequency with which we should celebrate the Lord's Supper. Since the Passover was an annual celebration, should the Lord's Supper be likewise infrequent? Historically, that has been the practice in some Reformed churches, especially in Scotland. It has sometimes been argued that this approach ensured the special solemnity of the event, and certainly it was a very special occasion. However, the same people would not argue that prayer, or worship, or

---

10. Milgrom, *Leviticus 1-16*, 188-9.

preaching, should be made equally special by only doing them once a year.[11] The Lord's injunction is to do this *whenever you eat this bread and drink this cup*, which seems to imply something more frequent than once a year, and thus a way in which the Lord's Supper is distinctly different from Passover. The early church's practice of breaking bread together at least weekly would tend to suggest that the Lord's Supper should be much more frequently celebrated, which is also the historic Reformed position. For example, the *Directory of Public Worship* of the Westminster Assembly says:

> The Communion, or Supper of the Lord, is frequently to be celebrated; but how often, may be considered and determined by the ministers, and other church-governors of each congregation, as they shall find most convenient for the comfort and edification of the people committed to their charge.

If the Lord's Supper is for our comfort and edification, the question is 'How often do we need to be comforted and edified?' Once a year or more frequently? In the same vein, the Westminster Larger Catechism 177 asserts:

> Q. Wherein do the sacraments of baptism and the Lord's Supper differ?
> A. The sacraments of Baptism and the Lord's Supper differ, in that Baptism is to be administered but once, with water, to be a sign and seal of our regeneration and ingrafting into Christ, and that even to infants; whereas the Lord's Supper is to be administered *often*, in the elements of bread and wine, to represent and exhibit Christ as spiritual nourishment to the soul, and to confirm our continuance and growth in him, and that only to such as are of years and ability to examine themselves (emphasis added).

Here there is a clear urging and encouragement towards having the Lord's Supper frequently, a desire that may have

---

11. Actually, outside internet discussion groups, it is very difficult to find anyone in the contemporary context who argues in favor of annual communion, so it is hard to represent fairly what such a view would assert.

been frustrated in actual historical practice at the time of the Reformation in Scotland by the shortage of ordained ministers to administer the sacrament.[12]

Third, there is the question of who may participate in the Lord's Supper: should the meal be open to baptized believers of whatever age or 'only to such as are of years and ability to examine themselves', as Westminster Larger Catechism 177 asserts? There has recently been a movement in favor of paedocommunion in some Reformed circles, often on the basis that since covenant children were admitted to the Passover meal, they should similarly be admitted to the Lord's Table, and that to do otherwise would be to 'excommunicate' our children.[13] In response to this movement, others have tried to drive a wedge between the Lord's Supper and the Passover as if they were really two entirely different meals, and the antecedents of the Lord's Supper lay elsewhere in the Old Testament.[14] Yet this is unnecessary, and misses the clear parallels between the two meals. In fact, there are continuities and discontinuities between the Lord's Supper and Passover that do not allow for simple equivalence between the two. Nonetheless, there are a number of aspects of correspondence between the Passover meal and the Lord's Supper that do not support the inclusion of infants and young children to the table.

Discerning the Body
In the first place, we should observe the fundamental differences that exist within the Old Testament between the rites of covenant

---

12. See W.D. Maxwell, *A History of Christian Worship: An Outline of its Development and Forms* (Grand Rapids: Eerdmans, 1982) 125. In 1567, there were only 289 ministers in the church in Scotland to serve around 1000 parishes; the remainder were normally attended by readers, who would not be permitted to administer the sacraments.

13. Peter Leithart, *Daddy, Why Was I Excommunicated? An Examination of Leonard J. Coppes' Daddy, May I Take Communion?* (Niceville, FL: Transfiguration Press, 1998). In my view, the title of the book is rather disingenuous, since any child who is theologically aware enough to ask and understand the answer to that question is probably ready to be examined by the elders for admission to the Lord's Table in any congregation.

14. Though it should be noted that not all advocates of paedocommunion see a strong link between Passover and Lord's Supper. C. John Collins locates the roots of the Lord's Supper in the peace offering, not in the Passover, yet still argues in favor of paedocommunion ('Eucharist as Christian Sacrifice,' 16-17).

initiation and covenant maintenance. In the Old Testament, the rite of covenant initiation is circumcision. The qualification for participation in that rite is either personal faith, in the case of converts from outside the community, or birth into a believing family on the part of a child. In the latter case, which is the primary situation in the Old Testament, it is clear that no comprehension is required of the human participant, since it was administered at the age of eight days. Paedobaptists like myself would argue that baptism functions similarly as a rite of covenant initiation within the New Testament: the faith of the covenant head of the family provides the grounds for marking the covenant child's admission into the community, without requiring personal faith in the child.

The Passover meal is different, however. At the Passover meal, everyone, even the most ardent supporters of paedocommunion, would agree that eight-day-old babies did not participate. So what is the qualification, then, for a member of the covenant community to partake in this meal of covenant maintenance? To put it crassly, is it the ability to chew and swallow solid food, or is it something else? The proponents of paedocommunion have rightly seen that the answer to this question doesn't just affect the admission of children to the Lord's Supper. On the other end of the age spectrum there is the analogous case of the person with Alzheimer's disease or other mental disorder. Should they be admitted to the Lord's Table or not? According to the paedocommunion view, as long as believers are physically able to process the elements, they must be encouraged to partake of the Lord's Supper.

What this approach misses is a crucial difference between the two sacraments within the Old Testament. The Passover was not a wordless sign, like circumcision. It was a sign that had explanation and comprehension built into its very structure. At the Passover meal, the children were expected to ask, 'What does this meal mean?' (Exod. 12:26), and then to receive an answer that they could presumably comprehend. In traditional Jewish Seders, it is the youngest child present who asks the four questions whose answers together explain how this night is different from all other nights.[15] There is thus a clear expectation of an ability to ask questions and to understand answers. They were to be told, 'It is the Passover sacrifice to the Lord, who passed over the houses of the Israelites in Egypt and spared our homes when he struck down the Egyptians' (Exod. 12:27). In other words, unlike circumcision, the Passover meal was recognized as a sacrament that worked through the understanding and not apart from it. It was clearly not a ritual that worked *ex opere operato* ('out of the power of the elements themselves'), but rather in conjunction with faith and understanding. We might even say that the Passover was received through discerning the significance of the body. Under the old covenant, children were not to be admitted to the Passover meal simply on the basis of the ability to swallow, but on the basis of the ability to ask and understand what the meal was about.

The same distinctions apply with even more force under the new covenant. We apply the covenant initiation sign of baptism to infants without regard to their comprehension of the sacrament. But according to 1 Corinthians 11, the Lord's Supper requires the additional element of discerning the body. In other words, there is some level of faith and comprehension required for the Lord's Supper to do its work effectively in our hearts. To be sure, we may discuss what level of faith and comprehension is required to participate. If no one under the age of sixty-five is going up to receive the elements, as has historically occasionally been the case in some reformed churches, there is something wrong with the picture. If others are asked why they are not partaking, and they respond, 'I'm not worthy; I'm not ready yet,' it suggests that the bar of admission is being set far too high. The Lord's Supper is for struggling sinners, not for perfected saints. In my church experience, we have admitted some nine-year-olds who partake on the basis of their profession of faith and their comprehension of the Lord's Supper. But on the other hand,

---

15. The four questions are these: 'Why is it that on all other nights during the year we eat either bread or matzo, but on this night we eat only matzo? Why is it that on all other nights we eat all kinds of herbs, but on this night we eat bitter herbs? Why is it that on all other nights we do not dip our herbs even once, but on this night we dip them twice? Why is it that on all other nights we sit straight or leaning, but on this night we are all seated leaning?'

my four-year-old niece who exclaimed as the elements went past her, 'Mommy, I'm hungry too, you know,' was not ready to be admitted to the Lord's Table. She was not able to discern the body and so for her, partaking of the elements would not have been the Lord's Supper; it would merely have been eating a snack.

What may we say, though, about the case of a person with Alzheimer's disease? Again, it is necessary to ask, 'How does the Lord's Supper work?' If it works *ex opere operato*, as in Roman Catholic teaching, no comprehension is required. All that is required is the ability to consume the elements. To take that view to the logical extreme, if some crumbs fell on the floor and a mouse ate them, we would have to acknowledge that the mouse had participated in the Lord's Supper.[16] But if the Lord's Supper requires faith and discernment in order for it to be the Lord's Supper and not something else, then I think it is appropriate for a church pastorally to inquire how a person is partaking. We may acknowledge that it is a sensitive pastoral issue that in individual cases may not be easy to resolve. Memory loss is a complex matter, and people with Alzheimer's disease and other mental disorders may sometimes remember and recognize old things when new things are not registered or understood. Sometimes people can remember the Scriptures and old hymns, even when they cannot remember their spouse's name or what they had for lunch. Rituals that have deep tracks in their memories still resonate long after other things have gone. That observation suggests that in some cases the Lord's Supper may genuinely communicate the gospel to people to whom preaching can no longer minister as effectively.

Yet if there is truly no comprehension of the significance of the elements at all, how is the person to be blessed in their partaking? The Lord's Supper is not magic: it works when combined with an active faith, which requires those partaking

---

16. This is not merely a hyperbolic statement. Such a concern over what we might call 'rodent communion' emerges already by the end of the second century in the writings of Hippolytus of Rome, who writes: 'All shall be careful so that no unbeliever tastes of the Eucharist, nor a mouse or other animal, nor that any of it falls and is lost. For it is the Body of Christ, to be eaten by those who believe, and not to be scorned' (*The Apostolic Tradition*, 32:2-4).

to be able to exercise that active faith. To be sure, balance is needed here. We don't want to emphasize the role of our active faith so much that we make our subjective response to the Lord's Supper the decisive element that makes it effective. We need to remember that there is an objective side of the Lord's Supper: God is actively at work through the sacraments as well. Yet there is something about the Lord's Supper that makes it possible to be physically partaking of the elements and nonetheless missing the spiritual reality, a sin for which Paul rebukes the Corinthians. These believers failed to receive the reality of the sacrament because, like their forefathers in the wilderness (1 Cor. 10:1-12), they didn't combine their eating with faith. This possibility of eating yet not partaking because of a failure to discern the true meaning of the sacrament makes the Lord's Supper strikingly different from baptism.

Conclusion

To conclude, then, we may say that the Lord's Supper is built on the Passover paradigm, yet it is not the same as it. Like the Passover, the Lord's Supper is a meal that reflects the limits of the visible covenant community as it invites us to renew our identification with Christ in his death and resurrection that was made at our baptism. It is a serious call to celebrate God's grace to us in the cross and live lives in line with the gospel we have received. It is not therefore something lightly to be received: indeed, Paul warns that some have become sick and even died in consequence of their failure to discern the true meaning of the feast (1 Cor. 11:30). The invitation to the Lord's Supper calls those who were once outsiders to the covenant community to come to Christ by grace alone, through faith alone, and taste ahead of time the glorious inheritance that is ours in Christ. Yet though the grace it offers is free, it is never cheap. It is grace that was paid for at a dear price, the price of the blood of the true Passover Lamb, the Son of God, shed for us on the cross. May we rightly value that sacrifice and the inheritance that it purchased for us as we partake of the Lord's Supper personally and as we administer it also to others.

3

'1 Corinthians 11:17-34: The Lord's Supper: Abuses, Words of Institution and Warnings[1] and the Inferences and Deductions with respect to Paedocommunion'

George W. Knight III

Introduction

1 Corinthians 11:17-34 is an important section in the letter to the Corinthians and therefore also an important section in the life and teaching of Presbyterian churches that adhere to the Westminster Standards and in their Books of Church Order, as well as that of other Reformed Churches.[2] The Confessional Standards refer to these verses more than fifty times and especially to the warning verses over twenty times.[3] It, therefore, demands our most careful attention.

This passage also merits our particular attention because it is the source for the warnings that are utilized by the Directory for Worship for warning people of their need to

---

1. This article appeared in its original form as a chapter in *The Auburn Avenue Theology, Pros and Cons: Debating the Federal Vision* edited by E. Calvin Beisner (Fort Lauderdale, FL: Knox Theological Seminary, 2004). It is utilized here in a reworked and revised form.

2. Compare, for example, the *Belgic Confession*, Article 35, the *Second Helvetic Confession*, XXI, esp. sections 9 and 11, and the *Heidelberg Catechism*, Q. and A. 81.

3. See page 44 of the *Scripture Index to the Westminster Standards* by Stephen Pribble (Dallas: Presbyterian Heritage Publications, 1994). Not included (because they are not part of the Westminster Standards) are equally relevant pages from the OPC and PCA Directories of Worship.

examine themselves and discern the Lord's body. The use of this passage to warn in this general way, and particularly with the understanding that young children are excluded by this warning, has been opposed by those who favor admitting covenant children to the Lord's Supper (because they are considered full members of the church because of their baptism and without requiring them to make a profession of faith before the elders), often referred to as the paedocommunion position.[4] Many of these see the opening section of 1 Corinthians 11, verses 17-22, and those mentioned in it, as the controlling factor in understanding Paul's warnings in verses 27-29. Thus they see the warnings only for those who have sinned like, or as grievously as, those mentioned in verses 21 and 22. Most commentators see the controlling element for understanding the warnings in verses 27-29 to be Paul's relating the account about the Lord's Supper in verses 23-26, and his drawing his remarks and warnings from the significance of that supper (note his introductory 'therefore' in verse 27). It is this view that is followed in the Westminster Standards and also in the Directory for Worship for the Orthodox Presbyterian Church and the one for the Presbyterian Church in America.

The account that follows will open up this and other matters in their context.

Outline

For us to understand well the teaching of 1 Corinthians 11:17-34, we need not only to outline the account, note the change in the persons addressed, but also to go through it in a careful way. The account divides itself into four parts. They are as follows:

1. Verses 17-22: The statement of the problem: some are eating their own supper and not sharing with others with the result that those others are hungry, and the Lord's Supper is not observed.

---

4. *Feed My Lambs, Why the Lord's Table Should Be Restored to Covenant Children* by Tim Gallant (Grande Prairie, Canada: Pactum Reformanda Publishing, 2002) is a representative of this view.

2. Verses 23-26: The Apostle Paul reiterates the words of institution with their emphasis on 'in remembrance of me'[5] (v. 25) and 'you proclaim the Lord's death until he comes' (v. 26), as the basis for his response to these and all other mishandlings of the Lord's Supper.

3. Verses 27-32: This section, with its introductory 'therefore' (v. 27), is drawn from verses 23-26, and states that one must 'examine himself' (v. 28) and 'discern the body' (of the Lord) as one eats, or one is in danger of eating and drinking 'judgment on himself' (v. 29). Thus it is based on the significance or intention of the Supper given in the prior section.

4. Verses 33-34: With its introductory 'then', these verses now return to verses 17-22 and give Paul's explicit instruction for overcoming the problem mentioned in verses 17-22. They are 'to wait for one another' 'when they come together to eat' (v. 33).[6] This is the section which most particularly returns to the original problem found in verses 17-22.

Persons in View

The previous four-fold outline is also undergirded by a change in the person(s) and number(s) of the people in view in each section.

1. Verses 17-22: This section uses primarily the second person plural 'you' (vv. 17-20 and 22), interspersed with Paul's own first person singular 'I' (vv. 17-18 and 22 at the end), and a third person singular (v. 21). In this first section Paul is interacting with their abuses that he has mentioned.

2. Verses 23-26: Paul reports Jesus instituting the Supper with Jesus' own third person singular 'he' throughout (vv. 23-26). This restating of the account shows that it was originally given to the 'you' who were present with Jesus,

---

5. The translation quoted is that of the English Standard Version (ESV). When other translations are quoted, or my rendering is utilized, this will be noted.

6. I am partially indebted to G. D. Fee, in his commentary on *The First Epistle to the Corinthians*, The New International Commentary on the New Testament (Grand Rapids: Eerdmans Publishing Company, 1987), 532, for this outline, which has, however, been revised.

and now, since it is being retold to the Corinthians, to them as well (cf. v. 23: 'For I received from the Lord what I also delivered to you...') and also to those who read and heed, including ourselves and his church 'until he comes' (vv. 23-26, the quote from v. 26). Paul introduces the account with his 'I' (v. 23).

3. Verses 27-32: Paul applies the account of the words of the Lord's Supper and their meanings and significances. Here we find two steps on his part.
    (a) Paul begins by giving his warning in general terms to all, who did then or do now, read or hear his account (vv. 27-29). This is evidenced by his expressing himself in such a way that his warnings apply to all, that is, with such constructions that are rendered in English as, 'whoever' (v. 27), 'a person' (v. 28), 'anyone' (part of a participial construction, v. 29) that apply to any and every one[7], and with verb forms in the third person singular throughout verses 27-29 directing his comment to each one (he or she that reads), with the first one being in the future tense (v. 27, 'will be guilty'), and specifying 'himself' (v. 29, referring back to the 'anyone' that begins v. 29) to make certain that the individual realizes that he or she is to heed this warning. (It is also for these reason that these words of warning have been utilized by Presbyterian and Reformed Churches in the warnings that ministers are called on to give to everyone at every serving of the Lord's Supper.)
    (b) Paul writes this section (vs. 30-32) to the Corinthians in particular with the second person plural 'you' (v. 30), now understood to refer back to the original 'you' in verses 17ff., and with his transitional words 'that is why...', as well as the specific words 'many of you...' and 'some [of you, understood]...', which 'you[s]' are then changed into a 'we' in which he then includes himself with them (vv. 31-32).

4. Verses 33-34: in these verses Paul applies this teaching even more particularly to those who have committed the abuses

---

7. The NASB renders these constructions with 'whoever' (v. 27), 'a man' (v. 28) and 'he' (v. 29), also NKJV (likewise KJV except 'whosoever' for 'whoever', and NIV also except 'anyone' for 'he in verse 29).

in verses 17-22. The language here is primarily second person plural 'you' (vv. 33-34), made even more specific by a third person 'anyone' and 'him' (v. 34). The whole section closes with Paul saying that he will give further directions when he comes, using the first person singular 'I' (v. 34).

Abuses at the Lord's Supper (vv. 17-22)

This first section is devoted to Paul's bringing the abuses to their attention. He begins the section by saying immediately that he is not commending them in the following instructions (v. 17, as he had in v. 2, and he comes back to this lack of commendation in v. 22), because with reference to the Lord's Supper they are not following what he had taught but rather 'when you come together it is not for the better but for the worse' (for further comments on this statement see the end of the discussion of this section).

The significance of this 'worse' 'not for the better' is given in verse 18, namely, that in their coming together there are 'divisions'. He adds the interesting caveat 'and I believe it in part'. This is an oral report that he has heard. His caveat indicates that he is still inclined to believe what he has heard, even if only some of it may be true.

His referring to 'divisions' with the same Greek word as found in 1:10,[8] may make us think that Paul is saying that the abuses of the Lord's Supper are caused by that same party spirit that is dealt with in the first chapters. However, it is doubtful that this is true for several reasons: (1) the former divisions were further defined as 'quarrels' and 'jealousy' (1:11; 3:3-4), which is missing from this section, and here the divisions are along sociological lines (vv. 21-22; 33-34); (2) 1:12 mentions four names, here there are only two groups, and there is no anti-Pauline quarrel as there was in the first chapters; (3) the divisions are related here to their coming together (v. 18), not to false allegiances to their leaders (cf. 1:11-12); (4) 'I believe it

---

8. The Greek word *schisma* is used by Paul in 1 Corinthians 1:10; 12:25 and here. The word is used elsewhere in the New Testament in Matthew 9:16 and Mark 2:21 and in John 7:43; 9:16; and 10:19.

in part' (v. 18) does not fit the situation described in 1:10–4:21, but it does fit this situation.[9]

Paul recognizes that the divisions are brought about by evil men (v. 18), but that they are used by God's good sovereignty and providence for a good end: 'for there must be factions among you in order that those who are genuine among you may be recognized' (v. 19).

In verses 20-22 Paul deals with why there are divisions when they come together to eat. He does so by using several phrases: (1) 'come together' (vv. 17, 18, 20); (2) 'eat' (vv. 20-22); and (3) 'divisions' or 'factions' 'among you' (vv. 18-19, cf. vv. 21, 22).[10]

Paul says categorically that they are not eating the Lord's Supper when they come together (v. 20). The reason for this absolute statement to them is given in the next verse, indicated by the introductory 'for': 'For in eating each one goes ahead with his own meal. One goes hungry, another gets drunk' (v. 21). Going ahead 'with his own meal' with its terrible consequences is not communing with the Lord and one another in his Supper. This is further explicated by a series of rhetorical questions in verse 22, the centerpiece of which is the question: 'Or do you despise the church of God and humiliate those who have nothing?'

Although this section began with Paul using the word 'you' in a general sense to address the entire congregation (see especially verse 18: 'you come together as a church,... there are divisions among you'), he gradually begins to use the 'you' to refer to those that he is charging with abuse. We are led to this conclusion from three facts in his discourse. First, those he is rebuking are distinguished from those who are hungry (v. 21), who are not being rebuked. Second, those who are being rebuked are the ones making the divisions and factions and they are distinguished from 'those who are genuine among you [who] may be recognized' (v. 19). Third, the questions asked are directed to the abusers who in verse 22 are distinguished from those they are humiliating because they 'have nothing'.

---

9. The overview of the argument is from Fee, *1 Corinthians*, 527, but changed considerably.

10. Again from Fee, *1 Corinthians*, 535, but presenting the material slightly differently.

Therefore, the statement of Paul in verse 17 that 'when you come together it is not for the better but for the worse' may be intended primarily for those abusing the Lord's Supper.

Verses 21 and 22 taken together give the essence of Paul's outrage at them. It is that those that have their own meals do not share it with those who have nothing ('goes ahead with his own meal,' v. 21). The outcome is that the 'have-nots' are 'hungry' and the 'haves' are sated to such a degree that Paul may even say that they get drunk. The theological outcome of this selfishness is that there is no shared Lord's Supper for them, and 'the church of God' is 'despise[d]' and those who 'have nothing' are 'humiliate[d]' (v. 22).

Paul concludes this section by writing, 'What shall I say to you? Shall I commend you in this? No, I will not' (v. 22). And by this he means the ones abusing the Lord's Supper.

The Words of Institution and Their Significance (vv. 23-26)

Since the abusers are not keeping the tradition which Jesus gave to Paul and which Paul gave to them, he feels constrained to repeat it in this section. And he draws their attention to this institution by his opening 'for' (v. 23). In giving the institution in Jesus' own words, he is confronting them with our Lord's own words and intentions. Paul will then draw upon these intentions in his general words of warning in verses 27-29, as is evidenced by the transitional word 'therefore' (v. 27).

The purpose of this chapter does not require a detailed consideration of these words which are so well-known and highly esteemed. It is, however, important to note that in the words of institution those partaking are charged by our Lord with a command to 'do this' (twice over, verses 24 and 25). This in and of itself makes a distinction between baptism and the Lord's Supper. In baptism, especially for infants, the recipient is passive with regard to the water applied to him and to the words said about him. Here the recipient is active, he (or she) takes the bread and wine and eats and drinks them. Also, whereas baptism is once given and received, the Lord's Supper is continually given and received. Baptism symbolizes God's regenerating work, and is not to be repeated, the Lord's Supper symbolizes God's sanctifying grace given to us to receive by faith, and thus faith is necessary for those receiving it, and it is therefore to be repeated. The Westminster writers drafted a statement in the Larger Catechism about these differences of the two rites, and accordingly, and appropriately, said of the Lord's Supper that it is to be given 'only to such as are of years and ability to examine themselves', because, as they stated it, 'the Lord's Supper is to be administered often..., to represent and exhibit Christ as spiritual nourishment to the soul, and to confirm continuance and growth in him...'[11] Only those united to Christ as evidenced by their fulfillment of that Apostolic injunction are qualified to take the Supper and thus only those may have the Lord's Supper administered to them.

The two intentions given in the words of institution, as well as the words of institution themselves, are referred back to with the 'therefore' beginning verse 27. Because these words are given not just for the Corinthian church but for every church and believer, what we learn from them applies to us and our church as well.

The first item is the statement by our Lord that the Supper is to be taken 'as often as you drink it,' 'in remembrance of me' (v. 25). This teaching of our Lord, as is demonstrated in the words 'as often as you drink it', must govern our every reception of the Lord's Supper as an act 'in remembrance of me'. Every receiving of the Supper must be a receiving of the Supper from Christ, and in so receiving it we must remember him in all his graciousness in laying down his life for us to satisfy God's justice (cf. Rom. 3:24-26). Just as they needed to be reminded to remember Christ, so must we, because these words are not just given by our Lord to the Corinthians, but in Paul and also in Luke they are the words of Christ to all who partake (cf. Luke 22:19, where it is stated after the bread,

---

11. *Larger Catechism* 177, 'The sacraments of baptism and the Lord's Supper differ, in that baptism is to be administered but once, with water, to be a sign and seal of our regeneration and ingrafting into Christ, and that even to infants, whereas the Lord's Supper is to be administered often, in the elements of bread and wine, to represent and exhibit Christ as spiritual nourishment to the soul, and to confirm continuance and growth in him, and that only to such as are of years and ability to examine themselves.'

'Do this in remembrance of me'). In this passage Paul restates the words of institution (given to every church and believer) so that it may be used in his warnings to all, as well as for this particular church's problem. We all need to acknowledge in our actions that we know what these words require of us. That is why Paul calls on each one to examine himself and also why he says that one must discern the body.

The second item is the words of verse 26: 'For as often as you eat this bread and drink the cup, you proclaim the Lord's death until he comes.' Here we have the reminder that remembering our Lord Jesus Christ in this Supper is also a proclamation of his death and that until he comes. The Greek word 'proclaim,' (*katangellō*), is used only in the New Testament by the Apostle Paul and in the Book of Acts.[12] It means generally to make known in public and thus here it is accurately translated 'proclaim'. The proclamation takes place when, or as often 'as you eat this bread and drink the cup.' The partaking of this remembrance of our Lord's death does itself ensure that his death is thereby proclaimed.

Since every partaking of the Lord's Supper is to be done in remembrance of him and particularly is a proclamation of his death, the Supper may not be partaken of in an unworthy manner.

The Application of the Intention of the Supper: First, in General, to 'Whoever' with the words of Warning (vv. 27-29) and, then, to the Corinthian Situation (vv. 30-32)

The Words of Warning – to 'Whoever' (vv. 27-29)
The first sentence in this section is very much taken up with what has been said in the preceding section. The Supper is in view with the words about eating the bread and drinking the cup and the guilt in view in doing so 'in an unworthy manner' is 'profaning the body and blood of the Lord' (v. 27).

---

12. The Greek word *katangellō* is found eleven times in the Book of Acts and seven times in Paul (1 Cor. 2:1; 9:14; 11:26; Rom. 1:8; Phil. 1:17, 18; and Col. 1:28). It means to make known in public, with implication of broad dissemination, and in the New Testament is usually rendered in English as 'proclaim' (as here) or 'announce'.

Not only the contents, but also the transitional word 'therefore,'[13] connects the contents of this verse with the words of institution and its intentions and thereby points to what follows as the consequence of that connection.

Furthermore, the relative pronoun 'who'[14] is combined with a particle 'ever'[15] so that it is properly translated 'whoever'. The meaning of this combination is given by the well-known Greek-English Lexicon (BDAG) in rather technical language (see footnote).[16] In summary form it may be said that the statement indicates that whenever this action is done in an unworthy manner by anyone, it will mean that that one will be guilty of the body and blood of the Lord.

The qualification 'in an unworthy manner' is the important element in this warning of the Apostle Paul. Here Paul uses an adverb to describe the activity (not the person's own inherent standing before God; for Paul's 'unworthy manner' is not speaking about the person but about his action or way of partaking) as a partaking by him in an 'unworthy' or 'careless'[17] manner, and thus the translation of this one word is rendered with the phrase 'in an unworthy manner'. The unworthy manner is explicated by Paul in verse 28 as requiring him to 'examine himself' and also in verse 29 as not 'discerning the body', that is, there are two dimensions to this unworthy manner of partaking, within oneself which demands examination, and concerning the body

---

13. The Greek word *hoste* introduces independent clauses and means 'for this reason, therefore, [or] so' according to W. Bauer, F. W. Danker, W. F. Arndt, and F. W. Gingrich, in *A Greek-English Lexicon of the New Testament and other Early Christian Literature*, 3rd ed. (Chicago: University of Chicago Press, 2000), 1107. Hereafter referred to as BDAG.

14. The Greek word *hos*.

15. The Greek word *an*.

16. The two Greek words *hos an* taken together with a subjunctive mood in the verb forms a relative clause that is virtually the protasis [the first part] of a conditional sentence. With the future tense of the verb in the apodosis [the second part], as here, it shows that the condition spoken of [in an unworthy manner] is thought of, as here, as resulting in a future guilt [i.e., he will be guilty of the body and blood of the Lord], BDAG, 56, sections I, (b) and *a*.

17. BDAG, 69. The Greek word is *anazios* and it occurs only here in the NT (except for a later, and variant, reading found in verse 29 in the Majority text, and therefore also in the new and old KJV. This variant is an understandable scribal addition for its inclusion makes clear the sense rightly understood).

which demands discernment.[18] If the person partakes in an unworthy manner he 'will be guilty of profaning',[19] in the sense of liable for, the body and blood as if he had committed the deed of death against that one, and thus must give an account of his actions. It is very clear that this guilt is seen with reference to the Lord's Supper and to what it represented, i.e., the giving of Christ's body and blood in his death.

There are those that would argue that the unworthy manner means only that kind of action of which the Corinthians have been found guilty in verses 17-22. They, in effect, want to restrict the application to them or at least to the kind of sins that they were guilty of and to nothing else but those. Calvin takes up this argument in his commentary on 1 Corinthians 11:27:

> Some restrict it to the Corinthians, and the abuse that had crept in among them, but I am of opinion that Paul here, according to his usual manner, passed on from the particular case to a general statement, or from one instance to an entire class. There was one fault that prevailed among the Corinthians. He takes occasion from this to speak of every kind of faulty administration or reception of the Lord's Supper.... To *eat unworthily*, then, is to pervert the pure and right *use* of it by our *abuse* of it. Hence there are various degrees of this *unworthiness*, so to speak; and some offend more grievously, others less so.

---

18. It is important to note that there are two dimensions to this unworthy manner of partaking, that which is within (to 'examine himself') and that which is outside of oneself ('discerning the body'), and not just one which is acquired by asserting that verse 29 explains what verse 28 means. On this misunderstanding, to 'examine himself' is said to mean that one must discern the body and no examination of oneself is required other than that. One can understand how this misunderstanding may arise because the two elements are tightly knit together with one another as is indicated by Paul's beginning verse 29 with 'for' (*gar*) (or, because). Thus the reason why one must examine himself is given in verse 29 in that he is partaking of that which represents the Lord's body. And, in so doing, he correlates these two distinct and interrelated matters to one another, but he does not thereby make them one and the same.

19. The translation of the ESV of the Greek word *enochos*. The NIV (& the NKJV) renders this by 'will be guilty of sinning against', and the NASB (& the KJV) renders the same section with the words 'shall be guilty of' (all without either 'sinning against' or 'profaning'); all renderings are followed by 'the body and (the, NASB) blood of the Lord'. BDAG (338 f.) renders this phrase of 1 Corinthians 11:27 with 'sin against the body and the blood'.

I think that Calvin's argument is a significant one[20] and even more so when it is connected with the general or generic tone of this section with its use of 'whoever' and the third person singular verb forms and also with the future tense verb ('will be guilty,' v. 27) which looks beyond the Corinthians' time frame to those in the future who also need to hear this warning lest they will be guilty too.

Paul's instructions move on to verse 28 which is introduced by a particle, which is appropriately translated by the ESV as 'then',[21] that is, this 'then' is the appropriate action demanded by the preceding requirement. This verse is very instructive. It reads 'Let a person[22] examine himself, then, and so eat of the bread and drink of the cup.' The instruction is very personal and very direct. It calls on each human being (every 'person') to engage in this examination of himself.[23] And it uses the verb *dokimazō*, which expresses that in the third person singular 'let him, i.e., a human being ("a person"), examine himself.' Each person individually is to look into his own being to determine if he or she is taking the Lord's Supper in a worthy manner, and not an unworthy manner.

Paul gives no specific guidelines for this action of examining oneself. The only guidance that we can ascertain is the meaning of the verb 'examine'.[24] BDAG indicate that the verb in this place, *dokimazō*, is used with the general meaning of 'to make a critical examination of someth[ing] to determine genuineness';

---

20. As do a number of renowned commentators. For a partial list see footnote 28.

21. The NASB utilizes 'but', and the NIV does not translate the Greek word *de*.

22. The word used by Paul is *anthropos*; it is a word that means here 'a human being' (or, as the ESV renders it, 'a person').

23. The Greek word is *heauton* which means that the one who is requested to do the examining is to do that with reference to his own self.

24. The Greek verb *dokimazō* is used twenty-two times in the New Testament: three times in Luke, seventeen times in Paul (Rom. 1:28; 2:18; 12:2; 14:22; 1 Cor. 3:13; 11:28; 16:3; 2 Cor. 8:8, 22; 13:5; Gal. 6:4; Eph. 5:10; Phil. 1:10; 1 Thess. 2:4 (2x); 5:21; 1 Tim. 3:10), once in 1 Peter 1:7; and once in 1 John 4:1. In 1 Corinthians it is used three times, and in 2 Corinthians it is used three times. BDAG put 1 Corinthians 11:28 and 2 Corinthians 13:5 together because in these two instances the verb is followed by the reflexive pronoun *heautou*. They list Galatians 6:4 next because there the reflexive pronoun is also used to qualify one's own works. The ESV translates Galatians 6:4 passage as follows: 'But let each one test his own work...'

thus they offer 'put to the test, examine'.[25] Paul uses the verb in 2 Corinthians 13:5 in the context where one's faith is examined ([our verb is rendered by 'test' not by 'examine' in this statement]): 'Examine yourselves, to see whether you are in the faith. Test yourselves. Or do you not realize this about yourselves, that Jesus Christ is in you? – unless indeed you fail to meet the test!') and in Galatians 6:4 where one's work is examined ('But let each one test his own work...; cf. 1 Corinthians 3:13). Thus both faith and work in oneself are subject to examination, as well as sin that may impinge upon either or both (cf. 1 Timothy 3:10: 'And let them also be tested first; then let them serve as deacons if they prove themselves blameless'). Whatever else one may say about this admonition to examine oneself ('himself'), it is certainly a looking into oneself to ascertain whether he is partaking in an unworthy manner, that is, in a manner that would make the person guilty of profaning the body and blood of the Lord. There are certainly more ways of doing that than were manifested in the Corinthian errors of 1 Corinthians 11:17-34, as are seen in 2 Corinthians 13:5, Galatians 6:4 and 1 Timothy 3:10, and Presbyterian and Reformed churches have sought to lay that out in various statements that instruct one as one is examining oneself.[26]

---

25. BDAG, 255.

26. Particular exception has been taken to the phrase found in the *Directory for Worship of the Orthodox Presbyterian Church* on page 148, i.e., 'and those who secretly and impenitently live in any sin' (which in the revised form is slightly changed into 'are living willfully and impenitently in any sin'). Several remarks can be made in response to this criticism. First, this is not the first or the only remark that is made in the fencing of the table, but rather the last. And in this last comment the authors are trying to follow our Lord in moving from external sins to internal sins, as our Lord does in the Sermon on the Mount as he unpacked and applies the teaching of the Ten Commandments. It is also stated with qualifying words that are significant, namely 'secretly', hid from others, and most importantly, 'impenitently', unwilling to repent of this, or any sin, in contrition to God. Secondly, the dire consequences of this way of stating the matter, as charged by the criticizers, are all removed by the words that are found in the next sentences, i.e., the 'Nevertheless' and all that is stated after this warning flag. Those words say that 'this warning is not designed to keep the humble and contrite from the table of the Lord' 'as if the supper were for those who might be free from sin'. The following sentence begins with 'On the contrary' and continues by saying that those who are invited to the table come 'as guilty and polluted sinners without hope of eternal life apart from the grace of God in Christ'. The last statement of the warning encourages us 'to the end that we may partake' of the table. It is my considered judgment that those who take the entire account into consideration should not be opposed to the statement as it is found in the context of the warning and as it should be considered in the

The examination is to be done with a view to taking the Supper. This is made evident in the text by the word 'so'[27] following the 'and' so that the two words taken together give us the usual, and meaningful, 'and so,' (or the 'so' may be rendered with 'therefore,' or 'for this reason'). An examination is called for, but it is to be followed, as the hoped for result, by the partaking ('and so eat of the bread and drink of the cup'). After examining oneself a person may 'thus' (or, 'so'), that is, after having done so, one is for that reason encouraged to eat and drink. The two verbs used for eating and drinking are in the imperative so that they underline the sense already gathered from the 'and so'. This perspective is caught in the NASB translation that properly renders the verbs 'let him eat ... and drink' in the rendering, 'But let a man examine himself, and so let him eat of the bread and drink of the cup.'

Before we delve into verse 29, we must note the differences between the King James Version of this verse (and the NKJV) and that of the more modern translations (such as NIV, NASB, ESV), or between the Byzantine or Majority Greek text and the older Greek text. The Majority Text (and thus the KJV) adds for clarification after the first reference to eating and drinking the understood word 'unworthily' and with the word 'body' the understood word 'Lord's' so that it reads 'for he that eateth and drinketh unworthily,... not discerning the Lord's body.' The older Greek texts do not include these understood words and so the translation following them reads without these words as follows: 'For anyone who eats and drinks without discerning the body eats and drinks judgment on himself.' We are utilizing this shorter text found in our translation because we believe that it more likely reflects Paul's writing since it is found in the oldest manuscripts. We can, however, understand why the words giving the appropriate clarifications to the verse may have been added by scribes copying the text.

---

context of the teaching of the Word of God. Cf. also the Q and A of the *Larger Catechism* 172 about one that doubts, especially 'of his due preparation', it is said in the final analysis that 'he may and ought to come to the Lord's supper, that he may be further strengthened.'

27. The Greek word *hoste* is used to introduce independent clauses with the meanings 'for this reason, therefore, or so' (cf. BDAG, 1107).

With the 'For'[28] that begins verse 29, Paul wants to indicate that in examining himself one must particularly be concerned about 'discerning the body'. The text reads 'For anyone who eats and drinks without discerning the body eats and drinks judgment[29] on himself.' Two important items are contained herein. The need for 'discerning the body' before one eats and drinks, and the solemn warning that a failure to do so will result in the chastisement of the Lord which is here designated 'judgment'.

This verse, just as the two that preceded it (vv. 27 and 28), is an application of the words of institution concerning 'whoever' reads these words of Scripture. Just as the words of Jesus speak of his body (v. 24), so the very first verse of this warning warns us not to be 'guilty of profaning the body and blood of the Lord' by partaking 'in an unworthy manner' of the bread and cup (v. 27). And right after Jesus spoke of his 'body', he also urged them to 'Do this in remembrance of me' (v. 24). Therefore our remembrance of him is to be done in the midst of partaking of that which signified his body, namely, the bread. That is why people will be guilty of profaning the body and blood of the Lord who take the bread or the cup in an unworthy manner (v. 27). Furthermore, the examination of oneself that is called for in verse 28 is to be done just because they are in the midst of

---

28. The Greek word *gar*.

29. The Greek term is the noun *krima* which is rendered in most modern translations as 'judgment' (e.g., NASB, NIV, ESV), but in the KJV as 'damnation' (NKJV has joined other translations by rendering the word as 'judgment'). Why has this change come about? Probably it was for two reasons. First, the other terms used in the context are from the same Greek root form, that is, they also have the basic form of *kri*. And these other expressions of the root are translated by the word 'judge' in the KJV and the modern translations (see verse 31 and the first part of verse 32: 'But if we *judged* ourselves truly, we would not be *judged*. But when we are *judged* by the Lord…'). It seemed right to the translators to carry through on this usage of Paul and translate with the same root form so that the reader might see and understand how Paul is expressing himself. Secondly, the translators probably thought that 'damnation', at least in our day, had become too strong a term to render the 'judgment' which they were experiencing, because verse 32 states, 'But when we are judged by the Lord, we are disciplined so that we may not be condemned along with the world,' that is, that God delivers them from the 'judgment' that they were experiencing when they were taking the Lord's Supper unworthily so that they would not be condemned (or, 'damned') along with the world. So that 'judgment' cannot appropriately be rendered 'damnation' or 'condemnation', even though it is grievous, for God has spared them from that 'condemnation' by even causing some to die (v. 30).

partaking of the Lord's Supper ('Let a person examine himself, then, and so eat …'). This is all involved in the fact that the Supper is a remembrance of the Lord Jesus and a proclamation of his death. So likewise in this verse 29. The body of our Lord Jesus that has been mentioned in verses 24 and 27 is surely the body in view in verse 29.[30]

Insight into the meaning of the word 'body' and into the significance of the phrase itself, 'discerning the body', is also to be sought in determining the meaning of the Greek word translated by 'discerning'.[31] The evidence of the Greek lexicon (BDAG) indicates that 'recognize' or 'discern' are the correct understandings in this context. We are to recognize that the body represented in the Lord's Supper is that of Jesus indeed and that the Lord's Supper is distinct and different from an ordinary meal. We will then escape the judgment warned in this verse, if we do not take the meal in an unworthy manner. We will therefore need to discern the body of our Lord signified by the elements in the Lord's Supper.

The 'judgment' referred to in this verse is an awesome word to be given in a warning, but fortunately it is not as awesome as one

---

30. Quite a number of commentators on 1 Corinthians understand the reference to the body in this sense at this place in the text (cf., e.g., C. K. Barrett, F. W. Grosheide, David Garland, Charles Hodge, Simon Kistemaker, Leon Morris, Archibald Robertson and Alfred Plummer, A. C. Thiselton, and Geoffrey Wilson). Gordon Fee is one of the exceptions among commentators. He takes it as referring to the body of Christians in Corinth and cites 1 Corinthians 10:17 as his warrant. It needs to be noticed that even there the preceding verse, which gives rise to verse 17, refers to 'the body of Christ'. But even if the reference in 10:17 might seem to give some warrant, it is too far removed. Furthermore, the reference back to the words of institution is that which is at hand and it is being utilized in this section which is building on it (cf. verses 24-26, esp. 'my body', and then 'the body and blood of the Lord' in verse 27, which is followed by 'the body' in verse 29). Barrett writes tersely and to the point: 'That **body** is not to be interpreted here as equivalent to *church* is shown by the addition of **blood**' (*First Epistle*, 273, has been drawn to my attention by Anthony C. Thiselton. *The First Epistle to the Corinthians*, NIGTC [Grand Rapids: Eerdmans, 2000], 890). Furthermore, Garland states about referring to the church as the body of Christ, 'as attractive as this view is, it is difficult to make it fit the basic meaning of the verb…' (David C. Garland, *1 Corinthians*, Baker Exegetical Commentary on the New Testament [Grand Rapids: Baker Academic, 2003], 552).

31. The Greek word in the text is a participle form from the verb *diakrinō*. This Greek verb means generally in this place, according to BDAG, 231, 'to evaluate by paying careful attention to', or specifically 'evaluate' or 'judge.' Thus more precisely in our verse 'recognize the body.' The Greek word occurs nineteen times in the New Testament, three times in the Gospels (Matthew and Mark), four times in Acts, seven times in Paul (Rom. 4:20; 14:23; 1 Cor. 4:7; 6:5; 11:29; 11:31; 14:29), three times in James and twice in Jude.

might take it to be.[32] Yes, it does result in the significant situation of many of them being weak and ill, and also of some having died (v. 30). That is indeed awesome. But the full meaning of this word is not grasped until one understands it in the light of the words of verses 30-32, especially verse 32. There we see that the judgment results in the chastening or disciplining of the Lord to keep us from being 'condemned along with the world'. And when put in this perspective we realize that the judgment evokes God's gracious action to keep us from that condemnation.

What Paul has been calling us, 'whoever' we may be, to do in these three general verses is to exercise that judgment on ourselves and with reference to the body so that we would not partake in an unworthy manner, with the result that we would not have to be judged by God (as verse 31 indicates, 'But if we judged ourselves truly, we would not be judged').

To the Corinthians (vv. 30-32)

With verses 30-32 Paul turns from his general and generic warning, based on the words of institution, and turns back again to the Corinthians and their particular abuses. He applies what he has just said in verses 27-29 to them in verses 30-32. First, in verse 30, he delineates his apostolic perspective on that which they have suffered with the words, 'That is why,' indicating why these things have happened to them (notice the second person plural ['you'] in this verse in distinction from the third person singular of verses 27-29).

He urges upon them the very judging or discerning in view in their self-examination ('but if we judged ourselves,' v. 31), and in their discerning of the body, so that they will not be judged by the Lord. But now in verse 31 and also verse 32 he includes himself with them and uses the first person plural ('we').

Then finally, in verse 32, he points out that being 'judged by the Lord' is done 'so that we may not be condemned along with the world'. This judgment, although very serious, is designed to keep them from the condemnation in view for the world of unbelievers.[33]

---

32. See also footnote 27.

33. This judgment is very gracious even as it is severe. It is brought about by the Lord himself (v. 32: 'But when we are judged by the Lord') on those who are misusing or abusing

Explicit Instructions to Overcome the Problem at Corinth (vv. 33-34)
Paul continues with the second person plural ('you') giving explicit instructions to those who needed it among the Corinthians so that they may overcome their problem which he had raised in verses 17-22. He harkens back, for the first time, to the specific abuses mentioned in verses 17-22, and does so with the same Greek word as found at the beginning of verse 27, but now translated as 'then', (*hoste*) (see footnote 13).

Paul does two things at once in verses 33 and 34. He designates them (i.e., the haves, or, the abusers), with the gracious phrase 'my brothers', and continues by saying that when they come together to eat they should 'wait for one another' (v. 33). The Lord's Supper is to be a communion of believers with the Lord and with each other. It needs to be taken and enjoyed together. And if someone says he is hungry, or even has brought his own meal (cf. v. 21), Paul says that if 'anyone' is hungry he should 'eat at home' (v. 34). Only by waiting for one another and not eating before one another can they avoid the judgment that will fall on them if they do not heed his warnings and admonitions ('so that when you come together it will not be for judgment,' v. 34).

Finally, Paul indicates that he will 'give directions when [he] come[s]' 'about the other things' (v. 34). What these other things are, when he gave this instruction and what it consisted of, we do not know because we have not been told. All that this verse teaches us is that he promised to give directions on these matters when he came.

Conclusion

What we do know is that he gave instructions to all those, 'whoever' they may be, who partake of the Lord's Supper,[34] as

the Lord's Supper ('... without discerning the body eats and drinks judgment on himself,' v. 29, followed by 'That is why ...' of verse 30 and the statements of judgment). Cf. the excellent treatment of the blessings and curses of the Lord's Supper by Herman Ridderbos in his *Paul: An Outline of His Theology* (Grand Rapids: Eerdmans, 1975), 425-28. His conclusion is excerpted as follows: '...blessing and curse are not automatically given with the elements nor are both joined to them in an equally essential way, but it is the living Lord himself who ... deals with the church according to his gracious and righteous redemptive will' (427).

34. Compare several noteworthy commentators, namely, Leon Morris on *The First Epistle of Paul to the Corinthians*, Tyndale New Testament Commentaries (London: Tyndale Press, reprinted 1964) at 163 in the first full paragraph under iii., and especially Simon Kistemaker on 1 Corinthians 11:28 in the following words: 'Is Paul counseling the Corinthians to conduct

well as returning to the several particular and explicit matters of which the Corinthians were themselves guilty. The matters that we need to heed as a general rule are contained in the three verses of 27-29. We are not to partake 'in an unworthy manner' and thus be 'guilty of profaning the body and blood of the Lord' (v. 27). We are 'then' (or, therefore) called to 'examine himself' (ourselves) so that we may indeed eat but not in an unworthy manner (v. 28). We are also called on to discern the body (of the Lord, understood) so that we will not be judged by God (v. 29). It is these matters that we are warned about in the 'fencing of the table'. These words of warning (and invitation) are given to us by our standards for use at the Lord's Supper. We will do well to practice these fencings and heed these warnings. There are good and necessary consequences which have also been drawn from these words of instruction and incorporated in the Confessional Standards, for example, the latter part of answer 177 of the Larger Catechism, which indicates that the Lord's Supper is to be administered 'only to such as are of years and ability to examine themselves'. I think that since they are both good and necessary they too should also be heeded.

The conclusion above has summarized for us that which we may positively deduce from this chapter and its application to us. But in this context we should also ask what we may deduce from this teaching in response to those that want to insist, contrary to our standards, that baptized children of all ages should also be allowed to partake of the Supper because baptism has brought them into the church and the Supper is, from their perspective, for all those in the church.

First, baptism should not be looked upon as if it worked automatically and therefore everyone that is baptized is born again and therefore must be invited to partake. Our Confession

---

self-examination before coming to the Lord's table? Should a pastor exhort the parishioners to examine themselves before they celebrate Communion? The answer to these two queries is a resounding yes. Here are the reasons' (see his *Exposition of the First Epistle to the Corinthians*, New Testament Commentary [Grand Rapids: Baker Books, 1993], 401). An excerpt is as follows: ' First, ... Paul prescribes self-examination for everyone who desires to partake of the bread and the cup of the Lord. He understands the word *man* generically to exclude no one. Next, the meaning of the verb *to examine* is applicable both to the original readers of this epistle and to the members of the church universal.... This holds true for all Christians everywhere....'

summarizes the biblical data on this issue when it denies 'that all that are baptized are undoubtedly regenerated' (WCF 28, 5; cf. Acts 8:13, 23; cf. further the WCF 28, 6 statement on the efficacy of baptism, and also its denial that the efficacy is tied to the moment it is administered but rather to God's will and his appointed time).

Second, those partaking are doing so in response to God's invitation (cf. the twice repeated 'do this' in 1 Corinthians 11:24, 25 followed by the offering of the bread and the wine which the participants take and eat and drink – see each of the verses of 1 Corinthians 11:24-29 and the explanation given earlier in this chapter). Babies cannot so partake by doing this themselves.

Third, those partaking are to do so 'in remembrance of me [Christ]' (1 Cor. 11:24-25). Babies cannot so partake 'in remembrance of me [Christ]'. Furthermore, this remembrance can only truly be done by those who have saving faith.

Fourth, those partaking ('whoever') are to do so in a worthy manner (and not in 'an unworthy manner,' 1 Cor. 11:27). They partake worthily when each one 'examine[s] himself' (1 Cor. 11:28), and discerns the Lord's body represented in the Supper (1 Cor. 11:29). Babies cannot fulfill these apostolic requirements for all those who are to partake. Only those who have saving faith can truly fulfill these requirements.

Fifth, those partaking are participating in the nurturing of their faith (cf. 1 Cor. 10:16; see particularly the treatment of the Lord's Supper and Baptism earlier in this chapter dealing with verses 23-26). The institution of the Lord's Supper is given to his disciples and it is reiterated by Paul to the church to be practiced in the church by those who have believed and who can be so instructed and warned. Thus faith, by implication, is necessary for those partaking to participate in the nurturing of that faith (cf. WCF 29.7, 'Worthy receivers, outwardly partaking ... do then also, inwardly by faith ... spiritually, receive, and feed upon Christ crucified ... present to the faith of believers in that ordinance... '). Therefore, only those who have made a public profession of their faith are to be admitted to the table.

This means that the table is open only to those children who have made such a public profession of faith and who are able to understand and act upon Paul's instruction.[35] It also means that children who have been baptized but have not so professed their faith are not yet ready to receive the Lord's Supper and its benefits for believers.

The result of this analysis of the Lord's Supper, as it is presented in 1 Corinthians 11:17-34 together with the positive and negative consequences, provide a rather clear reason why the church of the Lord Jesus Christ, in obedience to His Word, has not admitted children to the Lord's Supper solely on the basis of their baptism and without a profession of faith.

---

35. If this requirement of faith, indeed, a public affirmation of faith, is not required for the children, in a couple of generations, unless non-believers are evangelized and brought into the church, the church will contain no one who has confessed his (or, her) faith!

4

'Not a Particle of Sound Brain' – a theological response to paedocommunion

Derek W. H. Thomas

The Lord's Supper is to be administered... only to such as are of years and ability to examine themselves (Westminster Larger Catechism, 177).

Exegetical arguments *against* the participation of young (non-confessing[1]) children in the Lord's Supper have almost exclusively been drawn from the traditional understanding of Paul's words in 1 Corinthians 11:28: 'Let a person examine himself, then, and so eat of the bread and drink of the cup', as well as the exhortation of our Lord at the inauguration of the

---

1. There is a need to be clear as to the use of the term 'paedocommunion.' By it, we do not mean the inclusion/exclusion of children from participation at the Lord's Table as such; rather, we refer to the inclusion/exclusion of children from the Lord's Supper *who have not made a credible profession of faith*. To put the matter in a different form: should all members of the 'covenant community' (believers and their children *of any age from birth onwards*) be admitted to the Lord's Table? The problem with the nomenclature is that it suggests two types of communion: one for adults and one for children, a distinction that cannot possibly stand. Some have therefore suggested 'covenant communion' to dispel any notion that the essence of the communion itself is changed by the fact that children partake of it. Similarly, defenders of the historic view sometimes define it as 'credo-communion'. It is unfair and tendentious for advocates of paedocommunion to employ the term 'covenant communion' as though any other view was somehow less than covenantal in its understanding. Cf. *mutatis mutandis*, the use of 'credo-baptism' in the title of Fred Malone's book, *The Baptism of Disciples Alone: A Covenantal Argument for Credobaptism Versus Paedobaptism* (Cape Coral, FL: Founders Press, 2003).

Supper: 'Do this in remembrance of me' (Luke 22:19). The seeming assumption underlying these passages of a conscious ability to 'discern' something of the meaning and purpose of the occasion rules out the very possibility of paedocommunion. Clearly, infants are incapable of anything approaching discernment by any standard of definition and are therefore not within the purview of those eligible to participate in the Supper. Typical of such forthright conclusions is John Calvin, who dismisses the practice of paedocommunion this way:

> [The Lord] does not ... hold forth the Supper for all to partake of, but only for those who are capable of discerning the body and blood of the Lord, of examining their own conscience, of proclaiming the Lord's death, and of considering its power. Do we wish anything plainer than the apostle's teaching when he exhorts each man to prove and search himself, then to eat of this bread and drink of this cup [1 Cor. 11:28]? A self-examination ought, therefore, *to come first*, and it is vain to expect this of infants.[2]

Referencing the exhortatory *anamnesis* (remembrance) of the Supper's institution in Luke 22:19, Calvin writes with evident conviction:

> What remembrance of this thing, I ask, shall we require of infants when they have never grasped it? What preaching of the cross of Christ, the force and benefit of which their minds have not yet comprehended? None of these things is prescribed in baptism. Accordingly, there is a very great difference between these two signs, as we have noted in like signs also under the Old Testament. Circumcision, which is known to correspond to our baptism, had been appointed for infants [Gen. 17:12]. But the Passover, the place of which has been taken by the Supper, did not admit all guests indiscriminately, but was duly eaten only by those who were old enough to be able to inquire into its meaning [Exod. 12:26]. If these men had a particle of

---

2. John Calvin, *Institutes of the Christian Religion*, trans. Ford Lewis Battles, 2 vols., Library of Christian Classics, 20-21 (Philadelphia: Westminster, 1960), 1352-53 (IV: xvi: 30), CO 2:997-98. Emphasis added.

sound brain left, would they be blind to a thing so clear and obvious?[3]

And again,

> For everyone to be admitted to the Lord's Supper, without distinction or selection, is a sign of contempt that the Lord cannot endure. The Lord himself distributed the supper to his disciples only. Therefore anyone not instructed in the doctrine of the gospel ought not to approach what the Lord has instituted. No one should be distressed when his Christianity is examined even down to the finest point when he is to be admitted to the Lord's Supper. It should be established as part of the total state and system of discipline that ought to flourish in the church that those who are judged unworthy should not be admitted.[4]

Clearly, the Reformer showed no sympathy with the practice of paedocommunion and antipathy to the practice should not be considered as contrary to the spirit of the Reformation.

It is not our intention in this chapter to examine the exegetical validity of the traditional interpretation of 1 Corinthians 11:28;[5] this is more than ably done elsewhere in this volume. Rather, we will consider some of the theological issues that undergird the case for and against the practice of participation in the Lord's Supper by infants, and therefore those who have made no outward/credible profession of saving faith in Jesus Christ. In particular, three strands of argumentation will be considered: sacramental, covenantal, and ecclesiastical.

---

3. Ibid. Notwithstanding Calvin's colorful language, some have argued that the Corinthian text is not as 'clear and obvious'. See, Jeffrey J. Meyers, 'Presbyterian, Examine Thyself: Restoring Children to the Table,' in *The Case for Covenant Communion*, ed. Gregg Strawbridge (Monroe, LA: Athanasius Press, 2006), 19-34.

4. See *Calvin's Ecclesiastical Advice,* Ed. John H. Leith, trans. Mary Beaty and Benjamin W. Farley (Louisville, KY: Westminster-John Knox Press, 1991), 155. CO 10:255-66.

5. Advocates of paedocommunion have argued that the Corinthian text is irrelevant since it addresses a pathological situation unique to Corinth (as much else in the Corinthian correspondence does). It is therefore inappropriate to draw general conclusions from the specific apostolic application in 1 Corinthians 11:17-34 given to an errant body in Corinth. See, Jeffrey Myers, 'Presbyterian, Examine Thyself: Restoring Children to the Table,' in *The Case for Covenant Communion*, 19-34.

Sacramental administration in the Old and New Covenant: Similarity or Contrast?

Calvin's reference to baptism in the citation above is significant because he found no anomaly in drawing a contrast between the administrations of baptism on the one hand and the Lord's Supper on the other. As a paedobaptist, Calvin argued *for* self-examination and conscious remembrance at the Supper, but not at the sacrament of baptism – at least, not by the participant, even though, of course, he would have argued that it was required of at least one of the child's parents.[6] For Calvin, and for mainstream Reformed Christendom subsequently, there is no problem in drawing an administrative distinction as to the participants in sacramental observance: infants may and should participate in the one (baptism) but not in the other (the Lord's Supper/communion). However, for recent advocates of paedocommunion, this is precisely the weakness of its argument: should we not expect participation in *both* sacraments by all those who are members of the church? Should there not be a similarity, or *symmetry*, of administration rather than a contrast on the part of the participants?

The argument for the expectancy of symmetry is based, in part, on what is assumed to be a similarity of administration in the Passover[7] of the Old Covenant and the Supper of the New Covenant: while credo-communicants argue that infants did *not* participate in the Passover, defenders of paedocommunion argue that they did.[8] Again, it is not my aim to prove whether

---

6. I am assuming a particular understanding of 1 Corinthians 7:14 in suggesting the validity of infant baptism (and the covenantal status of the child) based on the profession of only one parent. I am also assuming an argument of asymmetry in the sacraments in the case of infant participation. Calvin did, of course, believe in baptism upon profession of faith in the case of adult converts who had not received baptism as children. In such instances, a conscious discernment was necessary and no asymmetry resulted.

7. We will not take time to argue here that the Lord's Supper takes the place of Passover, merely to point out that even those who have argued that the Lord's Supper is equivalent to the covenant meal eaten by Moses, Aaron, Nadab and Abihu, and the seventy elders of Israel on the top of Mount Sinai (Exod. 24:1-11), rather than Passover, have not been drawn to argue in favor of paedocommunion.

8. Jim Jordan, for example, makes the point abundantly clear in summary statements regarding the observance of *all* religious meals in the Old Testament: '... there is no passage anywhere in the Bible that commands, hints, or shows that children need to go through some *ritual* before they are included at any religious meal... there is no passage anywhere in

or not infants participated in the Passover (see elsewhere in this book); rather, the point we are examining is the *inconsistency* of the argument that insists that infants *do* participate in baptism but *do not* in the Lord's Supper. An inconsistency exists if faith is required of the participant as an antecedent to the one (Supper) but not the other (baptism).[9]

Those who have made most of the inconsistency involved in the administration of the sacraments have largely been Baptists.[10] The following is typical:

> The Lord's Supper is reserved for believers who have been baptized, but many paedobaptists do not allow children to partake of the Lord's table until the children have expressed personal faith. But such a divide between baptism and the Lord's Supper cannot be sustained from the NT, for it is clear that those baptized participated in communion.[11]

Malone in defense of credobaptism protests too much. He must make the case that such inconsistency was also absent from old covenant administration of the sacraments, a case that cannot be made either exegetically or historically. Whether or not infants participated in the Passover and whether Passover forms the proper old covenant antecedent to the Lord's Supper are both moot points (though Malone assumed that infants did participate in the Passover meal),[12] but if Baptists insist on a principle

---

the Bible that commands, hints or shows that children need to be *catechized or instructed* in order to make them eligible for any religious meal' ('Children and Religious Meals,' in *The Case for Covenant Communion*, 50).

9. In the case of baptism, faith *is* required as an antecedent on the part of one or more of the infant's parents.

10. See Fred Malone's personal testimony over this issue in *The Baptism of Disciples Alone*, 23. Cf. John Murray, *Christian Baptism* (Nutley, NJ: The Presbyterian and Reformed Publishing Company, 1974), 76-77.

11. *Believer's Baptism: Sign of the New Covenant in Christ*, eds., Thomas R. Schreiner & Shawn D. Wright, NAC Studies in Bible & Theology, Series ed., E. Ray Clendenen (Nashville, TN: B & H Academic, 2006), 5.

12. Robert Letham, for example, has argued that the clearest connection of the Lord's Supper with the Old Testament lies not in the Passover but in the covenant meal eaten by Moses and Aaron, Nadab and Abihu, and the seventy elders of Israel on the top of Mount Sinai (Exod. 24:1-11). Robert Letham, *The Lord's Supper: Eternal Word in Broken Bread* (Phillipsburg, NJ: P & R Publishing, 2001), 4-5, 55-57. Paul Bradshaw has also argued that even if the Supper has Passover roots, 'no exclusively paschal practices seem to have been

of consistency within new covenant administration of baptism and the Lord's Supper, they must also argue for it under the old covenant – a more difficult conclusion to achieve since circumcision (apart from the case of Abraham and cases of its neglect[13]) was self-evidently done to infants. Under both administrations then, one sacrament functioned as initiatory (with infants in mind) and another as confirmatory (with professing believers in mind).

Making a case for infant participation in the Passover is a very difficult one. More likely is the scenario that participation at Passover, following the first occasion of its celebration, was restricted to males as Jerusalem became the centralized location of its administration. Not only did this make it difficult for infants to be there, it also restricted the presence of women. The arguments are difficult and complex but our point here is simply to argue that complete consistency of administration between the Lord's Supper and baptism on the one hand, and the Lord's Supper and Passover on the other, will always be difficult to prove.[14]

Christian L. Keidel (a paedobaptist) admits that it was this issue – the Baptist charge of inconsistency – that led him to write that '…pedobaptists (sic.) are indeed guilty of the charge of inconsistency in not allowing their baptized infants and children to participate in the Lord's Supper.'[15] By advocating paedocommunion, Keidel hoped to strengthen the case for paedobaptism and lead Bapists to consider it more sympathetically. In a rejoinder, Roger Beckwith expressed his doubts over Keidel's vision for credo Baptist/paedobaptist ecumenicity,[16] expanding

retained in the primitive Church's Eucharistic celebrations.' See, *The Search for the Origin of Christian Worship* (New York: Oxford University Press, 1992), 205.

13. I have in mind such cases as the son of Moses and Zipporah (Exod. 4:24-26) and the incident at Gibeath-haaraloth (Josh. 5).

14. See the extensive discussions in Roger Beckwith, 'The Age of Admission to the Lord's Supper,' *Westminster Theological Journal*, XXXVIII:2 (Winter 1976), 130-34.

15. Christian L. Keidel, 'Is the Lord's Supper for Children?,' *Westminster Theological Journal*, XXXVII:3 (Spring 1975), 305. Keidel admits to being influenced by the charges of inconsistency leveled against paedobaptists by Paul Jewett and David Kingdon. See, Jewett's *Infant Baptism & the Covenant of Grace* (Grand Rapids, MI: Eerdmans, 1978), 206-07, and Kingdon's *Children of Abraham* (Foxton: Carey Publications, 1973), 48f5; 71.

16. Expressing his doubt whether Baptists would consider paedobaptism more sympathetically, Beckwith wrote, 'they might rather be shocked and repelled seeing

his response to deny the claim that 'if baptism is a ceremony suitable to infants, the Lord's Supper is a ceremony equally suitable.'[17]

But to return to the point at hand, why should inconsistency of administration at the point of those who participate be viewed with such concern? After all, *some* inconsistency is unavoidable whichever viewpoint is adopted. Baptism, as a sign and seal of the covenant of grace, is a sacrament of incorporation, 'for the solemn admission of the party baptized into the visible church ... of his ingrafting into Christ, of regeneration, of remission of sins, and of his giving up unto God, through Jesus Christ, to walk in newness of life.'[18] As such, baptism 'is but once to be administered unto any person'.[19] The Lord's Supper, on the other hand, 'is frequently to be administered.'[20] One is a sacrament of initiation. The other is a sacrament of nourishment and growth. In one (Baptism) the participant is passive (in the case of an infant); in the other (the Lord's Supper) the participant is active.

It is not, however, the inconsistency of *frequency* of administration of baptism and the Lord's Supper, or the testamental divergences between Passover and the Lord's Supper, that raises a problem so much as the inconsistency of the requirement of a profession of faith on the part of the participant. The uniform testimony of all Reformed confessions is that infants may

---

candidates being admitted to all the ordinances of Christianity without having made any profession of repentance and faith, or indeed of being capable of doing so.' 'The Age of Admission to the Lord's Supper,' 123.

17. Ibid., 124, 127-28. Beckwith's arguments against paedocommunion at this point focus on the impropriety of giving bread (unleavened and therefore akin to a dry biscuit) and intoxicating wine to an unweaned infant, adding his belief that weaning may have been delayed in the first century until the child was three years old.

18. WCF, 28:1. The Confession leaves unanswered at this point the question of whether such 'solemn admission in the visible church' presupposes the fact that children born to at least one believing parent are *already* members of the visible church by virtue of birth (or even conception), in which case the baptism is a formal declaration of an existing reality.

19. WCF 28:7. Technically, in the historic debates as to whether (say) Roman Catholic baptism is considered valid, those who have argued for re-baptism are in fact stating that the initial 'baptism' was invalid and therefore not a baptism at all. No re-baptism therefore has taken place.

20. The Directory for the Public Worship of God (1645), 'Of the Celebration of the Communion, or Sacrament of the Lord's Supper.'

participate in the Lord's Supper *following* a suitable (credible) attestation of faith in Jesus Christ, something which is not required for the baptism of infants.[21]

Covenant Communion

Proponents of paedocommunion state that their insistence upon the right of infants to participate in the Supper is derived from the covenant status of the meal. The title to Gregg Strawbridge's book, *The Case for Covenant Communion*, is meant to be significant. If devotees of covenant theology are meant to infer the practice of infant baptism through covenantal considerations, they are equally meant to infer the practice of infant communion from such covenantal considerations. But the matter is not quite as simple as that.

Though it is more than possible to over-argue the case, the sacrament of inclusion under the old covenant (circumcision) was based upon a parent-and-child solidarity, and Paul's linking of circumcision with baptism (Rom. 4:11-12; Col. 2:11), as well as his insistence that under the new covenant a believer's children are 'holy' along with their parent(s) (1 Cor. 7:14), makes the argument for infant baptism based on the faith of the *parent(s)* look right.[22] On this basis, Calvin argued:

> He who is an unbeliever, sprung from impious parents, is reckoned as alien to the fellowship of the covenant until he is joined to God through faith. No wonder, then, if he does not partake in the sign when what is signified would be fallacious and empty in him! Paul also writes to this effect: that the Gentiles, so long as they were immersed in their idolatry, were outside the covenant [Ephesians 2:12]. The whole matter, unless I am mistaken, can be clearly disclosed in this brief

---

21. The only notable exception in Reformed theology came from Wolfgang Musculus (1497–1563) in his *Loci communes theologiae sacrae* (Basel: Heruagiana, 1567), 471-73, cited by Herman Bavinck, *Reformed Dogmatics*, 4 vols. Ed. John Bolt, trans. John Vriend (Grand Rapids, MI: Baker Academic, 2008), 4:583. Richard Muller describes Musculus as one of the 'important second-generation codifiers of the Reformed faith', alongside Calvin, Vermigli, and Hyperius. *Post-Reformation Reformed Dogmatics*, 4 vols. (Grand Rapids, MI: Baker Academic, 2003), 1:31.

22. See, J. I. Packer, *I Want to be a Christian* (Eastbourne, Sussex: Kingsway Publications, 1985), 110.

statement. Those who embrace faith in Christ as grown men, since they were previously strangers to the covenant, are not to be given the badge of baptism unless they first have faith and repentance, which alone can give access to the society of the covenant. But those infants who derive their origin from Christians, as they have been born directly into the inheritance of the covenant, and are accepted by God, are thus to be received into baptism.[23]

The ground for baptism is thereby the same for both adults and for children: covenantal inclusion, the parent on the basis of professed faith; the child on the basis of familial solidarity.

Why, then, is this argument of familial solidarity not employed when the issue under consideration is the Lord's Supper rather than baptism? Why not argue that the basis for participation in the sacrament of the Lord's Supper is covenantal inclusion: the parent on the basis of professed faith, and the infant on the basis of familial solidarity? Why do the majority of paedobaptists employ 1 Corinthians 7:14 in the case of baptism but not in the case of the Lord's Supper? Is not this, yet again, a glaring example of inconsistency?[24] But this somewhat begs the question. A better question would be: is the basis for participation in one sacrament (Baptism, circumcision) *the same* as the basis for participation in another (the Lord's Supper, Passover)? 1 Corinthians 7:14 establishes the principle of familial solidarity but it does not establish the basis for paedocommunion any more than it establishes (by itself) the basis for paedobaptism. All it establishes is a pattern of consistency with regard to circumcision and baptism on the basis of familial solidarity. But familial solidarity is not sufficient as a basis for participation in either the Passover or the Lord's Supper. The latter is established by the fact that Christ instituted the Lord's Supper among his disciples (all

---

23. Institutes IV. xvi.24, CO 2:993. Cf. Pierre Marcel, *Baptism: Sacrament of the Covenant of Grace* (Cherry Hill, NJ: Mack Publishing Company, 1953), 198-220.

24. Peter Leithart, *Daddy, Why Was I Excommunicated?* (Niceville, FL: Transfiguration Press, 1992 [1998]), 68. Leithart is responding to Leonard J. Coppes, *Daddy, May I Take Communion? Paedocommunion vs. The Bible* (published by the author, Thornton, CO:1988), 254-55.

professing faith, including Judas), saying 'Take, eat and drink.' It presupposes they took the bread and wine from his hand. And Paul's insistence on self-examination prior to participation in the Supper at Corinth in 1 Corinthians 11:26-29 presupposes a measure of conscious ability to discern the Lord's body and thereby safeguard the participant from unworthily eating and drinking.[25] Denial of these implications for credo-communion involves radically different interpretations of the Corinthian command for self-examination.[26]

Any consideration of the covenantal nature of the sacraments requires us to consider two subsidiary issues: the *meaning* and the *efficacy* of the sacraments.

As to the meaning of the sacraments, the Corinthian passage, it is argued, is consistent with the view that the sacraments are 'signs and seals of the covenant of grace'. Baptism and the Supper function in the same way that the rainbow, circumcision, the Sabbath and the Davidic Kingship did under the old covenant, functioning as they did as signs and seals of the covenants with Adam (the Tree of Life, Gen. 2:9), Noah (the rainbow, Gen. 9:12), Abraham (circumcision, Gen. 17:11), Moses (the Sabbath, Exod. 31:16-17), and David (the house of David, Ps. 89:29). Thus, in similar fashion, baptism and the Supper function as signs and seals of the new covenant, as the Westminster Confession states:

> Sacraments are holy signs and seals of the covenant of grace, immediately instituted by God, to represent Christ, and His benefits; and to confirm our interest in Him: as also, to put a

---

25. I leave the exegetical considerations for such assumptions in the interpretation of the Corinthian passage to others in this volume to prove.

26. Tim Gallant, for example, is typical of those paedocommunion proponents who argue that the 1 Corinthian 11 passage is used selectively by credocommunicants. There are passages in Scripture which insist on prior faith and repentance in the case of baptism, for example, but credocommunicants insist that these refer only to adults and in no way detract from the rightness of the argument in favor of infant baptism. Why cannot the same be said for 1 Corinthians 11:27-29? Could this not be a special case where Paul is addressing adults but not providing the basis for participation in the Lord's Supper generally? *Feed My Lambs. Why the Lord's Table Should be Restored to Covenant Children* (Grande Prairie, Alberta: Pactum Reformanda Publishing, 1992), 96. See also, Keith A. Mathison's cautious agreement with this view in *Given For You: Reclaiming Calvin's Doctrine of the Lord's Supper* (Grand Rapids, MI: P & R Publishing, 2002), 319-320.

visible difference between those that belong unto the Church, and the rest of the world; and solemnly to engage them to the service of God in Christ, according to His Word.[27]

Sacraments are therefore seen as signs of the gospel. Baptism is the first sign of God's love for us. In these signs God speaks in 'visible words'.[28] The two sacraments do not bring blessings different from the Word. Their function is to guarantee the promises of the Word. And because sacraments guarantee the promises of the Word, they function as seals. As Calvin makes clear:

> The seals which are attached to government documents and other public acts are nothing taken by themselves, for they would be attached in vain if the parchment had nothing written on it. Yet, when added to the writing, they do not on that account fail to confirm and seal what is written.[29]

In restoring sinners into a right relationship with himself, God appends holy signs and seals. Baptism is a sign of what God does in the new covenant, by union with Christ and cleansing from sin. The two baptisms in the Old Testament to which the New makes reference are both water ordeals related to God's forging of a new covenant relationship with Noah (1 Pet. 3:20-21) and Moses (1 Cor. 10:2).[30] Christ, too, like Noah and Moses, has a baptism to be baptized with in order to forge his covenant between God and man. Interestingly, Paul, in Romans 15:3, views Psalm 69 as a Messianic Psalm, beginning as it does with a description of a water ordeal: 'Save me, O God! For the waters have come up to my neck. I sink in deep mire, where there is no foothold; I have come into deep waters, and the flood sweeps over me' (Ps. 69:1-2).[31] In Christ's baptism we share his baptism

---

27. Westminster Confession of Faith, 27:1.

28. 'The word is added to the element, and there results the Sacrament, as if itself also a kind of visible word.' Augustine, *Treatise of the Gospel of John*, LXXX, 3. Nicene and Post-Nicene Fathers, *First Series*, 14 vols., ed. Philip Schaff , Vol. 7 (Peabody, MA: Hendricksen Publishers, 2004), 344.

29. John Calvin, *Institutes of the Christian Religion*, 1281 (4.14.5). CO 2:944.

30. Cf. Meredith G. Kline, *By Oath Consigned* (Grand Rapids, MI: Eerdmans, 1968), 65-73.

31. Kline, op. cit., 59.

into divine judgment. Ours is no longer a water-ordeal, but a sign of cleansing and acceptance with God.

Likewise, the Supper is a covenant symbol. Christ's broken body as the judgment-bearing Passover lamb is set before us (1 Cor. 5:7). The cup Christ drinks is symbolic of the judgment curse of God of which the prophets spoke (Isa. 51:17; Jer. 25:15; Ezek. 23:32; Hab. 2:16). In turn he gives to his disciples the cup of blessing (1 Cor. 11:25; 10:16).

The sacraments are distinctively covenantal in the way they operate as signs and seals. They underscore that Christ's work is a covenantal work. He is the substance of the covenant, and his work is the fulfillment of its promise. When they are responded to in living faith, they are visible ways by which the blessings of the gospel are communicated to us, in just the same way as when the 'heard' word is grasped by faith its promised blessings are communicated to us. If we respond by unbelief we remain under the covenant curse. As such, the sacraments are not signs and seals *of* faith but *to* faith and *of* grace. They do not in themselves point to something within us. Their focus is on Christ. This objectifying of the sacraments is in stark contrast to views that tend to focus on the individual participant's faith rather than on what the sacrament is designed to do – draw our attention to Christ and his covenantal work on behalf of his people.

Covenant Signs and Seals

Another question is raised at this point: in what sense are the sacraments efficacious, communicating what they signify? In so far as they are signs and seals of the covenant of grace, they communicate that covenant (of which Christ is the substance) no less really and efficaciously than does the proclamation of the Word. Sacraments are not efficacious in an *ex opere operato* fashion. They do not function by some spiritual (or magical) power innate within themselves as though the mere celebration of them is sufficient. They communicate Christ *covenant-ally*, which means that they may be effectual for salvation or condemnation, blessing or cursing. It is what Paul suggests in

1 Corinthians 11:29: 'For anyone who eats and drinks without discerning the body eats and drinks judgment on himself.' As Calvin comments, 'the promise no less threatens wrath to unbelievers than offers grace to believers.'[32]

As gospel ordinances, the sacraments are designed to bring us to Christ through faith. And, as Robert Bruce expressed it in the sixteenth century in Edinburgh (though often viewed controversially):

> You get a better grip of the same thing in the Sacrament than you got by the hearing of the Word. That same thing which you possess by the hearing of the Word, you now possess more fully. God has more room in your soul, through your receiving of the Sacrament, than He could otherwise have by your hearing of the Word only. What then, you ask, is the new thing we get? We get Christ better than we did before. We get the thing which we had more fully, that is, with a surer apprehension than we had before. We get a better grip of Christ now, for by the Sacrament my faith is nourished, the bounds of my soul are enlarged, and so where I had but a little of Christ before, as it were, between my finger and my thumb, now I get Him in my whole hand, and indeed the more my faith grows, the better grip I get of Christ Jesus. Thus the Sacrament is very necessary, if only for the reason that we get Christ better, and get a firmer grasp of Him by the Sacrament, than we could have before.[33]

Neither baptism nor the Supper is instrumental in justification. Paul's insistence in Romans is pertinent here. Salvation is appropriated without recourse to sacraments as the case of Abraham shows (Rom. 4:12; Gal. 3:12-18). Had it been otherwise it is difficult to see how Paul could say with such conviction, 'I thank God that I baptized none of you' (1 Cor. 1:14). Salvation is received *by* the instrumentality of faith. And it is in the nature of faith to be non-contributory. Indeed, in one sense,

---

32. Institutes 4.14.14.

33. Robert Bruce, *The Mystery of the Lord's Supper: Sermons on the Sacrament preached in the Kirk of Edinburgh in A.D. 1589*, trans. & ed. by Thomas F. Torrance (London: James Clarke & Co. Ltd., 1958), 84-85.

there is no such 'thing' as faith, as though it were viewed as something akin to a gas. Faith is the outstretched hand pleading for mercy, the fixed 'look' of the eye upon an object it desires.

Arguments in favor of paedocommunion argue that the sacraments, as covenantal signs and seals, do not necessitate faith on the part of the participant – not in the case of the Supper any more than in baptism. They function covenantally in both instances, as signs and seals *to* faith and not *of* faith. The argument is a strong one but essentially flawed. It is true that baptism does not require faith on the part of the participant (in that sense it is a passive sacrament). Typical, therefore, is the conclusion drawn by Bavinck:

> Baptism is the sacrament of regeneration, a sacrament in which a human is passive; the Lord's Supper is the sacrament of maturation in communion with Christ, the formation of a spiritual life, and presupposes conscious and active conduct on the part of those who receive it.[34]

This inconsistency of admitting infants in covenant membership to one sacrament (Baptism) but not to the other (the Supper) was decisive in Fred Malone's journey away from paedobaptism:

> Why is New Testament regulation sufficient to define the subjects of the Lord's Supper but not infant baptism? … What has changed in the application of the covenant family concept from the old covenant to the new covenant? Why does the household child participate in the Passover and not in the Lord's Supper? Has the new covenant child of believers less blessings than the household old covenant child?[35]

Noting that Malone assumes that infants did participate in the Passover, his conclusion is to highlight *discontinuity* between old and new covenants at the point of both sacraments. John Murray went in the opposite direction, even if he ultimately brakes with accepting paedocommunion: 'less would be at stake

---

34. Bavinck, *Reformed Dogmatics*, 4:583.

35. Fred Malone, *A String of Pearls Unstrung: A Theological Journey Into Believers' Baptism* (Cape Coral, FL: Founders Press, 1998), 12.

in admitting infants to the Lord's Supper than would be at stake in abandoning infant baptism.'[36] Noting this concession on Murray's part, Gregg Strawbridge argues for a principle of *continuity* and *similarity* in the administration of baptism and the Supper[37], but Murray is, in fact, insistent on *discontinuity* at this point, arguing:

1. There is no evidence whatsoever that infants partook of the Passover;

2. Baptism signifies what lies at the basis and inception of a state of salvation, namely, union with Christ, and cleansing from sin's pollution and guilt;

3. The Supper presupposes what is sealed in baptism, requiring an ability to recognize Christ in order to commemorate him and commune with him;

4. Baptism is performed once, whereas the Supper is received frequently;

5. Whereas washing is appropriate for an infant, eating bread and drinking wine is not.[38]

Whatever concession Murray is making to the principle of consistency, the facts overwhelmingly convince him otherwise than to move in the direction of paedocommunion. The one sacrament (Baptism) is a sign and seal of covenant inauguration, and the other (the Supper) a sign and seal of covenant life.

Ecclesiastical Membership

Another argument in favor of paedocommunion is based on a corollary drawn on the basis that since covenant children are regarded as members of the church they ought therefore to enjoy *all* the privileges that such membership of the church entails, including therefore participation in the Lord's Supper.

---

36. John Murray, *Christian Baptism* (Philadelphia, PA: The Presbyterian and Reformed Publishing Company, 1974), 77.

37. Gregg Strawbridge, 'The Polemics of Infant Baptism,' in *The Case for Covenant Communion*, 150.

38. Murray, op. cit., 77-79.

Although reformed liturgy is not always consistent at this point, covenant children are baptized on the basis that they already are members of the visible church.[39] Baptism is the sign and seal of their covenant status and is not the initiator of it. Believers' children are members of the church and therefore should be baptized. They are not baptized *in order to initiate* church membership.

The infants of believers are members of the kingdom of God. 'Then children were brought to him that he might lay his hands on them and pray. The disciples rebuked the people, but Jesus said, "Let the little children come to me and do not hinder them, for to such belongs the kingdom of heaven"' (Matt. 19:13-14). The infants in question, as the parallel in Luke makes clear, were in fact *infants* (*brephē*), that is to say, little infants. By employing the *demonstrative* pronoun 'to such,' Jesus intends to underline that the kingdom belongs to actual infants and not just those with 'infant-like dispositions.' As John Murray put it:

> The pronoun (*toioutoi*) means 'of this kind, sort, or class.' It is necessary to note the class of which Jesus had been speaking; it is distinctly and only of the infant class. This class alone provides us with the antecedent of the *toioutōn* and not at all the class of those who are of childlike and humble spirit. Of the latter Jesus had not spoken. Neither were they in the focus of attention. The disciples were not forbidding such nor did Jesus here say of such, 'Suffer them to come to me.'[40]

The basis of the inclusion of covenant children in the community of the visible church is not their presupposed regeneration, either actual or eternal or prospective; rather, it is the fact of their covenantal status. Paedobaptism rests on the

---

39. Reformed books of church order have been vague on this point, for example see the PCA Book of Church Order at 56.4g or the OPC Book of Church Order and Directory for the Public Worship of God at 3.B.2.

40. John Murray, *Christian Baptism*, 64. Note John Gill's (the famous Baptist Systematic theologian) remarks at this point: 'Such who are comparable to children for modesty, meekness and humility.' Was he a bachelor? John Gill, *Exposition of the Old and New Testaments: Complete and Unabridged*. 9 vols. (Paris, AK: Baptist Standard Bearer, 2006), commentary, ad. loc.

claim that the transition from the 'old' to the 'new' covenant marks a point of continuity and not discontinuity at the point of the inclusion of infants within the covenant. This principle of solidarity is underlined by the fact that the New Testament deliberately chooses baptism as the new covenant representation of circumcision (Rom. 4:11-12; Col. 2:11). Without the express signal of discontinuity the early (Jewish) church would have presupposed that the newness of God's covenant they now enjoyed did not signal *less* than what the old covenant had promised. Surely, this is what Peter's Jewish audience at Pentecost heard when he said, 'For the promise is to you and for your children and for all who are afar off, everyone whom the Lord our God calls to himself' (Acts 2:39).

The children of believers are, in God's providence, born into the covenant and therefore into the visible church, the covenant community. Paul makes clear in 1 Corinthians 7:14 that even the children born of marriage where only one partner has become a Christian are considered relationally and covenantally 'holy.' These children are dedicated to and are accepted by God in company with their one Christian parent. Hence they are members of Christ's body, kingdom and (visible) church and enjoy the privileges of the covenant community, including the sacrament of baptism. The right of a covenant infant to baptism is not founded on that infant's personal state of grace and regeneration (personal, real, inchoate, or prospective) but rather on the basis of how God defines covenant membership in the covenant of grace in both Old and New Testaments; that is, on the principle of 'professing believers and their children'. Thus the Westminster Confession comments:

> The efficacy of Baptism is not tied to that moment of time wherein it is administered; yet, not withstanding, by the right use of this ordinance, the grace promised is not only offered, but really exhibited, and conferred, by the Holy Ghost, to such (whether of age or infants) as that grace belongeth unto, according to the counsel of God's own will, in His appointed time.[41]

---

41. WCF 28:6

In other words, we do not baptize infants on the basis of any real exhibition of grace signed and promised in baptism in every person (infant or adult) who receives it. Rather, God really exhibits and confers that grace to such as that grace belongs, according to the mystery of his will and choice, and when he chooses to do so.[42]

Tim Gallant asks the somewhat obvious question at this point: 'If believers' children are full members of the kingdom of heaven, and objects of Christ's self-giving love, who can deny that they are included in His body, the church? Such a denial, surely, would be thoroughly implausible.'[43] The question, however, assumes too much and differentiates too little. It all depends on what is meant by the expression 'full members of the kingdom'! It is not denied that covenant children are members of the kingdom and therefore entitled to the benefits of baptism but it begs the question to suggest that (1) such are members of and entitled to all the benefits of the invisible church, and (2) that such entitlement includes not only the sign and seal of membership in the covenant community (baptism) but also of regenerate life and communion (the Supper).

Historically, the reformed churches have distinguished between 'baptized members' and 'communicant members' of the visible church. Those in favor of paedocommunion sometimes employ intemperate language at this point, suggesting that the historic position in effect 'excommunicates' covenant children by denying them access to the Supper. Indeed, when the Supper is viewed as conveying grace in some way, to deny them access to the means of grace is none other than excommunication.[44]

There is more than one response which may be given to such a charge. First of all, it is a high view of the Supper that suggests that more can be obtained by partaking of the Supper

---

42. Murray's ambivalence over the visible-invisible church distinction at this point is decidedly unhelpful. See *Christian Baptism*, 34-57.

43. Tim Gallant, 'The Kingdom of God and Children,' in *The Case for Covenant Communion*, 43.

44. Note the title of Peter J. Leithart's book cited above, *Daddy, Why was I Excommunicated?*

than can be obtained through the proclaimed Word. Unless we hold to a position that advocates the Supper operates *ex opere operato*, a view that Reformed theology has steadfastly resisted, it is difficult to see what this 'grace' may be that comes only through the Supper and not through the Word. The effect of withholding the Lord's Supper is not the same as withholding the Word. The divine means of imparting faith is the Word alone; the Lord's Supper is an additional means to nourish and strengthen that faith which already exists. Requiring a credible profession of faith on the part of those who participate in the Supper is consonant with the supportive role of the covenant sign and seal of the Supper.[45]

Conclusion

Our study of paedocommunion has shown that it faces a number of insurmountable theological difficulties. It is built on the unstable foundation of a presupposed notion that the Old Testament celebration of Passover included infants and that a certain view of the covenant as inclusive of infants argues in favor of infant participation in *both* sacraments. Both the data of the Old Testament regarding Passover and the understanding of the operation of the covenant of grace under its administration cannot be made to argue such a case with any conviction. Furthermore, in arguing for consistency of application of baptism and the Supper, it fails to distinguish the significance of the two sacraments, the one as initiatory and the other as confirmatory. One, baptism, is designed for the point of entry; the other is designed with progressive sanctification and growth in mind, requiring faith, knowledge and understanding – as much in the practice of the Passover of the old covenant as in the Supper of the new covenant.

The adoption of paedocommunion has a tendency to foster sacramentalism. The failure to insist on the need for a

---

45. The issue of what age is suitable for 'communicant membership' is an important one but does not affect the argument being made here. Even if some argue for a younger age than others, the issue remains one of a *credible profession*. Paedocommunion is not concerned to argue for any profession at all.

credible profession of faith on the part of covenant children at the Supper encourages a view that the sacrament operates by some mystical power inherent within itself. The same might be said of baptism but, as with circumcision, parental representation functions in this sacrament in a way that it does not in the Passover/Lord's Supper.

There remains a suspicion that the practice of paedocommunion makes certain assumptions regarding the regeneration of the participant. Those who have argued for a profession of faith as a prerequisite for participation in the Supper have viewed the occasion of initial participation as a rite of passage requiring some kind of examination on the part of the church. Consequently, it 'forces' self-examination on the part of the participant. Charles Hodge, for example, writes:

> The Apostle, therefore, argues that as those who partook of the Jewish altars did thereby profess to be Jews... so those who partake in the Lord's Supper, do thereby profess to be Christians. But to be a Christian a man must have a competent knowledge of Christ and of his gospel. He must believe the record which God has given of his Son. He must believe that Christ died for our sins; that his body was broken for us. He must accept of Christ as He is thus offered to him as a propitiation for sin. All this, or, the profession of all this is involved in the very nature of the service.[46]

The need to evangelize covenant children is as necessary now as it evidently was when Jesus said to Nicodemus, a covenant child, 'Truly, truly, I say to you, unless one is born again he cannot see the kingdom of God' (John 3:3; cf. 3:5). This may raise the charge of pietism but it is a vacuous charge when the need for evident piety as a pre-requisite to participation in the Supper is the point at issue. The practice of paedocommunion, in the end, leads to an unconverted church for it removes the very means of ensuring the piety of its covenant-membership – the practice of self-examination

---

46. Charles Hodge, *Systematic Theology*, 3 vols (London: James Clarke & Co. Ltd, 1960), 3: 623.

and profession of faith required before participating in the Supper.[47]

---

47. It is interesting to compare our discussion here with the 'Half-Way Covenant' introduced into the puritan churches in New England in 1662 by Samuel Stoddard. Noticing that the second generation puritans were less pious than the first-generation settlers, and that 'full-membership' in the church required a conversion experience, Stoddard proposed that some means be adopted allow such to participate in the Supper if not be entitled to vote. See, Sydney Ahlstrom, *A Religious History of the American People*, vol. 1 (Yale Press, 1975). Chapter 10: 'Tensions in the New England Way.'

5

Paedocommunion and the Reformation Confessions

Cornelis Venema

Though churches of the Reformation are committed to the principle of *sola Scriptura,* which requires that the Scriptures be regarded as the supreme standard for their faith and practice, they are not indifferent to the lessons of church history. Nor are they indifferent to the tradition of Scriptural interpretation that is embodied in the confessions of the church. These confessions have an authority that is subordinate to Scripture, but they nonetheless represent an acknowledged consensus regarding what the Scriptures teach. When it comes to the question of paedocommunion, it is not enough to consider the practice of the churches throughout history. It is also necessary to study what the Reformed churches have confessed regarding the proper recipients of the sacrament of the Lord's Supper. Before turning to the Scriptures' teaching regarding the proper recipients of the Lord's Supper, therefore, it is necessary to complete the consideration of the history of the church by turning attention to the Reformed confessions.

In the classic confessions of the Reformed churches, which were written during the period of the Reformation in the sixteenth century and the early seventeenth century, there is compelling evidence that the Reformed churches believe the Lord's Supper ought to be administered only to professing believers. These confessions express a comprehensive understanding of the sacraments as an indispensable means whereby the grace of Christ is communicated to his people. They affirm that the children of believers, together with their parents, are recipients of the gospel promise and ought accordingly to receive the sacrament of baptism, which is a sign and seal of their incorporation into Christ and membership in the covenant community of the church. However, they also insist that such children, prior to their reception at the Table of the Lord, require instruction in the Christian faith in order that they might be prepared to receive properly the body and blood of Christ in the sacrament. Advocates of paedocommunion often argue that there is an inconsistency in this practice of admitting children into the covenant community through baptism, while withholding the sacrament of the Lord's Supper until such children have been instructed in and professed their faith before the church. In the opinion of proponents of paedocommunion, the insistence that covenant children profess their faith before they are received at the Table of the Lord denies to them a privilege that ought to be extended to every covenant member.

In order to evaluate the claims of advocates of paedo-communion, it is necessary to have a clear understanding of the Reformed confessions' teaching that bears upon the subject of the proper recipients of the sacraments. As shall be seen in the summary of the confessions, their position on this subject derives from a more comprehensive view of the sacraments' role as means of grace that accompany the preaching of the gospel. The advocacy of paedocommunion not only touches upon the question of the proper recipients of the sacrament of the Lord's Supper, but it also touches upon the more basic issues of the nature of the sacraments and the obligations they place upon those who receive them. Indeed, the notion that children should be admitted to the sacrament of the Lord's Supper, which is the principal interest of those who advocate paedocommunion, has more far-reaching implications than many paedocommunionists often admit. Whether these implications are consistent with essential features of the Reformed view of the sacraments remains to be seen. Here it need only be observed that the question of paedocommunion cannot be isolated from the broader framework of traditional Reformed teaching regarding the sacraments.

Our summary of the Reformed confessions on the subject of paedocommunion will begin with a review of their understanding of the nature and use of the sacraments in general. Within this framework of the doctrine of the sacraments, the particular question of the proper recipients of the sacraments, especially the Lord's Supper, will then be taken up.

The Relation of the Word and Sacraments[1]

The doctrine of the sacraments belongs, in the structure of the Reformed confessions, to the doctrine of the church and her ministry. Those whom God the Father elects to save in Jesus Christ become beneficiaries of his saving work in no other way than through communion with the church. Though the ancient dictum of Cyprian, 'outside the church there is no salvation' (*extra ecclesiam nulla salus*), is not explicitly echoed in all of the Reformed confessions, they commonly affirm that saving fellowship with Christ does not ordinarily occur apart from the church's official ministry of Word and sacrament.[2] Christ's saving presence in the world is mediated through the church and the means of grace entrusted to her. Where the true church of Jesus Christ is manifest, there Christ is present gathering, defending, and preserving for himself a people chosen unto everlasting life.[3] Christ is pleased to communicate himself by the working of his Spirit through the administration of the Word

---

1. In my summary of the Reformed confessions' teaching regarding the sacraments, I am making free use of material that was first published in two articles on the confessions in the *Mid-America Journal of Theology*. See Cornelis P. Venema, 'The Doctrine of the Sacraments and Baptism according to the Reformed Confessions,' *Mid-America Journal of Theology* 11 (2000), 21-86; and 'The Doctrine of the Lord's Supper in the Reformed Confessions,' *Mid-America Journal of Theology* 12 (2001), 81-145.

2. Cyprian's dictum is used in The Westminster Confession of Faith, 25.2, which speaks of the church, 'out of which there is no ordinary possibility of salvation,' and the Belgic Confession, Article 28, which says that 'out of it [the church] there is no salvation.'

3. Heidelberg Catechism, Q. & A. 54.

of God in preaching and sacrament. Where the Word of God is faithfully preached and the sacraments rightly administered—the two marks of the true church uniformly stipulated in the confessions—there Christ is present by his Spirit imparting his saving benefits to his people.[4] The location of the doctrine of the sacraments in the confessions, therefore, confirms their importance as necessary marks of the presence of the true church of Christ and as indispensable means to communicate God's grace in Christ to his people.

In their exposition of the 'outward means' that Christ has appointed in the church for the purpose of communicating the 'benefits of his mediation', the confessions grant a priority to the preaching of the gospel in relation to the sacraments. The sacraments do not communicate anything other than the grace of God in Christ, the same grace that is firstly and primarily communicated through the preaching of the gospel. Apart from the Word of the gospel, the visible word of the sacrament would be empty and lifeless. In the confessions, there is a clear ordering of Word and sacrament, such that the sacrament follows upon or is 'added' to the Word as a kind of auxiliary means of grace. If the sacrament is to be administered properly, it must be preceded by an exposition of the biblical Word and promise that the sacrament signifies and seals. Failure to administer the sacrament in conjunction with the Word represents a misunderstanding of the nature of the sacraments as 'appendices' to the Word.[5] For this reason, it is permissible to speak of the preaching of the Word as the 'first' or 'preeminent' means of grace, and of the sacrament as the 'second' and 'subordinate' means of grace. This relative priority of preaching in relation to the sacraments is well expressed in the Heidelberg Catechism, which affirms that 'the Holy Spirit ... works [faith] in our hearts

---

4. Belgic Confession, Article 29.

5. The language of the sacrament as an 'appendix' to the Word stems from Calvin: 'Now, from the definition that I have set forth we understand that a sacrament is never without a preceding promise but is joined to it as a sort of appendix, with the purpose of confirming and sealing the promise itself, and of making it more evident to us and in a sense ratifying it' (*Institutes* IV.xiv.3). When the Reformed confessions insist that the administrant of the sacrament be a lawfully ordained minister, they are setting forth one of the implications of the intimate and necessary conjunction of the ministry of the Word and the sacraments.

by the preaching of the holy gospel, and confirms it by the use of the holy sacraments' (Q. & A. 65). Faith is *produced* by the Spirit's ministry through the Word; it is only *confirmed* by the proper use of the sacraments.

This raises a question that has been disputed in the history of the Reformed tradition: Are the sacraments necessary and indispensable to the communication of God's grace in Christ? Or is the preaching of the Word of God a sufficient means of grace, apart from the sacraments? The best answer to this question, and the one which most faithfully represents the doctrine of the Reformed confessions, must be that ordinarily the sacraments are necessary and indispensable. The indispensability of the sacraments, however, is not absolute, but consequent upon the Lord's appointment of the sacraments for the believer's benefit. Because the Lord has appointed the sacraments for the church's use and added them to the preaching of the Word, it would be disobedience to his will to neglect their use. Furthermore, because they have been added to the Word, in view of the believer's weakness and proneness to doubt the gospel promise in Christ, neglecting the sacraments would betray an ingratitude and false sense of security on the part of the church.[6] Though it may be necessary to posit (by way of exception in extraordinary circumstances)[7] the possibility of the grace of Christ being

---

6. Belgic Confession, Article 33: 'We believe that our gracious God, taking account of our weakness and infirmities, has ordained the sacraments for us, thereby to seal unto us His promises, and to be pledges of the good will and grace of God toward us, and also to nourish and strengthen our faith; which He has joined to the Word of the gospel, the better to present to our senses both that which He declares to us by His Word and that which He works inwardly in our hearts, thereby confirming in us the salvation which He imparts to us.'

7. For example, the Westminster Confession of Faith, 10.3, speaks of infants and others who may be elect and regenerated without the ordinary use of the means of grace, particularly the preaching of the Word. It is possible to imagine other circumstances where the sacraments could not be administered to believers or their children. For example, one reason the Reformed confessions were able to reject the practice of baptism by midwives was their assumption that the sacrament of baptism is not necessary to the infant's salvation. The Roman Catholic permission of baptism of infants by midwives reflects the teaching of the necessity of baptism for salvation. For a statement of this view, see Philip Schaff, *The Creeds of Christendom: The Greek and Latin Creeds* (reprint; Grand Rapids: Baker, 1985 [1931]), 'The Canons and Decrees of the Council of Trent,' Seventh Session, On Baptism, Canon V, 2:121. Though this teaching is also expressed in the Augsburg Confession (Art. IX), it has always been rejected by the Reformed churches. See Calvin, *Institutes* IV.xv.20-22. Sometimes Reformed theologians have distinguished, so far as the necessity of the sacraments is concerned, between a 'necessity of means' and a 'necessity of precept.' See Louis Berkhof, *Systematic Theology,* 4th edition (Grand Rapids: Eerdmans, 1941), 618-19.

communicated apart from the sacraments, the ordinary means Christ uses require the sacraments. To neglect the use of the sacraments represents a failure to appreciate the intimate conjunction of Word and sacraments in the divine economy of grace. For just as the sacraments require the preceding Word, so the Word calls for, by virtue of Christ's appointment, the accompanying sacrament.

The Distinctive Nature of the Sacraments

The typical definition of the sacraments in the Reformed confessions speaks of them as 'visible signs and seals' of an 'invisible grace'. What is peculiar to the sacramental communication of God's grace in Christ is the appointment or consecration of visible elements that represent to the eye of faith the truth of the believer's saving fellowship with Christ.[8] The water of baptism, for example, is a visible representation of the washing away of sins through the blood of Christ and the regeneration of the Holy Spirit. There is a divinely appointed correspondence between the visible sign and the grace to which it points. Moreover, the sacraments are given by God to confirm and attest the promise of the gospel. Not only are they signs that visibly represent, but they are also seals that authenticate and assure the believer of the truth of the gospel promise. The Reformed confessions are fond of insisting that the believer is assured by the visible sign and seal of the sacrament that the grace of God in Christ is for the one who receives it by faith. Though the sign and seal do not add anything to the promise, they do constitute a more 'full' or 'open' confirmation of the gospel so that the believer's faith is fortified.[9]

All of the Reformed confessions grope for words to express simultaneously the most *intimate conjunction* between the

---

8. See, e.g., Heidelberg Catechism, Q. & A. 66: 'The sacraments are holy, visible signs and seals ...'; Belgic Confession, Art. 33; Westminster Confession of Faith, 27.1, 'Sacraments are holy signs and seals of the covenant of grace ....'

9. To say the sacraments do not 'add' anything to the Word is only to say that their 'substance' is the grace of God in Jesus Christ, the same grace communicated through preaching. However, they do 'add' something, namely, a visible sign and seal of this grace. If I may use an analogy, a birth certificate does not 'add' anything to the evident fact of one's birth and subsequent life; but it does authenticate this fact in ways that are publicly credible and important.

sacramental sign and the grace signified, as well as the *necessary distinction* between them.[10] Consistent with the nature of sacraments, the Lord has appointed the sign as a visible representation and confirmation of the gospel. The visible representation and confirmation are not to be confused, however, with the spiritual reality to which they point. The water of baptism is not to be confused with the blood of Christ or the washing of the Holy Spirit.[11] The bread and wine of the Lord's Supper, likewise, are not to be confused with the body and blood of Christ.[12] In sacramental language, we may speak of the sign as though it were the reality, so intimate is the divinely appointed connection between them. But lest we fall prey to idolatry, worshiping the sacramental element rather than the mediator, Jesus Christ, to whom the element refers, we must distinguish between them. The 'substance' to which the sacramental sign points can only be Jesus Christ himself in all of his saving presence and power.

Furthermore, the confessions consistently teach that the power and efficacy of the sacraments require that they be received by faith. Since the sacraments do not add anything new to the grace of Christ promised in the gospel, and since the sacramental elements are not to be confused with the spiritual reality to which they refer, the sacraments require the same response as the Word. The administration of the sacrament can no more savingly communicate the grace of Christ than the preaching of the gospel, unless the gospel promise is believed or appropriated by an active faith on the part of its recipient.[13] The Holy Spirit who authors faith through the preaching of the Word, also uses the sacraments to confirm and nourish faith. The sacraments function instrumentally to communicate the grace of God in Christ, but only when the Holy Spirit works

---

10. See, e.g., Westminster Confession of Faith, 27.2, 'There is in every sacrament, a spiritual relation, or sacramental union, between the sign and the thing signified: whence it comes to pass, that the names and effects of the one are attributed to the other.'

11. See, e.g., Heidelberg Catechism, Q. & A. 72.

12. See, e.g., Heidelberg Catechism, Q. & A. 78.

13. See, e.g., Heidelberg Catechism, Q. & A. 67, 76, 81; Belgic Confession, Art. 33, 35; Westminster Confession of Faith, Chapter 27.3.

through them to strengthen the believer in faith. Consistent with this emphasis upon the believing reception of the sacraments, the Reformed confessions consistently oppose any doctrine of *sacramental regeneration* apart from the Spirit's working faith through the Word. The sacraments do not work simply by virtue of their administration (*ex opere operato*), so long as the recipient does not interpose any obstacle (*obex*) to the reception of the grace they confer.[14] Though they do genuinely serve, as means of grace, to *confer* and to *communicate* the grace of God in Christ, they do so only as the Spirit is working through them and as they confirm the faith required on the part of their recipients.[15]

---

14. See, e.g., Westminster Confession of Faith, 28.5, 28.6. The teaching that the sacraments effectively confer grace upon their recipients by virtue of their administration (*ex opere operato*) was affirmed by the Council of Trent, and continues to be the official teaching of the Roman Catholic Church. Cf. 'The Canons and Decrees of the Council of Trent,' Seventh Session, On The Sacraments in General, Canon VIII: 'If any one saith, that by the said sacraments of the New Law grace is not conferred through the act performed (*ex opere operato*), but that faith alone in the divine promise suffices for the obtaining of grace: let him be anathema' (quoted from Schaff, *The Creeds of Christendom*, 2:121). Though Catholic teaching does acknowledge the necessity of certain 'minimum conditions' (the absence of which constitutes an 'obstacle' to the reception of grace) in the adult recipient of the sacraments to the realization of their 'fruits,' in the particular case of the baptism of infants, baptism confers grace by the simple performance of the act. For a contemporary statement of the Catholic view, see *New Catholic Encyclopedia* (Washington, D.C.: The Catholic University of America, 1967), XII:806-816 (esp. 813); and *Catechism of the Catholic Church*, 292.

15. Jan Rohls, *Reformed Confessions: Theology from Zurich to Barmen* (Louisville, KY: Westminster John Knox Press, 1998), 181-85, argues that there is a subtle difference of emphasis regarding the efficacy of the sacraments in the Reformed confessions. Some of the confessions (e.g., the Belgic) affirm a fully 'instrumental' view of the sacraments as means of grace. In this view the sacraments confer grace at the time of their administration and through the means of the sacramental sign and seal itself. However, some of the confessions (e.g. the Westminster Confession of Faith) only affirm that grace is conferred 'in parallel' or alongside of the administration of the outward sign and seal. In this second view, there is a sharper disjunction between the 'external reception of the sign' and the 'internal reception of the signified substance.' I am not persuaded that this difference of emphasis is as significant as Rohls maintains. Though it is true that some of the confessions use stronger language in linking the sign with the thing signified, while others are more anxious to keep a distance between them, these differing emphases answer to different concerns. The former are anxious to stress the efficacy of the sacraments as God-appointed instruments for the communication of the grace of Christ to his people. The latter are anxious to stress that this efficacy requires a Spirit-authored believing reception of the sacrament, and that this believing reception finds the 'substance' of the sacrament in Christ himself, not the sacramental sign. All of the Reformed confessions, however, though they distinguish between the sign and the thing signified, affirm the power of the sacraments as genuine instruments or means of grace.

The Two Sacraments of the New Covenant

The sacraments are, in the nature of the case, visible signs and seals that the Lord alone can appoint for the use and benefit of the church. Because they require divine authorization, the church may not appoint as sacraments any church rite or practice, however useful, that she pleases. Just as in the old covenant, so also in the new, the Lord has appointed only two sacraments for the use of his people, holy baptism and the Lord's Supper.[16] The Roman Catholic doctrine that speaks of seven sacraments, therefore, represents an abuse of church authority and undermines its claim to be the true church of Jesus Christ. In order to appreciate the Reformed confessions' understanding of the proper recipients of the Lord's Supper, each of these sacraments must be considered specifically and the differences between them noted.

1. Baptism – A Sacrament of Incorporation

The first sacrament that Christ has appointed for the church is holy baptism. By the Lord's ordinance and appointment, the sacramental sign of baptism is pure water. Only a lawfully ordained minister of the Word is authorized to administer this sacrament, and he must do so using the words of institution given by Christ in Matthew 28:19. Though the mode of baptism may differ from place to place—whether through immersion, affusion (pouring), or sprinkling[17]—the validity of baptism requires the use of the Christ-appointed sign of water and the gospel Word regarding the baptized member's communion with the Triune God, Father, Son, and Holy Spirit.

The sacrament of baptism, which by its nature may be administered only once, serves to signify and seal to believers

---

16. See, e.g., Heidelberg Catechism, Q. & A. 68; Belgic Confession, Art. 33; Westminster Confession of Faith, 27.4.

17. See Westminster Confession of Faith, 28.3. For a thorough discussion of the Reformers' views on the mode of baptism, including a review of the history of the question in the Christian church, see Hughes Oliphant Old, *The Shaping of the Reformed Baptismal Rite in the Sixteenth Century* (Grand Rapids: Eerdmans, 1992), 264-82. Though some of the Reformers attempted to reintroduce the practice of immersion (e.g., Zwingli), the general consensus was that the mode was an *adiaphoron* and that sprinkling was, practically, the most expedient mode.

their adoption into the household of God and incorporation into Christ.[18] The water of baptism especially represents the washing away of sin through the blood of Christ and the Spirit of regeneration. By baptism believers are not only visibly distinguished from those who remain 'strangers' to God and Christ's church, but they are also assured of the grace of reconciliation with God and purification from the pollution and guilt of sin. Moreover, as those who are distinguished as members of Christ and the household of God, believers are also by baptism enlisted into the service of Christ, engaged to him as those who are his cherished possession, and called to live in love with all others who enjoy communion with Christ. Though the emphasis in the Reformed confessions falls upon the privileges of grace that are signified and sealed to believers in baptism, the *Westminster Larger Catechism* especially emphasizes these accompanying obligations of baptism.[19] Just as the required response to the Word of the gospel includes repentance and faith, so the required response to the visible Word of the sacrament includes corresponding responsibilities and privileges. These purposes of baptism are not restricted to the occasion of its administration. Rather, throughout the entire course of the believer's life, the sacrament of baptism serves powerfully and effectively to confirm faith and stimulate obedience. To use the language of the *Westminster Larger Catechism*, believers must be vigilant in the constant 'improvement' of their baptism, being reminded by this sacrament of their engagement to Christ and enrollment in the company of his people.

Though the Reformed confessions do not teach baptismal regeneration, they do ascribe a real efficacy to the sacrament of baptism in conferring the grace of God in Christ upon believers. A cursory reading of the descriptions of the function and effect of baptism in these confessions indicates that they affirm a real connection between the sacramental sign and the spiritual reality signified. Again and again, the sacrament of baptism is described as that which effects, or brings about, what is visibly

---

18. See, e.g., Heidelberg Catechism, Q. & A. 70; Belgic Confession, Art. 34; Westminster Confession of Faith, 28.1.

19. Q. & A. 167.

represented and pledged. As a divinely appointed instrument for the confirmation of faith, it could not be otherwise. For if the sacrament were of little or no effect as a means of grace—merely a visible testimony to the believer's subjective state and disposition toward God, and not a divinely given sacramental Word signifying and sealing divine grace in Christ—then it would not have been added to the Word as a more full confirmation of God's grace. Because God has been willing to join the spiritual grace communicated with its sacramental sign, the church must not weaken its understanding of the sacrament's power by 'breaking asunder' what God has joined together.

In their handling of the question, *Who should be baptized?*, the Reformed confessions consistently affirm that baptism should be administered not only to believers, but also to their children. The affirmation of the baptism of children of believing parents is treated more expansively in the later confessions of the Reformation era, which reflect the continuing and intensifying polemic against the Anabaptist repudiation of infant baptism.[20] According to the confessions, the children of believing parents must be baptized for the same reason as their believing parents: God is pleased to extend the gospel promise to them. The ground for the baptism of children of believers is their divinely promised inclusion in the church and covenant of Jesus Christ. As members of Christ and recipients of the gospel promise,

---

20. See, e.g., Heidelberg Catechism, Q. & A. 74; Belgic Confession, Art. 34; Westminster Confession of Faith, 28.4. It is well known that Karl Barth severely criticized the Reformed confessions' affirmation of the baptism of children of believing parents. See Karl Barth, *Church Dogmatics* (Edinburgh: T. & T. Clark, 1969), IV/4:264-94. According to Barth, the Reformers failed at this point to carry through consistently their insistence upon faith as necessary to the reception of the sacrament. The Reformers simply adopted a common social practice of the day and then invented ('necessity is the mother of invention'!) a theological justification for it. In this criticism, Barth fails to appreciate the Reformed view of the sacrament as essentially *God's sacramental signifying and sealing of his grace* to believers and their children. Though it is true that faith receives the grace the sacrament confers, it does so as a 'receptive' rather than 'constitutive' act. The children of believing parents who are baptized must believe, to be sure, but their believing is a response to the gracious promise previously signified and sealed to them in the sacrament of baptism. The argument of the Reformed confessions, which is a biblical argument based upon the doctrine of the covenant and God's sovereign initiatives in salvation, underscores the sheer graciousness of God's grace in the promise he makes to the children of believing parents. For a discussion of Barth's critique and a defense of the Reformed view, see G. C. Berkouwer, *Karl Barth en de Kinderdoop* (Kampen: J. H. Kok, 1947).

therefore, their baptism has the same meaning as the baptism of adult believers. Consistent with the Reformed understanding of the divine initiative in election and the communication of God's grace in Christ to his people, the baptism of children of believing parents attests to their adoption into the household of God, and the washing away of their sins through the blood of Christ and the Spirit of regeneration.

Several biblical considerations are adduced in the confessions to support the practice of the baptism of children of believing parents: God's gracious promise to them; their inclusion within the covenant people of God; the fact that the kingdom of God belongs to them; the Old Testament precedent of the sacrament of circumcision, which in the New Testament has been replaced by baptism; and the Old Testament practice of offering a lamb of purification at the birth of a child, which was a sacrament of Jesus Christ.[21] Children are not baptized on the basis of a presumed regeneration or any other subjective condition (such as an 'infant faith' or the faith of the parents in lieu of their own). Since the power and efficacy of the sacrament of baptism, as is the case with the sacraments generally, depend upon a believing reception of the sacramentally communicated Word of grace, the baptized children of believers are under the obligations to believe and repent that accompany the privileges of their baptism. Moreover, because the sacramental sign and seal are to be distinguished from the spiritual grace that they confirm, the efficacy of baptism may not be tied to the moment of its administration.[22] This does not diminish the efficacy of baptism, but only acknowledges that its power may not be immediately exhibited.[23]

---

21. See, e.g., Heidelberg Catechism, Q. & A. 74; Belgic Confession, Art. 34.

22. Westminster Confession of Faith, 28.6: 'The efficacy of Baptism is not tied to that moment of time wherein it is administered; yet notwithstanding, by the right use of this ordinance, the grace promised is not only offered, but really exhibited, and conferred, by the Holy Ghost, to such (whether of age or infants) as that grace belongeth unto, according to the counsel of God's own will, in his appointed time.'

23. The only Reformed confession that expressly addresses the issue of the validity of baptism in the Roman Catholic Church is the Gallican Confession of 1560 (Art. 28). The Gallican Confession expressly affirms the validity of Roman Catholic baptisms as a 'trace' of the true church remaining within that communion. This affirmation of the Gallican Confession represents, however, the predominant view of the Reformed churches at the time

2. *The Lord's Supper — A Sacrament of Nourishment*

The second sacrament that Christ has appointed for his church is the sacrament of the Lord's Supper. Unlike the sacrament of baptism, which is a sign and seal of incorporation into Christ and his church, the sacrament of the Lord's Supper is a sign and seal of God's grace in Christ that continually nourishes and strengthens the faith of its recipient.

With respect to the frequency of its administration and reception, the sacrament of the Lord's Supper is clearly distinguished in the Reformed confessions from the sacrament of baptism. Whereas baptism is a rite of initiation or incorporation into Christ and his body, the church, the Lord's Supper is a rite of continual confirmation, nourishment and strengthening of the faith of believers. Baptism is by its nature a one-time ordinance. The Lord's Supper is by its nature a sacrament that needs to be repeated and therefore continually used by believers. Though the Reformed confessions do not explicitly comment on the frequency of the administration of the Lord's Supper, they favor in principle a practice where the sacrament of the Lord's Supper ordinarily accompanies the preaching of the gospel.[24] Stated negatively, there are no clear confessional reasons that the sacrament of the Lord's Supper should not regularly be

---

of the Reformation and subsequently. The validity and efficacy of the sacrament does not depend upon the ministrant, but upon the presence of the gospel promise of communion with the Triune God and its accompanying sacramental sign and seal.

24. The desirability of a frequent use of the sacrament was already set forth in Calvin's 'Draft Ecclesiastical Ordinances' of 1537 (in *Calvin: Theological Treatises,* ed. J. K. S. Reid [Philadelphia: Westminster Press, 1954], 66): 'Since the Supper was instituted for us by our Lord to be frequently used, and also was so observed in the ancient Church until the devil turned everything upside down, erecting the mass in its place, it is a fault in need of correction, to celebrate it so seldom.' Cf. G. W. Bromiley, *Sacramental Teaching and Practice in the Reformation Churches* (Grand Rapids: Eerdmans, 1957), 74: 'The general view of the Reformers was that, considering scriptural precedent and the purpose and meaning of the sacrament, it ought to be administered each week, or monthly at the very least.' For a recent defense of a more frequent celebration of the Supper, which argues on the basis of Calvin's doctrine and the standpoint of the Reformed confessions, see Michael J. Horton, 'At Least Weekly: The Reformed Doctrine of the Lord's Supper and of Its Frequent Celebration,' *Mid-America Journal of Theology* 11 (2000), 147-69. It is an irony of history that, whereas several of the church orders of the Reformed churches stipulate the administration of the sacrament *at least* four times per year, this became the standard practice. Historically, this stipulation was a compromise intended to *increase* the frequency of participation in the face of the Medieval practice going back to the Fourth Lateran Council of 1215 requiring reception of the mass at least once per year (the normal practice of many).

appended to the administration of the gospel in preaching. The requirements for a proper participation in the Supper—self-examination and the guarding of the Table against its profanation by unworthy participation on the part of the unbelieving and impenitent—might well present practical impediments to the regular, even weekly, celebration of the Supper. But, with the possible exception of the *Westminster Larger Catechism*, which provides a detailed description regarding the preparation for and use of the sacrament, none of the great confessions of the Reformed churches offers any argument against frequent communion.

In the Reformed confessions the Lord's Supper is variously described and several of its purposes are identified.

Perhaps the most basic metaphor governing the descriptions of the Lord's Supper is that of *a sacred meal,* which was instituted to nourish believers in their communion with Christ.[25] The sacramental elements of bread and wine were consecrated to serve as tokens and pledges of Christ himself, whose body given and blood shed are the spiritual sustenance and life of believers. By sharing this sacramental meal, believers enjoy a rich communion with Christ and with all his members. They commune with Christ under the veil of the sacramental elements, and acknowledge him to be their food and drink unto life eternal. Reflecting this emphasis upon the sacrament as a nourishing meal, the Reformed confessions typically denominate the sacrament as 'the Lord's Supper' or 'the Lord's table.' Even as the physical body is strengthened by bread and wine, so the spiritual life of believers is strengthened by the eating and drinking of Christ, who is the spiritual food of those who belong to him by faith.

Consistent with the understanding of the Lord's Supper as a spiritual meal in which the believer enjoys communion with and is nourished by the Lord, the Reformed confessions also speak of the sacrament as *a memorial* of Christ's death and sacrifice upon the cross.[26] Though the sacrament of the Lord's Supper is

---

25. See e. g. Heidelberg Catechism, Q. & A. 75, 77, 79; Westminster Confession of Faith, 29.1.

26. Heidelberg Catechism, Q. & A. 75; Westminster Confession of Faith, 29.2.

not merely a memorial or occasion for thanksgiving to God—the Zwinglian doctrine of the sacrament is uniformly, though often only implicitly, repudiated as inadequate—through it the church commemorates and proclaims Christ's death until he comes again at the end of the age. For this reason, the sacrament is also an occasion for thanksgiving and praise—a Eucharistic meal whose character is not only one of reverent commemoration but also one of joyful thankfulness. When believers receive the elements as tokens of Christ's body and blood, they do so in gratitude to God for all of the benefits of salvation that are theirs through Christ.

The sacrament, which as a visible sign of an invisible grace confirms and strengthens faith in the promises of the gospel, also evokes thanksgiving by *assuring* believers of their participation in Christ and his saving work. To use the language of the confessions, as assuredly as believers take the bread and the wine from the hand of Christ's ministers, so assuredly may they believe that Christ's work was for them.[27] Indeed, it was for this reason that the Lord graciously and mercifully appointed the sacrament. Knowing the weakness and uncertainty that often characterize the faith of believers, the Lord instituted this sacramental meal as a visible representation of his work on their behalf. Lest the gospel promise, first announced through the preaching of the Word, be doubted, God has graciously condescended to our weakness in appointing this means to aid our faith.

Because the sacramental meal of the Lord's Supper is a *holy communion* with Christ, it also serves the purposes of uniting believers more intimately with him and calling them to a life of loving obedience and holy consecration. Believers, when they commemorate and proclaim the reconciling work of Christ in the sacrament, are reminded of their calling to be united to and reconciled with fellow believers. Those who are joined through the sacrament in communion with Christ are likewise joined with all who are his members. Furthermore, as members who enjoy the most intimate and full communion with Christ, they

---

27. Heidelberg Catechism, Q. & A. 75.

are engaged to a life that is marked by love and obedience to him. Those who share this meal with Christ are called to live in greater intimacy with Christ and his members. Failure to live in communion with Christ or to love those who share this communion with him is a manifest denial of the nature and significance of this sacred meal.

On the much-disputed question of the nature of Christ's *real presence* in the sacrament, the Reformed confessions typically affirm this presence in strong terms. But they do so with an accompanying denial of the explanations of that presence traditionally offered by the Roman Catholic Church or the Lutheran tradition.

According to the Reformed confessions, those who receive Christ through the sacrament with the mouth of faith genuinely partake of him. Believers enjoy through the sacrament a true participation in and reception of the body and blood of Christ. The sacramental signs of bread and wine, though not to be confused or identified with the actual body and blood of Christ, genuinely communicate Christ to believers. The sacramental acts of eating and drinking are instrumental to a communication of Christ *with* the sacramental signs. In several of the confessions, the language used to describe Christ's presence is quite robust. Believers are said to partake through the sacrament of 'the proper and natural body and the proper blood of Christ'.[28] The spiritual eating and drinking that takes place in the sacrament involves such an intimate participation in Christ that the believer becomes altogether one with him, bone of his bone, flesh of his flesh.[29]

However, when it comes to providing an explanation of the manner of Christ's presence in the Lord's Supper, the Reformed Confessions object vigorously to the Roman Catholic doctrine of transubstantiation and the Lutheran doctrine of consubstantiation. The Roman Catholic doctrine of transubstantiation improperly identifies the sacramental elements with the spiritual reality that they represent. The

---

28. Belgic Confession, Art. 35.
29. Heidelberg Catechism, Q. & A. 76.

earthly elements of the sacrament become the actual body and blood of Christ, though remaining under the form or appearance of bread and wine. Whether received by faith or not, the consecrated elements are objectively the body and blood of Christ, and remain what they have become until they are properly consumed.[30] Moreover, in this doctrine the eating and drinking of Christ is a physical act, an 'eating with the mouth' (*manducatio oralis*) that is a physical rather than a spiritual participation in Christ. Likewise, though the Lutheran doctrine of consubstantiation does not improperly identify the sacramental signs with the thing signified, nonetheless it teaches that the actual body and blood of Christ are *locally* present in the sacrament. This doctrine also affirms an 'eating with the mouth' (*manducatio oralis*) that fails to appreciate the spiritual nature of the believer's participation in Christ through the sacrament. Contrary to these doctrines of Christ's presence, therefore, the Reformed confessions simply affirm the believers' eating and drinking of the natural body and blood of Christ. This occurs through an inexpressible and incomprehensible working of the Spirit of Christ, who draws believers through the sacrament up to Christ who is in heaven in order that they might be joined in communion with him.

In their criticism of the Roman Catholic doctrine of Christ's presence in the sacrament of the Lord's Supper, the Reformed confessions typically express several key objections to the Roman Catholic doctrine of the mass. The objection to the doctrine of transubstantiation is not only addressed to the problem of the adoration of the consecrated elements, which is a form of idolatry and an inappropriate identification of the sign with the thing signified. But it is also addressed to the idea that Christ's presence

---

30. Heidelberg Catechism, Q. & A. 78, 80; Westminster Confession of Faith, Chapter 29.6. This kind of 'objectivism' in the understanding of Christ's presence in the sacramental elements is clearly expressed in the decisions of the Council of Trent on the sacrament of the mass. Cf. 'The Canons and Decrees of the Council of Trent,' Thirteenth Session, Decree Concerning the Most Holy Sacrament of the Eucharist, Canon IV (Schaff, *The Creeds of Christendom*, 1:137): 'If any one saith, that, after the consecration is completed, the body and blood of our Lord Jesus Christ are not in the admirable sacrament of the Eucharist, but only during the use, whilst it is being taken, and not either before or after; and, in the hosts, or consecrated particles, which are reserved or which remain after communion, the true body of the Lord remaineth not: let him be anathema.'

in the sacrament is the basis for the unbloody sacrifice of Christ in the mass. The priest who ministers at the altar in the Roman Catholic mass offers Christ himself as a propitiation and sacrifice for sin. Though this sacrifice is an unbloody re-presentation of Christ's sacrifice upon the cross, it obtains further grace and merit for those who participate and even for those who may not be present (the dead). Furthermore, the administration of the mass includes or permits a number of unbiblical practices: the elevation and adoration of the host, the withholding of the cup from the laity, the communing on the part of the priests or clergy without the presence or participation of the laity, and private masses for individuals or portions of the whole body of the church. These and a host of additional ceremonies constitute an affront to the exclusive priesthood of Christ, whose one sacrifice is sufficient to the needs of his people, and betray a superstitious and magical view of the working of the sacrament.

The Proper Recipients of the Lord's Supper

Though it might seem that this extended discussion of the Reformed confessions' view of the sacraments has traveled far afield of the specific question of paedocommunion, the position of the confessions on this question can only be understood within the broader framework of its doctrine of the sacraments in general. The insistence of the confessions that the recipients of the Lord's Supper be professing believers arises out of their general teaching regarding the nature and power of the sacraments. When the confessions insist upon the presence of faith on the part of the recipient of the Lord's Supper, they do so for reasons that correspond to their more comprehensive view of the sacraments.

As noted in the foregoing, the sacrament of the Lord's Supper, because it is a visible representation and confirmation of the gospel promise in Christ, *requires faith* on the part of its participants. Because the sacrament visibly signifies and seals the promises of the gospel, it demands the same response as the gospel. Neither the gospel Word nor the sacrament work merely by virtue of their administration (*ex opere operato*). Only by a spiritual eating and drinking by the mouth of faith does the sacrament work to communicate Christ to his people. Therefore, the Roman Catholic teaching of an objective presence of Christ in the sacramental elements, irrespective of a believing response to the gospel Word that the sacrament confirms, is rejected. Not only does this Roman Catholic view improperly identify the sacramental sign and the spiritual reality it signifies, but it also maintains that Christ is objectively present before, during, and even after the administration of the elements whether or not those participating (or not participating) actively accept the gospel in faith and repentance.

In the Reformed confessions, moreover, the kind of faith that is competent to remember, proclaim, and receive Christ through the Lord's Supper is carefully defined. Before members of the church may receive the sacrament, they have a biblical mandate to engage in self-examination. This self-examination requires that believers test their faith against the normative requirements of the Word of God. Essential to such faith are the acknowledgement of the believer's sin and unworthiness, the recognition that Christ alone by his mediatorial work has made atonement for the sins of his people, and a resolution to live in holiness and obedience to his will. In this way believers are called actively to embrace the promises of the gospel that the sacrament visibly confirms in the same way as they respond to the preaching of the gospel. Furthermore, it is the duty of the ministers and elders of the church to oversee the administration of the sacrament, preventing so far as they are able those from participating who are unbelieving or living an ungodly life. Since Christ has instituted the sacrament for the purpose of nourishing the faith of believers, it would violate the nature of the sacrament to invite the unbelieving or the impenitent to partake. Unworthy participation, that is, participation on the part of those who have not properly examined themselves or who are unbelieving, would profane the table of the Lord and be contemptuous of its ordained purpose.

Since this feature of the Reformed confessions' teaching touches directly upon the propriety of paedocommunion, we need to take particular note of the confessions' teaching regarding the proper recipients of the sacrament.

The Belgic Confession, after noting that the recipient of the Lord's Supper receives the body and blood of the Lord 'by faith (which is the hand and mouth of our soul),' speaks directly to this subject.

> We receive this holy sacrament in the assembly of the people of God, with humility and reverence, keeping up among us a holy remembrance of the faith and of the Christian religion. Therefore no one ought to come to this table without having previously rightly examined himself, lest by eating of this bread and drinking of this cup he eat and drink judgment to himself. In a word, we are moved by the use of this holy sacrament to a fervent love towards God and our neighbor. (Article 35)

According to the language of this article, the sacrament of the Lord's Supper requires the active engagement of its recipients. Only believers, who are capable of remembering the faith and the Christian religion, may come to the Table in order to be nourished and fortified in the way of faith and love. With an obvious allusion to the Apostle Paul's teaching in 1 Corinthians 11, this Confession also insists upon a proper preparation on the part of believers for the reception of the sacrament. Only those who have previously examined themselves should partake of the bread and the cup, lest they should eat and drink judgment unto themselves.

In its extensive treatment of the sacrament of the Lord's Supper, the *Heidelberg Catechism* also expressly addresses the question of those for whom the sacrament is instituted.

> Q. For whom is the Lord's supper instituted?
> A. For those who are truly displeased with themselves for their sins and yet trust that these are forgiven them for the sake of Christ, and that their remaining infirmity is covered by His passion and death; who also desire more and more to strengthen their faith and amend their life. But hypocrites and such as turn not to God with sincere hearts eat and drink judgment to themselves (Q. & A. 81).[31]

---

31. It should be noted that the Scripture proofs cited for this answer are 1 Corinthians 11:28, 29; and 10:19-22. In earlier questions and answers, additional passages

It is important to observe that the three marks of true faith, which are identified in this question and answer, are the same as the three general headings of the *Heidelberg Catechism*. This is not accidental, since the purpose of the Catechism is to provide an instrument for the instruction of the children of believers in the Christian faith. True faith always includes three elements: (1) a conscious awareness of the believer's sin and misery; (2) an understanding of the person and work of Christ, who satisfied for the believer's sins by his cross and passion; and (3) a Spirit-worked readiness on the part of the believer to live in gratitude to God. When the children of believing parents, who have received the sign and seal of incorporation into Christ through the sacrament of baptism, are instructed in these principal elements of the Christian religion, they are being invited to respond in faith to their baptism and to come believingly to the Lord's Supper. Though this is not the place to answer the objections of proponents of paedocommunion, the teaching of the *Heidelberg Catechism* does not seem to create an artificial and unnecessary barrier before children who might otherwise be received at the Lord's Table. All believers who are received at the Lord's Table come in the same way and with the same obligations. Consistent with the nature of true faith (cf. Heidelberg Catechism Q. & A. 21), all believers who come to the Table of the Lord in order to be nourished in faith are expected to come believingly. If the sacrament is to be used to strengthen faith, it is only appropriate that those who receive the sacrament do so as professing believers.

That this is the consensus view of the Reformed confessions is also evident from the Westminster Standards. In 29.7 of *The Westminster Confession of Faith*, the necessity of a believing participation in the Lord's Supper is clearly affirmed: 'Worthy receivers [of the Lord's Supper], outwardly partaking of the visible elements, in this sacrament, do then also, inwardly by faith, really and indeed yet not carnally and corporally but spiritually, receive, and feed upon, Christ crucified, and all

---

are cited to show that faith is required on the part of the recipient of the sacrament (e.g., John 6:35, 40, 47, 48, 50, 51, 53, 54).

benefits of his death.' Since the Lord's Supper is a sacrament that nourishes faith, it requires faith on the part of those who receive it. Perhaps the most relevant statement of the confessions in respect to the question of paedocommunion, is found in *The Westminster Larger Catechism*. In answer to a question about the difference between the sacraments of baptism and the Lord's Supper, the *Larger Catechism* states:

> The sacraments of Baptism and the Lord's Supper differ, in that Baptism is to be administered but once, with water, to be a sign and seal of our regeneration and ingrafting into Christ, and that even to infants; whereas the Lord's Supper is to be administered often, in the elements of bread and wine, to represent and exhibit Christ as spiritual nourishment to the soul, and to confirm our continuance and growth in him, and that only to such as are of years and ability to examine themselves (Q. & A. 177).

According to the *Larger Catechism*, baptism and the Lord's Supper differ in terms of what they signify and seal. Baptism signifies and seals to its recipients their regeneration and ingrafting into Christ. The Lord's Supper signifies and seals to its recipients their continuance and growth in believing union with Christ. Whereas baptism is administered but once to believers and their children, the Lord's Supper is administered often 'to such as are of years and ability to examine themselves'. Though the *Larger Catechism* does not spell out what it means by the expression 'of years and ability to examine themselves', it transparently reflects the confession and practice of the Reformed churches, which has historically required a public ceremony of profession of faith on the part of the children of believing parents prior to their reception at the Lord's Table. The purpose of such a profession of faith is to confirm publicly the kind of faith demanded by their baptism and to be the occasion for admitting them to the Lord's Table.

Summary
The uniform testimony of the Reformed confessions is that, though the children of believing parents ought to be baptized

as a sacramental sign and seal of their incorporation into Christ, they may only receive the sacrament of the Lord's Supper upon an attestation of their faith in the gospel promise. Even though the practice of paedocommunion is not expressly rejected in these confessions, their general understanding of the nature and purpose of the sacraments stands opposed to this practice. Two emphases in the confessions especially militate against the practice of paedocommunion.

The first emphasis is the confessions' insistence that the sacraments do not communicate the grace of Christ apart from the preaching of the gospel, in relation to which they are confirming signs. The principal means whereby Christ dwells among and communicates himself to his people is the preaching of the gospel. Through the preaching of the gospel, the Holy Spirit produces faith in the hearts and minds of believers. Indeed, the saving power of the gospel Word is only communicated to those in whom such faith lives by the working of the Holy Spirit. Because the sacraments are visible signs and seals of the gospel promise, their effectiveness—like that of the Word they visibly proclaim—also requires a believing reception on the part of their beneficiaries. Just as the gospel Word is received through faith, so the sacramental pledges and seals of the gospel require faith on the part of their recipients. Though the children of believers are to be baptized, since they together with their parents are included in the covenant community, their baptism summons them to the same believing response that the gospel Word demands. Baptism, just as with the Lord's Supper, does not work by its mere administration. It only serves to confirm and bolster faith, which is principally worked by the Holy Spirit through the gospel. Therefore, consistent with their emphasis upon the priority of the Spirit's use of the preaching of the gospel to produce faith, *the confessions insist that the route from the baptismal font to the Lord's Table can only be taken in the way of an active response of faith.* To argue that baptism alone is a sufficient basis for admitting the children of believers to the Lord's Table, would require a substantial change in the way the confessions understand the use and effectiveness of the sacraments in relation to the preaching of the Word.[32]

The second emphasis is the confessions' view of the difference between the sacraments of baptism and the Lord's Supper. Whereas baptism is a once-for-all sign and seal of incorporation into Christ and his church, the Lord's Supper is a frequently administered sign and seal of the gospel that nourishes faith, which the Spirit produces by means of the Word. Because the sacrament of the Lord's Supper is designed to nourish and strengthen faith, it requires a prior attestation of the presence of faith on the part of its recipients. Though the language may be a little misleading, the Lord's Supper, unlike baptism, requires for its proper reception an *active* and *believing* participation in Christ. Believers are summoned at the Table of the Lord to 'take, eat, remember, and believe.' The purpose of the catechetical instruction of children of believing parents is to prepare them to make a credible confession of faith, which in the traditional practice of the Reformed churches is effected by means of a 'public profession of faith'. Unless such faith has been publicly attested, the children of believers are not yet prepared to make proper use of the sacrament that Christ has appointed for the specific purpose of nourishing faith.

Admittedly, the Reformed confessions do not stipulate a particular age at which such a profession should be made. Nor do they spell out in detail the kind of instruction in the faith that ought ordinarily to precede a mature profession of faith and admission to the Lord's Table. They clearly insist, however, in keeping with the nature of the sacraments in general and of the sacrament of the Lord's Supper in particular, that the straight line leading from the baptismal font to the Lord's Table includes along the way a confirmation of the baptized believer's embrace of the gospel promise. Though baptism summons the children of believers to faith and therefore to the Table of the Lord, it

---

32. Perhaps it should also be noted here that the confessions' emphasis upon the pre-eminence of preaching belies the common paedocommunionist argument that, deprived of their reception at the Lord's Table, they are being spiritually malnourished. This would only be true, if they were deprived of the benefit of the preaching of the gospel and its application through catechetical instruction.

does not constitute a sufficient condition for their admission to the Table. Baptism summons its recipient to faith, whose presence must first be publicly attested before the believer comes to the Table of the Lord.

To state the matter in a different way, the admission of children to the Table of the Lord without a prior attestation of their faith would require a substantial change in the historic Reformed understanding of the nature and use of the sacraments. If advocates of paedocommunion are able to demonstrate that the teaching of Scripture demands such a change, then the confessions should be revised. This is the obvious implication of the church's confession that the Scriptures must always remain the supreme standard for the church's faith and practice. This consideration of the Reformed confessions, however, indicates that advocates of paedocommunion bear a significant burden of proof to show the basis for and extent of such revisions. No one should be under the illusion that anything less would be required.

6

Children at the Lord's Table in the Patristic Era

Nick Needham

Introduction

The attempt to reconstruct church life in the patristic era can be fraught with difficulties. Children's participation in the Lord's Supper is one of them. This is especially so when there is heated contemporary debate within significant sections of Protestantism over the admission of children to the Supper. In such a context, it is all too easy to search and interpret patristic sources with a polemical motive; slanted 'takes' on the evidence can be a more than usually pressing temptation. Perhaps, however, I can marginally reassure readers of this particular chapter by pointing out that its author has no theological or existential stake in the current intra-Protestant debate. As a British Baptist, I do not encounter in my own tradition the cluster of issues relating to the place of baptized infants at the Lord's Table, since we do not baptize infants. I trust I am not being over-charitable to myself if I therefore indulge the hope of assessing the patristic situation with a modicum of enlarged objectivity.

My confessional position itself, however, highlights a serious problem in this whole area: namely, we can hardly disentangle the two dominical sacraments from each other. Belief and practice about baptism and about the Lord's Supper are bound up with each other, both theologically and historically. Those who reject infant baptism are unlikely (to put it mildly) to endorse infant communion.[1] Were we to find evidence from the patristic era of a rejection of infant communion, therefore, we would have to ask whether this was itself posited on a rejection of infant baptism. If the connection holds, the important consequence would follow that this particular species of anti-paedocommunion would have no relevance to current debates within paedobaptist bodies concerning the admission of baptized infants to the Lord's table.

As it happens, there was a powerful strain of credobaptism in the patristic church, especially in the fourth century (or at least, it is especially documentable then). Christian parents often 'delayed' baptising their offspring until the children had reached early adulthood, and themselves volunteered for baptism as an expression of conscious commitment. The three Cappadocian fathers (Basil and the two Gregories), John Chrysostom, Jerome, and Augustine of Hippo all fit into this pattern: raised Christian, but not presented for baptism in childhood, and baptized only later as their own voluntary act. This reluctance of Christian parents to bring their children to the baptismal basin or pool seems generally to have been linked, in the parents' mind, with a fear that the grace of baptism would be squandered by their children's sins (notably after the onset of puberty); consequently it was thought better to delay baptismal initiation until the youngsters had personally committed themselves to serious Christian discipleship, after the initial shock of puberty was over. Gregory of Nazianzus, as an adult preacher, argued against this fairly common practice of delaying baptism (although it had been his own experience), and Gregory's argument reveals not only the existence of such delay but the reasoning behind it:

---

1. I use the term 'infant communion' rather than 'child communion', because it is possible, within a credobaptist framework, to baptize a child on confession of faith. That child could then be admitted to the Lord's Supper, since there seems no cogent reason to think that a child capable of a credible profession of faith should be admitted to one sacrament but not the other: in effect, to baptize a believer and then immediately excommunicate him/her. The term *infant*, however, refers historically to very young children, those not yet capable of confessing faith.

Have you an infant child? Do not let sin get any opportunity, but let him be sanctified from his childhood; from his very tenderest age let him be consecrated by the Spirit. Fearest thou the Seal on account of the weakness of nature? O what a small-souled mother, and of how little faith! Why, Anna even before Samuel was born promised him to God, and after his birth consecrated him at once, and brought him up in the priestly habit, not fearing anything in human nature, but trusting in God. You have no need of amulets or incantations, with which the Devil also comes in, stealing worship from God for himself in the minds of vainer men. Give your child the Trinity, that great and noble Guard.[2]

Since baptism was the gateway to the Lord's Table in the patristic era, the model of practice I have just sketched would necessarily have precluded infant communion. It does not count, however, as an argument against infant communion for those who practise infant baptism. What interests us here is the bond between baptismal and Eucharistic theology and practice in the case of the well-attested paedobaptist strain of patristic piety. Where Christian parents did present their infants for baptism, did this lead to the automatic inclusion of the infants in the Lord's Supper? If not, was there a universal delay in admission, or a diversity of practices?

The easiest aspect of this investigation is to locate evidence for the inclusion of baptized infants (with little or no delay) into the patristic Eucharist. Such evidence is palpable in the primary source literature. Let us consider it. My self-imposed timeframe here will cover the patristic age up to and including

---

2. *Oration on Holy Baptism* 17, in Philip Schaff (ed.), Nicene and Post-Nicene Fathers (Hendricksen: Peabody, Massachussets 1994), Second Series, vol.VII, p.365. Cf. *Baptism* 28: 'Be it so, some will say, in the case of those who ask for Baptism; what have you to say about those who are still children, and conscious neither of the loss nor of the grace? Are we to baptize them too? Certainly, if any danger presses. For it is better that they should be unconsciously sanctified than that they should depart unsealed and uninitiated. A proof of this is found in the Circumcision on the eighth day, which was a sort of typical seal, and was conferred on children before they had the use of reason... For this is how the matter stands; at that time they begin to be responsible for their lives, when reason is matured, and they learn the mystery of life (for of sins of ignorance owing to their tender years they have no account to give), and it is far more profitable on all accounts to be fortified by the Font, because of the sudden assaults of danger that befall us, stronger than our helpers' (ibid. p. 370).

Augustine of Hippo (d. 430). Such decisions are often arbitrary; my justification is that I wish to keep a relatively tight focus for this chapter (going all the way up to the traditional end of the patristic era in 787 – last of the ecumenical councils – would make the material unwieldy), and most readers of this book will recognise in the death of Augustine a natural landmark.

Cyprian

Cyprian of Carthage (d. 258) was the dominant voice of Catholic theology in Roman North Africa until the emergence of Augustine 150 years later.[3] Indeed Cyprian was so much 'the' African theologian, that when the Catholic-Donatist controversy broke out in the fourth century, a major Catholic embarrassment was the legitimacy with which Donatists could appeal to Cyprian for their view of rebaptism. Some of Augustine's strongest statements about the fallibility of post-apostolic theologians were inspired by this embarrassment in the context of debating the Donatists: Cyprian, though great, was only flesh and blood, and sadly liable to err.[4]

Still, in his own lifetime there can be no doubting Cyprian's stature as eloquent articulator of African Catholic tradition. He was undoubtedly a paedobaptist, as his 64th Letter forcefully demonstrates. Cyprian here recounts to bishop Fidus (otherwise unknown) a decision taken by the third council of Carthage in 253:

> But in respect of the case of the infants, which you say ought not to be baptized within the second or third day after their birth, and that the law of ancient circumcision should be regarded, so that you think that one who is just born should not be baptized and sanctified within the eighth day, we all thought very differently in our council. For in this course which you thought was to be taken, no one agreed; but we

---

3. I exclude the otherwise brilliant and influential Tertullian since subsequent generations did not consider him Catholic. His dallyings with Montanism overshadowed and increasingly wrecked his reputation.

4. 'I am not bound by the authority of this epistle, because I do not account the writings of Cyprian as canonical Scriptures, but I consider them to be outside of the canonical Scriptures. Whatsoever in Cyprian's writings agrees with the authority of the Holy Scripture, I receive with Cyprian's approval; but whatsoever does not agree with Scripture, I reject it with Cyprian's leave' (Augustine, *Contra Cresconium* 2.32 [in Migne PL 43.490]).

all rather judge that the mercy and grace of God is not to be refused to any one born of man...

But if anything could hinder men from obtaining grace, their more heinous sins might rather hinder those who are mature and grown up and older. But again, if even to the greatest sinners, and to those who had sinned much against God, when they subsequently believed, remission of sins is granted—and nobody is hindered from baptism and from grace—how much rather ought we to shrink from hindering an infant, who, being lately born, has not sinned, except in that, being born after the flesh according to Adam, he has contracted the contagion of the ancient death at its earliest birth, who approaches the more easily on this very account to the reception of the forgiveness of sins—that to him are remitted, not his own sins, but the sins of another.[5]

There is no evidence that the third council of Carthage was enacting anything revolutionary in its affirmation of infant baptism. The debate was not over whether infants should be baptized, but how soon after birth.

Given this sacramental setting, Cyprian made a number of statements in his treatise *On the Lapsed* about the participation of young children in the Eucharist which can scarcely be understood as indicating anything other than a contextually uncontroversial admission of baptized infants to the Lord's Table. Cyprian describes the apostasy of some Christians under persecution, not only partaking of Pagan sacrifice themselves, but including their young children in the ceremony:

But to many their own destruction was not sufficient. With mutual exhortations, people were urged to their ruin; death was pledged by turns in the deadly cup [of Pagan sacrifice]. And that nothing might be wanting to aggravate the crime, infants also, in the arms of their parents, either carried or conducted, lost, while yet little ones, what in the very first beginning of their nativity they had gained. Will not they, when the day of judgment comes, say, "We have done nothing; nor have we

---

5. Letter 58:2, 5, in Schaff, *Ante-Nicene Fathers*, vol. V, 353–54.

forsaken the Lord's bread and cup to hasten freely to a profane contact; the faithlessness of others has ruined us. We have found our parents our murderers; they have denied to us the Church as a Mother; they have denied God as a Father: so that, while we were little, and unforeseeing, and unconscious of such a crime, we were associated by others to the partnership of wickedness, and we were snared by the deceit of others?"[6]

Cyprian puts sentiments in the mouths of Christian infants here that make no sense unless their baptism placed them at the Lord's Table. 'We have not forsaken the Lord's bread and cup...' As the editor of the Schaff translation of Cyprian comments, 'The baptism of infants seems now to be general, and also the communion of infants.'[7]

Later in the treatise, Cyprian tells a cautionary story which has been taken as evidence for his superstition and credulity. For our purposes, however, it has more relevance to the practice of infant communion in the North African Catholic church of his day:

Learn what occurred when I myself was present and a witness. Some parents who by chance were escaping, being little careful on account of their terror, left a little daughter under the care of a wet-nurse. The nurse gave up the forsaken child to the magistrates. They gave it, in the presence of an idol whither the people flocked (because it was not yet able to eat flesh on account of its years), bread mingled with wine, which however itself was the remainder of what had been used in the immolation of those that had perished. Subsequently the mother recovered her child. But the girl was no more able to speak, or to indicate the crime that had been committed, than she had before been able to understand or to prevent it.

Therefore it happened unawares in their ignorance, that when we were sacrificing, the mother brought it in with her. Moreover, the girl mingled with the saints, became impatient of our prayer and supplications, and was at one moment shaken with weeping, and at another tossed about like a wave of the sea by the violent excitement of her mind; as if by the compulsion of a torturer the soul of that still tender child

---

6. *On the Lapsed* 9, in Schaff ANF vol.V, p.439.

7. Footnote 6, p.439.

confessed a consciousness of the fact with such signs as it could. When, however, the solemnities were finished, and the deacon began to offer the cup to those present, and when, as the rest received it, its turn approached, the little child, by the instinct of the divine majesty, turned away its face, compressed its mouth with resisting lips, and refused the cup. Still the deacon persisted, and, although against her efforts, forced on her some of the sacrament of the cup. Then there followed a sobbing and vomiting. In a profane body and mouth the Eucharist could not remain; the draught sanctified in the blood of the Lord burst forth from the polluted stomach.

So great is the Lord's power, so great is His majesty. The secrets of darkness were disclosed under His light, and not even hidden crimes deceived God's priest. This much about an infant, which was not yet of an age to speak of the crime committed by others in respect of herself.[8]

Comment seems superfluous. The entire incident is intelligible only on the supposition that infant communion was the norm (even to the point, according to Cyprian's testimony, where the officiating deacon thought it quite appropriate to force the Eucharistic elements into the child's mouth).

Hippolytus

Hippolytus (c.170–c.236) was a significant Greek-speaking theologian living in third-century Rome. He fell out with its bishop Callistus (217–22), set himself up as a rival bishop, but was later reconciled with the Roman congregation and died a martyr's death. The document now known as *The Apostolic Tradition* is widely attributed to Hippolytus.[9] It claims to record the established liturgical practices of the Roman church in the early third century. Since Hippolytus wrote before Cyprian, chronological order may seem to dictate that he be treated first; however, a good number of scholars think there is evidence of later redaction of the *Tradition*. I doubt whether this affects its substantial usefulness as a witness to early Roman liturgical practice, but it seems prudent not to

---

8. *On the Lapsed* 25-6, in Schaff, *Ante-Nicene Fathers*, vol. V, p.444.

9. See Everett Ferguson, 'Hippolytus', in Everett Ferguson (ed.), *Encyclopedia of Early Christianity*, (Garland Publishing, New York 1998), pp.531-2.

insist that the *Tradition*, in its present form, necessarily reflects the late second or very early third century – we may have to allow that some elements are a little later. That is why I have dealt with Cyprian prior to Hippolytus.

The passages in the *Tradition* relevant to our study, however, are completely consistent with Cyprian's testimony. Hippolytus clearly describes infant baptism:

> At dawn, prayer shall be offered over the water. The stream must flow through the baptismal tank, or pour into it from above when there is no lack of water. But if there is a lack, whether normally or suddenly, then use whatever water you can find. The candidates shall remove their clothes. First baptize the little ones; if they can speak for themselves, let them do so; if they cannot, their parents or other relatives shall speak for them. Next baptize the men, and finally the women; they must first unloose their hair and set aside any gold or silver ornaments they were wearing: no one must take any unfitting thing with them down to the water.[10]

This establishes the paedobaptist context of Hippolytus' Eucharistic teaching, which follows on from his description of the accompanying rites of baptism (chrism, laying on of hands, prayer). The account makes it clear that baptism leads directly into the first communion of the baptized:

> Then the deacons immediately bring the offering to the bishop, and by thanksgiving he shall make the bread into an image of Christ's body, and the cup of wine mixed with water according to the image of the blood, which he shed for all who believe in him. Also milk and honey mixed together to fulfil the promise to the fathers, which spoke of a land flowing with milk and honey; that is, Christ's flesh which he gave, by which those who believe are nourished like babes, for he sweetens the bitter things of the heart by the softness of his word. Also the water into an offering in a token of the washing, so that man's inner aspect, a living soul, may receive the same as the body. The bishop shall explain the reason for all these things to those who partake. When he breaks the bread and distributes the pieces,

---

10. *Apostolic Tradition* 21:1-5.

he shall say: "The bread of heaven in Christ Jesus." The recipient shall say, "Amen." And the presbyters—or the deacons, if there are not enough presbyters—shall hold the cups, and stand near with reverence and modesty, firstly the one who holds the water, next the milk, thirdly the wine. Those who receive shall taste of each three times. He who offers the cup says: "In God the Father Almighty"; and he who receives shall say, "Amen." Next: "In the Lord Jesus Christ"; and he shall say, "Amen." Then: "In the Holy Spirit and the holy church"; and he shall say, "Amen." This is how it shall be done to each.[11]

The argument for paedocommunion here is admittedly indirect. However, given that this whole section of the *Tradition* is a single narrative unit, with baptism leading on, through chrism, laying on of hands, and prayer, into the Eucharist, and given that Hippolytus includes infants in the baptismal rite, there is no reason to think he excluded them from the ensuing communion. Certainly there is no hint of such exclusion. The phrase that Christ's flesh is the spiritual nutriment 'by which they who believe are nourished like babes', although metaphorical, is nonetheless suggestive, especially since 'babes' have just been incorporated in the baptismal rite. The 'Amen' responses of communicants no more militates against their infant status than the posing and answering of questions at the preceding baptism, where Hippolytus clearly states of infants that 'if they can speak for themselves, they shall do so; if not, their parents or other relatives shall speak for them.'

Although we cannot give unhesitating credence to the *Apostolic Tradition*, then, as recording the very earliest traditions of the Roman church, it says nothing inconsistent with what we know from North Africa via Cyprian in the mid-third century.

The Apostolic Constitutions

The *Apostolic Constitutions* dates from the late fourth century (c.350–80), and seems to be of Syrian origin. It is a collection of church laws and liturgical customs. The compiler has been theologically identified as an Origenist (Semi-Arian) or

---

11. *Apostolic Tradition* 21:27-37.

Apollinarian, which has somewhat tainted the work's pedigree among the Nicene orthodox. However, he was not an original composer, but a compiler of already existing materials: the *Didache* (somewhere between late first and late second century), the *Didascalia Apostolorum* (third century), and the *Apostolic Tradition* of Hippolytus. These materials were themselves orthodox enough.[12] From a purely historical standpoint, then, the *Constitutions* offer a picture of church life in the latter part of the fourth century that is worth scrutiny, especially bearing in mind its nature as largely a compilation of earlier material.

The *Constitutions* is a paedobaptist document:

> For the Lord says: "Except a man be baptized of water and of the Spirit, he shall by no means enter into the kingdom of heaven." And again: "He that believeth and is baptized shall be saved; but he that believeth not shall be damned." But he that says, "When I am dying I will be baptized, lest I should sin and defile my baptism," is ignorant of God, and forgetful of his own nature. For "do not thou delay to turn unto the Lord, for thou knowest not what the next day will bring forth." Do you also baptize your infants, and bring them up in the nurture and admonition of God. For says He: "Suffer the little children to come unto me, and forbid them not."[13]

Later, in book 8, the *Constitutions* present material on the celebration of the Eucharist. Among other things we read:

> the deacon shall immediately say, "Let none of the catechumens, let none of the hearers, let none of the unbelievers, let none of the heterodox, stay here. You who have prayed the foregoing prayer, depart. Let the mothers receive their children; let no one have anything against any one; let no one come in hypocrisy; let us stand upright before the Lord with fear and trembling, to offer."[14]

---

12. See George Dragas, 'Apostolic Constitutions', in Everett Ferguson (ed.), *Encyclopedia of Early Christianity*, (Garland Publishing, New York 1998), pp.92-3.

13. *Apostolic Constitutions* 6:15, in Schaff ANF vol.VII, p.457.

14. *Apostolic Constitutions* 8:12, in Schaff ANF vol.VII, p.486.

This is ambiguous by itself; 'let mothers receive their children' could mean 'take them under control so that they do not disturb the worship', or it could mean 'take them so as to prepare them for communion'. The ambiguity, however, is removed in the next section:

> And let the bishop speak thus to the people: "Holy things for holy persons." And let the people answer: "There is One that is holy; there is one Lord, one Jesus Christ, blessed for ever, to the glory of God the Father. Amen. Glory to God in the highest, and on earth peace, good-will among men. Hosanna to the son of David! Blessed be He that cometh in the name of the Lord, being the Lord God who appeared to us, Hosanna in the highest." And after that, let the bishop partake, then the presbyters, and deacons, and sub-deacons, and the readers, and the singers, and the ascetics; and then of the women, the deaconesses, and the virgins, and the widows; then the children; and then all the people in order, with reverence and godly fear, without tumult.[15]

Then the children. The Apostolic Constitutions sees the baptized children of the church as simply one among various classes (bishop, presbyters, deacons, sub-deacons, readers, singers, ascetics, women, deaconesses, virgins, widows) who together partake of the Eucharist.

Augustine of Hippo

Augustine (354–430) needs no introduction. It is well-known that this greatest of the Latin fathers was a devout paedobaptist. Indeed, in the most historically momentous of his controversies, the one with Pelagius and Julian of Eclanum, Augustine appealed to infant baptism as proof of original sin. Why did the church baptize infants if (as the Pelagians maintained) infants were untainted by sin? Was baptism not a washing from sin? Why give baptismal washing to the clean? Pelagians must either stop baptizing infants, or else (the option they actually took) wriggle about trying to deny that baptism, in the case of infants, had anything to do with cleansing from sin.

---

15. *Apostolic Constitutions* 8:13, in Schaff ANF vol.VII, p.490.

Only let him [Julian] spare the infants, so as not to praise their condition uselessly, and defend them cruelly. Let him not declare them to be safe; let him suffer them to come, not, indeed, to Pelagius for eulogy, but to Christ for salvation.[16]

By 'suffering the infants to come to Christ for salvation', Augustine meant bringing them for baptism.

Here is Augustine speaking more generally about infant baptism:

And if any one seek for divine authority in this matter, though what is held by the whole Church, and that not as instituted by Councils, but as a matter of invariable custom, is rightly held to have been handed down by apostolical authority, still we can form a true conjecture of the value of the sacrament of baptism in the case of infants, from the parallel of circumcision, which was received by God's earlier people...

And as in Isaac, who was circumcised on the eighth day after his birth, the seal of this righteousness of faith was given first, and afterwards, as he imitated the faith of his father, the righteousness itself followed as he grew up, of which the seal had been given before when he was an infant; so in infants, who are baptized, the sacrament of regeneration is given first, and if they maintain a Christian piety, conversion also in the heart will follow, of which the mysterious sign had gone before in the outward body. And as in the thief the gracious goodness of the Almighty supplied what had been wanting in the sacrament of baptism, because it had been missing not from pride or contempt, but from want of opportunity; so in infants who die baptized, we must believe that the same grace of the Almighty supplies the want, that, not from perversity of will, but from insufficiency of age, they can neither believe with the heart unto righteousness, nor make confession with the mouth unto salvation. Therefore, when others take the vows for them, that the celebration of the sacrament may be complete in their behalf, it is unquestionably of avail for their dedication to God, because they cannot answer for themselves.[17]

---

16. *On Marriage and Concupiscence* 2:60, in Schaff NPNF First Series, vol.V, p.308.

17. *On Baptism, Against the Donatists* 4:24, in Schaff NPNF First Series, vol. IV, pp.461-2.

Augustine held equally robust views about infant communion. Often he expressed this once more in the framework of the Pelagian controversy:

> If anyone says that there is nothing in infancy for Jesus to save, they deny that Christ is "Jesus" for all believing infants. I repeat, if anyone says that that there is nothing in infancy for Jesus to save, they say exactly this, that for believing infants, those who have been baptized in Christ, the Lord Christ is not "Jesus." For what is "Jesus"? Jesus means Savior. Indeed, Jesus is the Savior! Those whom he does not save, if there is nothing in them to save – he is not "Jesus" for them. If you can bear the notion that Christ is not "Jesus" for some who have been baptized, I am not sure your faith can be accepted as harmonizing with the wholesome rule. They are infants, yet they belong to him. They are infants, yet they receive his sacraments. They are infants, yet they share in his table, that they may have life in themselves.[18]

In other words, just as baptism was necessary to wash away original sin, ergo infants must be baptized, likewise eating the flesh and drinking the blood of Christ was necessary to sustain spiritual life (according to Augustine's understanding of John 6:27ff.), ergo baptized infants must partake of the Eucharist. Here is Augustine's argument:

> Will, however, any man be so bold as to say that this statement ["Unless you eat My flesh and drink My blood you shall have no life in you", Jn. 6:53] has no relation to infants, and that they can have life in them without partaking of His body and blood—on the ground that He does not say, "Except *one* eat," but "Except *ye* eat"; as if He were addressing those who were able to hear and to understand, which of course infants cannot do? But he who says this is inattentive; because, unless *all* are embraced in the statement, that without the body and the blood of the Son of man men cannot have life, it is to no purpose that even the elder age is solicitous of it. For if you attend to the mere words, and not to the meaning, of the Lord as He speaks, this passage may very well seem to have been spoken merely to the people

---

18. Augustine, *Sermones ad populum* 5:261.

whom He happened at the moment to be addressing; because He does not say, Except *one* eat; but "Except *ye* eat."

What also becomes of the statement which He makes in the same context on this very point: "The bread that I will give is my flesh, for the life of the world?" For, it is according to this statement, that we find that sacrament pertains also to us, who were not in existence at the time the Lord spoke these words; for we cannot possibly say that we do not belong to "the world," for the life of which Christ gave His flesh. Who indeed can doubt that in the term *world* all persons are indicated who enter the world by being born? For, as He says in another passage, "The children of this world beget and are begotten." From all this it follows, that even for the life of *infants* was His flesh given, which He gave for the life of the world; and that even they will not have life if they eat not the flesh of the Son of Man.[19]

Catholic theology was not in fact to endorse Augustine's view of the absolute necessity of the Eucharist for salvation, but our concern here is otherwise situated; we are exploring Augustine's historical testimony to the fact of infant communion, rather than his theological rationale for the practice.[20]

It seems, then, that there is solid evidence for the practice of infant communion in the patristic era. Cyprian, Hippolytus, the *Apostolic Constitutions*, and Augustine all testify to the practice. The silence of other sources is no argument against the existence of infant communion; it may merely mean that a context was lacking in which the practice deserved or demanded commentary.

Countervailing Evidence

Is there, however, competing evidence that witnesses against infant communion? Some have thought so.[21] For example,

---

19. *A Treatise on the Merits and Forgiveness of Sins, and on the Baptism of Infants* 1:27, in Schaff NPNF First Series, vol.V, p.25.

20. See *Catholic Encyclopedia*, 'Communion of Children', for the erroneous character of 'absolute necessity' as applied to the Eucharist. A lesser category, 'moral necessity', is preferred: see *ibid.*, 'Holy Communion'. Available online at http://www.newadvent.org/cathen/index.html, accessed 30/6/10.

21. For example, the distinguished Anglican scholar Roger Beckwith, who states the case with pithy force in 'Age of Admission to the Lord's Supper,' *The Westminster Theological Journal*, Vol. XXXVIII, No. 2 [Winter 1976], pp. 125-27.

appeal has been made to Origen (c.185–c.254). In his *Homilies on Judges*, the illustrious Alexandrian says the following:

> Before we arrive at the provision of the heavenly bread, and are filled with the flesh of the spotless Lamb, before we are inebriated with the blood of the true Vine which sprang from the root of David, while we are children, and are fed with milk, and retain the discourse about the first principles of Christ, as children we act under the oversight of stewards, namely the guardian angels.[22]

The heavenly bread, Lamb's flesh, and Vine's blood, have been interpreted as the Eucharist, and the children as those baptized but of young age, who are first 'fed with milk' (rudimentary teaching) under the oversight of angels (pastors) before being admitted at some later stage to the Lord's Table. If so, Origen becomes an historical witness to the practice of the Palestinian churches in the mid-third century (the *Homilies on Judges* were written in Palestine). It may be doubted, however, whether we can clearly read so much into the richly allegorical phraseology of this passage; it is strongly reminiscent of Galatians 3:19–4:7, where we have the same language of elementary principles, stewards, angels, children, and coming to maturity, with quite different implications than anti-paedocommunion. So while Origen *could* be saying that in the Palestinian churches of his day, baptized children did not share in the Eucharist, his words are sufficiently metaphorical to leave doubt.

Appeal has also been made to the *Didascalia Apostolorum*, from third-century Syria:

> But do you honour the bishops, who have loosed you from sins, who by the water regenerated you, who filled you with the Holy Spirit, who reared you with the word as with milk, who bred you up with doctrine, who confirmed you with admonition, and made you to partake of the holy Eucharist of God, and made you partakers and joint heirs of the promise of God.[23]

---

22. *Homilies on the Book of Judges* 6:2, in Migne PG 12:975, available online at http://books.google.com/books?id=sLpDsFbzv2wC, accessed 7/1/10.

23. *Didascalia* 9, available online at http://www.bombaxo.com/didascalia.html accessed 7/1/10.

The argument is that the *Didascalia* here presents a historical sequence in the Christian life: loosing from sins, baptism, infilling with the Spirit (perhaps chrismation), being nourished and matured by the milk of teaching and admonition, and finally being admitted to the Eucharist. In that case, it is argued, infants who are baptized are not admitted to Holy Communion until they have first been made mature through the milk of teaching.

There are, however, problems with this interpretation. The sequence does not end with the bishop making the Christian a participant in the Eucharist, but making him or her 'partaker and joint heir of the promise of God'. Does that mean that baptized children, within the church and under instruction, are not partakers or co-heirs of God's promise until, much later, they are admitted to the Eucharist? Perhaps the *Didascalia* is not actually setting out a strict sequence here. After all, how is the bishop envisaged as 'loosing from sins' (the first thing mentioned) if not through baptism (mentioned second)? And what is the sequential difference between 'reared you with the word as with milk', 'bred you up with doctrine,' and 'confirmed you with admonition'? The passage is, I think, too loosely rhetorical to be construed as a sort of systematic theology of initiation.

We ought to remember that in the case of adults – and a large number of initiates in the third century would have been converted adults – the teaching actually *preceded* their baptism by way of the catechumenate. The order would then have been, 'reared you with the word as with milk, bred you up with doctrine, confirmed you with admonition, loosed you from sins, by the water regenerated you, filled you with the Holy Spirit, and made you to partake of the holy Eucharist of God.'

Given what seems plausibly to be the imprecise rhetorical construction of the passage, I doubt whether it can serve as a knock-down proof of the exclusion of baptized infants from the patristic Eucharist. I suspect its real intent is to say that bishops must not be despised because they are the instruments through whom God effects the whole process of Christian initiation, by which we are made 'partakers and joint heirs of the promise of God' (the last phrase in the passage is not, then, the last act in a chronological sequence, but a summing up of the whole).

Conclusion

Evidence from patristic sources is thin, but what there is demonstrates an acceptance of infant communion in at least some sections of the church, certainly from the mid-third century. This is not to say that the practice was geographically universal; if one accepts that the disputed passage in Origen refers to the exclusion of baptized infants from the Eucharist, it would mean that the Palestinian churches had a different custom from the North Africans. Diversity of practice would not, I think, be an intolerable conclusion; if embraced, it would leave paedocommunionists and anti-paedocommunionists alike in the position of having ancient precedent for their practice, so that the disagreement would need to be settled on biblical and theological grounds.

Suppose, however, that we remain purely with the historical evidence. The least robust conclusion we can form on the basis of the source material is that in some quarters of the patristic church, the communion of baptized infants was an accepted practice from the middle of the third century (possibly even earlier, depending on how one assesses the composition of *The Apostolic Tradition*). The countervailing evidence of infant exclusion from Origen and the *Didascalia* is weaker because of interpretive problems.

7

'Only for His Believers': Paedocommunion and the Witness of the Reformed Liturgies

Joel R. Beeke

The form and content of public worship was a high priority for the Protestant Reformers, since public worship is the context in which, by the preaching of the gospel, 'the Holy Ghost works faith in our hearts'[1] and 'the kingdom of heaven is opened to believers'.[2] Such worship must be the true and acceptable worship taught in God's Word, since we may not 'worship Him in any other way than He has commanded in His Word'.[3]

Thus the Reformers took care to draw up orders of worship, forms of prayer, and other liturgical documents and directories. The Reformed liturgies and the Reformed confessions, together with the writings and sermons of the Reformers, are primary sources for identifying and interpreting the faith and practice of the Reformation.

The Reformers took care to provide forms for the administration of the sacraments, knowing that the most deadly corruptions of the Roman Catholic Church centered in her system of sacraments. With Calvin, the Reformers regarded the Roman Catholic mass as the 'head of all abominations', in which 'every

---

1. Heidelberg Catechism, Q. 65. I wish to thank Ray B. Lanning for his assistance in writing this chapter.

2. Ibid., Q. 83.

3. Ibid., Q. 96.

imaginable kind of gross profanity is perpetrated'.[4] The Reformers understood that they had a huge task in restoring a right understanding of the sacraments, according to Christ's institution, and to re-educate their congregations about the true function and use of the sacraments in Christian nurture.

These forms show that the Reformers explicitly opposed the practice of giving Holy Communion to baptized persons – whether infants, children, or adults – who had not made public profession of faith in Christ. However much they perceived the biblical warrant, meaning, and value of infant baptism, the Reformers did not consider baptism enough to qualify someone to partake of the sacrament of the Lord's Supper.

These forms, and the catechetical context in which they were used, show that for the Reformers, the Lord's Supper is a means of grace only to baptized persons with the maturity, knowledge, and faith to examine themselves, repent of their sins, cling to Christ as Savior, and resolve to live a godly life. Good order in the church, therefore, requires that the sacrament be given only to those baptized persons who have made public profession of their faith and whose lives are known to be consistent with that profession.

The Roman Catholic Background

'For whom is the Lord's Supper instituted?'[5] The Reformers were not the first Christians to ask this question. It is well to consider the Roman Catholic background common to all the Reformers and the congregations they served.

The Roman Catholic Church historically taught that those who wished to receive Holy Communion as dispensed in the Mass must meet four requirements:[6]

1. They must be baptized persons, since thereby their original sin is wholly remitted.

---

4. John Calvin, 'On the Shunning of the Unlawful Rites of the Ungodly,' in *Calvin's Tracts*, trans. Henry Beveridge (Edinburgh: Calvin Translation Society, 1861), 3: 360.

5. Heidelberg Catechism, Q. 81.

6. 'Holy Communion,' *A Catholic Dictionary*, ed. Donald Attwater (New York: MacMillan Company, 1931), 115.

2. They must be in a state of grace, and not in the state of sin, i.e., guilty of having committed any mortal sin that deprives the soul of sanctifying grace.

3. Ordinarily, they must fast from the preceding midnight onward.

4. They must or at least ought to have 'dispositions of charity'.

Holy Communion is only given to infants (defined as baptized persons not yet seven years of age) who are in danger of death, and even they must 'realize that it [Communion bread] is different from ordinary bread, and that they reverently adore it. Otherwise a fuller knowledge of Christian doctrine and careful preparation are required of children before they are admitted to the sacrament.'[7]

The practice of giving Holy Communion to baptized minors (by definition, children seven years of age and older) before they were confirmed was revived in the Roman Catholic Church only after 1910.[8] The medieval practice was to give Holy Communion only to those baptized persons who had been confirmed and met the other requirements stated above.

This background accounts in part for the interest the Reformers took in the question of who could partake of the Lord's Supper. No matter what was attributed to the sacrament of baptism, it was by no means sufficient by itself to qualify a person to receive Holy Communion. Such had been the rule even in a church as corrupt as Rome.

Calvin's Catechism and Liturgy (c.1541)[9]

The Catechism of the Church of Geneva
In his catechism, John Calvin provides a helpful context in which to interpret his form for administering the Lord's Supper.

---

7. Ibid., 269.

8. 'Quam Singulari,' *A Catholic Dictionary*, 439.

9. Calvin's catechism and liturgy may both be found in Vol. I of *Calvin's Tracts*, trans. Henry Beveridge (Edinburgh: Calvin Translation Society, 1861), reprinted as *Treatises on the Sacraments* (Grand Rapids: Reformation Heritage Books, 2002). Another translation of 'The Manner of Celebrating the Lord's Supper' may be found in Charles W. Baird, *Presbyterian Liturgies* (originally published as *Eutaxia*, 1855; reprinted, Grand Rapids: Baker, 1957), 49-58. The exact date of the introduction of Calvin's liturgy in Geneva appears to have been lost.

He raises a number of questions relating to the sacraments in general and to the sacrament of the Lord's Supper in particular. First, he asks this question concerning the efficacy of the sacraments:

> Master: How then, and when does the effect follow the use of the sacraments?
>
> Scholar: When we receive them in faith, seeking Christ alone and his grace in them.

Second, Calvin raises the question of 'the right and legitimate use' of the Lord's Supper:

> Master: What is the right and legitimate use of this Sacrament?
>
> Scholar: That which Paul points out, 'Let a man examine himself,' before he approach to it (1 Cor. 11:28).
>
> Master: Into what is he to inquire in this examination?
>
> Scholar: Whether he be a true member of Christ.
>
> Master: By what evidence may he come to know this?
>
> Scholar: If he is endued with faith and repentance, if he entertains sincere love for his neighbour, if he has his mind pure from all hatred and malice.

Third, Calvin asks if all baptized persons should be given the sacrament of the Lord's Supper:

> Master: But ought pastors, to whom the dispensing of it has been committed, to admit all indiscriminately without selection?
>
> Scholar: In regard to baptism, as it is now bestowed only on infants, there is no room for discrimination; but in the Supper the minister ought to take heed not to give it to any one who is clearly unworthy of it.
>
> Master: Why so?
>
> Scholar: Because it cannot be done without insulting and profaning the sacrament.

Note Calvin's stress on the command of the Apostle Paul, 'Let a man examine himself' (1 Cor. 11:28). This same emphasis appears in subsequent Reformed catechisms and liturgies. Where there is no evident capacity for such self-examination, there is no possibility of partaking of the Supper in a worthy manner. Without such self-examination, a person comes to the table unprepared and therefore unqualified to receive the sacrament. To give the sacrament to persons 'clearly unworthy of it' is heinous sin on the part of the one who administers it and of the person receiving it.

Form of Administering the Sacraments

In his 'Manner of Administering the Lord's Supper', Calvin says certain persons are to be excluded from the privileges of the table, by way of public announcement a week prior to the administration of the sacrament:

> The Sunday before the Supper is dispensed it is intimated to the people: first, in order that each may prepare and dispose himself to receive it worthily and with becoming reverence; secondly, that young people may not be brought forward unless they are well instructed, and have made a profession of their faith in the Church; thirdly, that if there are strangers who are still rude and ignorant, they may come and present themselves for instruction in private.[10]

Furthermore, on the day that the sacrament is dispensed, 'the minister adverts to it at the end of his sermon, or indeed, if he sees cause, makes it the sole subject of [the] sermon, in order to expound to the people what our Lord means to teach and signify by this ordinance, and in what way it behooves us to receive it.'[11] Before the sacrament is administered, the Apostles' Creed ('the Confession of Faith') is said or sung 'to testify in the name of the people that all wish to live and die in the doctrine of Christ.'[12]

---

10. *Calvin's Tracts,* 1:119.

11. Ibid., 119.

12. Ibid., 119.

The exhortation that precedes Holy Communion has been faulted for being overly didactic. What is less frequently noted is that Calvin took pains to emphasize the intimate relationship between Christ as Lord, Savior, and Master, and the communicants as disciples, believers, and faithful members of his household. Calvin repeatedly draws a circle of intimacy around the sacrament, saying:

> We have heard, brethren, how our Lord makes his Supper among his disciples, and thereby shows us that strangers—in other words, those who are not of the company of the faithful—ought not to be admitted.
>
> Our Lord Jesus Christ gives [the sacred viands] only to his household and believers.
>
> If we have this testimony in our hearts before God, let us have no doubt at all that he adopts us for his children, and that the Lord Jesus addresses his word to us to invite us to his table, and present us with this holy sacrament which he communicated to his disciples.

In exhorting people to examine themselves according to Paul's mandate, Calvin enlarges on what he says in his catechism: 'Let each prove and examine his conscience, to see whether he has truly repented of his faults, and is dissatisfied with himself, desiring to live henceforth holily and according to God; above all, whether he puts his trust in the mercy of God, and seeks his salvation entirely in Christ, and whether, renouncing all enmity and rancour, he truly intends and resolves to live in concord and brotherly charity with his neighbours.'[13]

The First Prayer Book of King Edward VI (1549)[14]

Thomas Cranmer, the principal author of the *Book of Common Prayer*, helped make clear how the Prayer Book service repudiates the Roman Catholic ideas of transubstantiation of the elements

---

13. Ibid., 120.

14. *The Booke of the Common Prayer and Administracion of the Sacramentes, and Other Rites and Ceremonies of the Churche after the use of the Churche of England* (first published 1549; reprinted as *The First Prayer-Book of King Edward VI* [London: Griffith Farrar Browne & Co., 1910]).

and a continuing sacrifice for sins. Cranmer is also credited as author of the teachings that prefaced the administration of the sacrament of the Lord's Supper, although these exhortations would in aftertimes fall into disuse and be eliminated from modern editions of the Prayer Book.

The order for the Lord's Supper[15] says that those intending to partake of Holy Communion must 'signify their names' to the local curate,[16] either the night before or first thing in the morning on the day the sacrament is to be administered. Even those people were not to be given the sacrament indiscriminately, however. The curate was obliged to call upon any who were 'open and notorious evill livers,' warning them not to come to the Lord's table until they publicly declared their repentance and amendment of life; and likewise, 'those betwixt whom he perceiveth malice and hatred to reign,' until he knew them to be reconciled.[17]

During the service, the curate was charged to deliver a sermon or read a homily, exhorting the people to the worthy receiving of the sacrament; or else to read an exhortation provided in the liturgy for that purpose, calling attention to the apostle Paul's charge 'to all persones diligently to trie and examine themselves before they presume to eate of that breade, and drink of that cup.' The basic requirements for worthy receiving of the sacrament were 'a truly penitent heart and lively faith'. There is great benefit in the worthy receiving of the sacrament, but, as the order goes on to say, 'so is the daunger great, yf wee receive the same unworthily; for then we become gyltie of the body and bloud of Christ our savior; we eate and drinke our owne damnacion, not considering the Lordes bodye. We kindle God's wrathe over us, we provoke him to plague us with diverse diseases and sondery kyndes of death.' Impenitent sinners are asked not to come to the holy table but to bewail their sins. Those who would be worthy receivers are advised: 'Let your mynde be without desire to synne, repent you truly for your

---

15. 'The Supper of the Lorde and the Holy Communion, Commonly Called the Masse,' *The Booke of the Common Prayer*, 193-211.

16. Used in its older sense, referring to the minister of the local parish.

17. Ibid., 193.

sinnes past, have an earnest and lyvely faith in Christ our savior, be in perfect charitie with all men.'[18]

An even stronger exhortation is to be used in parishes where the people are neglecting the sacrament: 'My duetie is to exhorte you … to consider the greatnes of the thing, and to serche and examine your owne consciences, and that not lightly more after the maner of dissimulers with GOD: But as they whiche shoulde come to a moste Godly and heavenly Banket, not to come but in the marriage garment required of God in scripture, that you may (so muche as lieth in you) be founde worthie to come to suche a table.'[19]

As for baptized children, the order for confirmation states, 'Whan the children come to the yeres of discretion and have lerned what theyr Godfathers and Godmothers promised for them in Baptisme, they may then themselves with their owne mouth, and with theyr own consent, openly before the churche ratify and confesse the same.'[20] The confirmation order concludes by stating, 'And there shal none be admitted the holye communion: until suche time as he be confirmed.'[21]

No matter how differently he approached the formulation of the liturgy, Cranmer clearly shared Calvin's view of what is required for the worthy partaking of the sacrament. From that time until the latter part of the twentieth century, the churches of the Anglican Communion administered Holy Communion only to those baptized persons who had made public profession of their faith in the rite of confirmation.

John Knox's Genevan Service Book (1556)[22]
Though it is called 'Mr. Knox's liturgy,' others worked with John Knox, first in Frankfort and later in Geneva, to produce

---

18. Ibid., 196.

19. Ibid., 197.

20. Ibid., 228.

21. Ibid., 232.

22. *The Forme of Prayers and Ministration of the Sacraments, etc., Used in the Englishe Congregation at Geneva: and Approved by the Famous and Godly Learned Man, John Calvyn,* originally published in Geneva, 1556; reprinted in William D. Maxwell, *John Knox's Genevan Service Book* (Edinburgh: Oliver and Boyd, 1931).

the Genevan service book of 1556. The book was intended to be something of a compromise between the post-Reformation usages of the Church of England, distilled in the *Book of Common Prayer*, and the liturgy of John Calvin, whom Knox and his fellow refugees so greatly admired. The Marian exiles took Mr. Knox's liturgy with them when they returned home to England and Scotland at the end of the reign of 'Bloody Mary'. England's Puritans made use of it as an alternative to the *Book of Common Prayer*. And the liturgy became the first service book of the Church of Scotland. It was used down to the time of the adoption of the *Westminster Directory* (see below).

Knox's liturgy draws heavily on both Calvin and Cranmer. For example, the pre-Communion exhortation splices together roughly the first half of Cranmer's exhortation, referred to above, and the second half of Calvin's. It should also be noted that Calvin's catechism was printed with the liturgy and served the same purpose as an introduction or commentary on the contents of the liturgy itself.

The sacrament of the Lord's Supper was administered in the context of the Lord's Day service, at precisely the same point as in Calvin's liturgy, namely, after the sermon and the 'Prayer for the Whole Estate of Christes Churche,' concluding with the Lord's Prayer and the Apostles' Creed. This order made the sacrament another act of faith in response to God's Word.

In the exhortation, having advised various kinds of sinners not to come to the holy table, the minister says:

> Judge therefore your selves bretherne, that ye be not judged of the lorde: repent you truly for your sinnes paste, and have a lyvely and stedfast faith, in Christ our saviour, sekinge onely your salvation in the merits of his death and passion, from hensforth refusinge, and forgettinge all malice and debate, with ful purpose to live in brotherly amytie, and godlye conversation, all the dais of your life.[23]

In concluding the prayer of consecration and having rehearsed the benefits of salvation, the minister makes a confession of faith

23. Ibid., 122-23.

on the part of the communicants who are now seated at the table, ready to receive the sacrament:

> And these moste inestimable benefites, we acknowledge and confesse to have received of thy free mercie and grace, by thy onely beloved sonne Jesus Christ, for the which therefore we thy congregation moved by the holy sprite render thee all thankes, prayse, and glorie for ever and ever.[24]

From this order, it appears that Knox did not differ from Calvin or Cranmer in offering the sacrament only to those who were 'saints by profession' and 'conversation,' or manner of life.[25]

The Dutch Reformed Liturgy (1556)[26]

Authorship of the Liturgy of the Reformed Churches in the Netherlands is customarily assigned to Petrus Dathenus (1531–1588), but the actual history of its various forms is more complicated. Dathenus was responsible only for giving the text its final form in 1556, with the exception of things that were later emended or added by the Synod of Dort (1618–1619). Charles W. Baird says, 'Composed originally by Calvin in French, translated by Polanus into the English, rearranged by Johannes a Lasco in Latin, then translated by Utenhoven into the Dutch, and abridged by Micronius, it was finally reviewed by Dathenus and adopted in 1556 as the standard of worship in the Reformed Church of Holland.'[27] So the father of the Dutch liturgy was actually John Calvin, for much of his liturgy is retained, especially in the sacramental and marriage forms. Still, credit for its clarity of structure and completeness of statement must be given to the several men through whose hands the liturgy passed.

The history of English versions of the Dutch Reformed liturgy is almost as complicated. The most widely used translation

---

24. Ibid., 126.

25. For the way in which that profession was made in Geneva and later in Scotland, see 'Note on Confirmation,' Maxwell, *John Knox's Genevan Service Book,* 120.

26. 'Formulier om het Heilig Avondmaal to houden,' *De Liturgy der Gereformeerde Kerken in Nederland* (Dordrecht: Gereformeerde Bijbelstichting, n.d.).

27. Baird, *Presbyterian Liturgies,* 214.

was produced by John Livingston in 1767 for use in the Reformed Church in America, revised somewhat by the Christian Reformed Church (CRC) in 1914, and printed with editions of *The Psalter* (1912) for use in the CRC and other Dutch Reformed bodies in North America.[28] The CRC replaced the 1914 revision with a new translation published in the *Psalter Hymnal* of 1934, while the Canadian Reformed Churches began work on a version of their own in 1954, which appears in their *Book of Praise* (1984).

The most substantial parts of the Dutch Reformed liturgy are the 'Form for the Administration of Baptism' and the 'Form for the Administration of the Lord's Supper'. These forms, whether in Dutch or English, continue to be used by several Reformed denominations rooted in the Dutch tradition down to the present time, something that cannot be said of any other Reformation-era liturgy.

In the 'Form for the Lord's Supper', communicants are addressed as 'beloved in the Lord Jesus Christ', 'dearly loved brethren and sisters in the Lord', and 'beloved in the Lord'. Such expressions are borrowed from the New Testament epistles and are used in reference to those 'believers' for whom the Supper is appointed (see below).

The practice of self-examination is necessary to 'celebrate the Supper of the Lord to our comfort'. This practice is described as a three-fold inquiry:

> A personal ('everyone by himself') consideration of one's own sins, the curse of God upon them, and the punishment of them in the person of Christ, in the death of the cross.
>
> An examination of one's own heart, with respect to faith in God's promise of salvation in Christ, and in particular, one's faith in the imputation of Christ's righteousness as a covering for one's own sins, so complete ('perfect') that it is 'as if he had satisfied in his own person for all his sins, and fulfilled all righteousness.'

---

28. English citations are all taken from the 'Form for the Lord's Supper' as currently published in *Doctrinal Standards, Liturgy, Church Order*, ed. Joel R. Beeke (Grand Rapids: Reformation Heritage Books, 1999), 136-40.

An examination of one's own conscience, regarding one's purpose in life as a believer, 'to show true thankfulness to God … and to walk uprightly before Him,' and the righteous character of his relationships with his fellow human beings.

Having thus identified what is required for the worthy partaking of the Supper, the implications for unbelievers are: 'Those who do not feel this testimony in their hearts, eat and drink judgment to themselves.'

Accordingly, a long list of persons 'defiled' with various sins is given, and all such persons are admonished 'to keep themselves from the table of the Lord', with the further declaration that 'they have no part in the kingdom of Christ'. The reason given for excluding such persons is that 'Christ hath appointed [this meal] only for the faithful.' The original Dutch is more specific: 'Christus [deze spijze] alleen voor Zijn gelovigen verordineerd heft' ('Christ has appointed this food only for His believers'). The form goes on to say, 'This is not designed … to deject the contrite hearts of the faithful [Dutch: *gelovigen,* 'believers'], as if none might come to the supper of the Lord but those who are without sin.'

Furthermore, to remember Christ by partaking of the Lord's Supper, 'the end for which Christ hath ordained and instituted the same,' the communicant must be 'confidently persuaded' that Christ was sent into the world for our salvation, assumed our nature, fulfilled all righteousness, bore our punishment in his sufferings and death, and 'confirmed' the covenant of grace with the shedding of his blood as 'the new and eternal testament'.

The communicant must also 'firmly believe' that he belongs to this covenant of grace; indeed, the Supper was instituted to confirm this very faith, and to nurture it in the believer. Hence, the Holy Supper confirms the unity of all 'who by a true faith are ingrafted in Christ', as 'altogether one body, for Christ's sake.' The Apostles' Creed is not a preliminary to the celebration of the sacrament but incorporated into the prayer of consecration, thus tightening the connection between profession of faith and partaking of the sacrament.

Finally, in the same manner as Calvin, the form exhorts communicants to feed on Christ in faith by lifting their hearts 'up on high in heaven where Christ Jesus is our Advocate at the right hand of his heavenly Father ... not doubting but we shall ... certainly be fed and refreshed in our souls through the working of the Holy Ghost, with His body and blood.'

From first to last, all that is said and done in administering the sacrament of the Lord's Supper is based on the premise that those who come to the table are believers, blessed with the knowledge of Christian truth, moved to heartfelt repentance from sin, capable of performing acts of faith, and fully aware of their covenantal standing, privileges, and duties, as confessing members of Christ's church.

The Westminster Directory (1644)[29]

The Westminster Directory for Public Worship was supposed to replace the *Book of Common Prayer* in England and Ireland. Within a year of its publication, the Directory replaced Knox's Genevan service book in Scotland, by act of the General Assembly of the 'Kirk' or Church of Scotland and the Scottish Parliament. As a result, the Directory was later carried to many other parts of the world, where it became the first liturgical manual for many churches founded, wholly or in part, by Scottish Presbyterians.

Much as the Divines wished to change the liturgical practice of the Church of England, they were also eager to bring that practice into closer accord with that of the Reformed churches in Switzerland, France, Germany, the Netherlands, and elsewhere. A study of the Directory therefore reveals an obvious discontinuity, or change in outward forms, superimposed on a deeper continuity, or unity of understanding, faith, and practice, with the wider Reformed community.

As with Calvin, the Divines furnish an extensive commentary on their Directory in the form of the *Westminster Confession of Faith* and its two Catechisms, Larger and Shorter. It should be

---

29. *The Directory for the Publick Worship of God; Agreed Upon by the Assembly of Divines at Westminster, with the Assistance of Commissioners from the Church of Scotland, as a Part of the Covenanted Uniformity in Religion betwixt the Church of Christ in the Kingdoms of Scotland, England, and Ireland; with an Act of the General Assembly, and Act of Parliament, Both in Anno 1645, Approving and Establishing the Said Directory,* originally published in 1644 (reprinted together with the *Westminster Confession of Faith* in the volume of the same name, Glasgow: Free Presbyterian Publications, 1995).

noted that, first, the Confession of Faith defines the visible, catholic church as consisting of 'all those throughout the world that profess the true religion; and of their children' (25.2). Furthermore, 'not only those that do actually profess faith in and obedience unto Christ, but also the infants of one or both believing parents, are to be baptized' (28.4). These statements incorporate both parents and children in the body of the church but clearly distinguish between professing members, or believers, and non-professing members, or members by baptism, of the church (see also *Larger Catechism*, 61, 62).

Likewise, the Confession distinguishes between 'saints that are united to Jesus Christ their head by His Spirit and by faith' (26.1) and those who are 'saints by profession' (26.2). The latter may not necessarily be the former because there may be hypocrites in the body of the visible church. Even those who are 'saints by profession' may be excluded from the sacrament, their profession of faith notwithstanding, if they 'are found to be ignorant or scandalous' (LC. 173).

Third, the Lord's Supper was instituted, *inter alia,* for 'the sealing of all benefits [of Christ's death] to true believers' (29:1), and the crucified body and blood of Christ are present, 'not corporally or carnally, in, with, or under the bread and wine; yet, as really, but spiritually, ... to the faith of believers in that ordinance' (29:7). The sacrament can therefore be of no help to unbelievers or ignorant persons; it can only harm hypocrites and ungodly men.

Fourth, the *Larger Catechism* provides a brief manual for communicants, describing their duties before they come to the Lord's Supper, in the time of receiving it, and after receiving it (171–174). The first duty is for such persons to examine themselves 'of their being in Christ' (171). Their chief duty during the time of administration is to 'stir up themselves to a vigorous exercise of their graces' (174). Their duty afterwards is, 'if they find quickening and comfort, to bless God for it' (175).

Finally, the *Larger Catechism* compares baptism with the Lord's Supper (177). Baptism may be administered 'even to infants', but the Lord's Supper 'only to such as are of years and ability to examine themselves'. Such was the confessional and practical framework within which the Divines went on to give direction for 'the Celebration of the Communion, or Sacrament of the Lord's Supper.'

Like Calvin and the 'reformed Churches abroad', administration of the sacrament is judged 'convenient to be done after the morning sermon', i.e., on the Lord's Day. While it is not administered on any stated basis (or 'frequently'), a public 'warning' is to be given 'the sabbath-day before', and on that day, or some other day preceding the sacrament, 'something concerning that ordinance, and the due preparation thereunto, and participation thereof, be taught.'

When administering the Supper, a word of 'exhortation, warning, and invitation' is addressed to the congregation. Communicants are told to come to the sacrament 'with knowledge, faith, repentance, love, and with hungering and thirsting souls after Christ and his benefits.' Ignorant, scandalous, profane, and impenitent persons are warned not to come. An invitation is given, nonetheless, to 'all that labour under the sense of the burden of their sins, and fear of wrath, and desiring to reach unto a greater progress in grace than yet they can attain unto, to come to the Lord's table' (cf. LC 172).

In the prayer of consecration, the minister, on behalf of the communicants seated 'about or at' the table, is 'to profess that there is no other name under heaven by which we can be saved, but the name of Jesus Christ.' Once again, a connection is forged from profession of the Christian faith, in perhaps its oldest and simplest form, to partaking of the sacrament.

Finally, before the sacrament is concluded with thanksgiving, the minister addresses the communicants once more, putting them in mind 'of the grace of God in Jesus Christ, held forth in this sacrament'; and exhorting them as to their duty 'to walk worthy of it', the duty of those who profess to be Christ's disciples, the partakers of a heavenly calling (Eph. 4:1, Heb. 3:1).

The Westminster Communion service is a simplified version of Calvin's liturgy. The forms are reduced to directions. The recitation of the Ten Commandments, the Lord's Prayer, and the Apostles' Creed are omitted; but the Divines did not deny to any minister liberty to include these forms in conducting public worship, administering the sacraments, or giving instruction to catechumens. For that reason these particular forms were 'annexed' to the Shorter Catechism for use as forms of instruction, direction, or devotion (see also LC 187).[30]

However, the Westminster service matches its predecessors in requiring knowledge, understanding, discernment, repentance, and faith of all who would partake of the sacrament in a worthy manner. All the essential acts and duties required of the communicants are acts of faith (Confession, 14.2), and all the benefits of Holy Communion are promised to believers (29.7). Hence it is fitting that the privilege of receiving the sacrament be restricted to those only who are 'saints by profession' and walk in a godly life.

Conclusions

The liturgical documents just reviewed span the distance of one hundred years and reflect the beliefs and practices of men and churches of various nations, languages, times, and customs. The unity of belief and uniformity of practice is all the more extraordinary in that light.

The witness of these Reformation era liturgies and directories is a reliable and helpful guide in determining whether or not some proposed innovation in public worship or administration of the sacraments is authentically Reformed. Those who wish to alter or discard some part of our Reformation heritage should at least be compelled to admit that they are doing so.

Specifically, these liturgies and directories show that 'paedo-communion' had no place in the beliefs or practice of the Reformers or the Westminster Divines. As clearly as they perceived and affirmed the validity of infant baptism, the Divines insisted, with equal clarity, that the Lord's Supper is a privilege accorded only to 'saints by profession'.

Children of the covenant, though heirs of the promise and included in the body of the church, do not possess in infancy

---

30. These 'annexed' forms, and the note accompanying them, are omitted from many American printings of the Shorter Catechism.

or childhood the faith with the requisite knowledge and powers of judgment to answer the demand of the Apostle Paul for self-examination and spiritual discernment. By the Spirit's blessing, so long as they are safeguarded by the love and prayers of the church and fed with the milk of the Word, their spiritual needs are well provided for as lambs of the flock. So long as they cannot receive the sacrament of the Lord's Supper with heartfelt faith in Christ, the sacrament cannot do them good and may possibly do them harm. Calvin, Cranmer, Knox, the fathers of the Dutch Reformed Church, and the Westminster Divines insist with one voice that 'Christ has appointed this food only for His believers'.

8

Where Do We Go From Here?
Some Pastoral Reflections on the Covenant of Grace, the Children of the Church, and the Lord's Supper

Guy Prentiss Waters and J. Ligon Duncan III

Introduction

The contributors to this volume have been addressing the question of paedocommunion. Advocates of paedocommunion claim that the children of believers, by virtue of descent from at least one believing parent, may partake of the Lord's Supper. We have seen that the Scripture offers no support for this practice. Furthermore, the church over much of her history has heeded the Scripture in acknowledging that the Lord's Supper is only for qualified recipients, those who are 'of years and ability to examine themselves'.[1]

In the church today, it is important to provide a reasoned response to paedocommunion. Such a response has been the objective of this book. More than a response, however, is needed. In this chapter, we, the editors, will consider some of the practical questions broached by the paedocommunion debate. While these practical questions are broached by paedocommunion, they are of themselves independent of paedocommunion. In other words, whether or not paedocommunion were before us, we would still need to reflect on these questions in order to

---

1. Westminster Larger Catechism, Q & A 177.

minister effectively in the church. It will be helpful to set the stage for our discussion by introducing at least three interrelated questions raised by paedocommunion.

First, what are the terms of admission to the Lord's Supper? What precisely is required of one for him to approach the Lord's Table? Is covenantal membership enough, or does the Scripture require that the recipient be both sufficiently mature and spiritually qualified to partake? The essays in this work have argued the latter from Scripture, particularly from Paul's words in 1 Corinthians 11. Mere covenantal membership is not enough to warrant one's coming to the Lord's Table.

Second, what is the nature of the Lord's Supper? Advocates of paedocommunion frequently characterize the Supper's significance in terms of a community meal. This emphasis correlates well with what is said to be the capacity of all recipients – young and old – to profit from the sacrament. Even the youngest of recipients, it is argued, can grasp what it means to be included within this meal of the church family.

There is no debate that believers, in the Lord's Supper, 'testify and renew ... their mutual love and fellowship each with the other as members of the same mystical body.'[2] But what of the Scripture's teaching that the Supper is preeminently a display of the atoning and sacrificial death of Jesus Christ? What of the Scripture's teaching that in the Supper, worthily partaking believers 'feed upon [Jesus'] body and blood, to their spiritual nourishment and growth in grace'?[3] If the Supper so represents the death of Christ to the faith of believers, and if this representation lies at the heart of what the Supper is, then surely this fact speaks to the question of who may approach the Lord's Table. The Table is for believers who are prepared, with understanding and self-examination, to commune, by faith, with Christ spiritually in the sacrament.

Third, how are we to understand membership in the visible church? Some paedocommunion proponents urge that the classical distinction between communing membership and

---

2. Westminster Larger Catechism, Q & A 168.

3. Ibid.

non-communing membership in the church must be revisited. They argue that membership in the church is undifferentiated, and that all members of the church are entitled to exercise alike the privileges of membership. Consequently, the church membership of infant children of believers is said to warrant these young members' partaking of the Lord's Supper.

Affirming the membership of the children of the church, however, does not necessarily entitle them to the exercise of all privileges of membership.[4] This state of affairs means that we need to think deliberately and carefully about the children of the church. We will consider in more detail below what the Scripture has to say concerning this matter. Does the Bible regard the children of believers as members of the church? If so, what privileges belong to them (or not)? If they do not have the immediate or automatic exercise of the privilege of approaching the Lord's Table, what must happen in order for them to be able to approach?

This observation raises a related and final set of questions. Some have urged that covenant children are inwardly renewed by the Spirit at baptism and, as such, are qualified to partake of the Lord's Supper. The Westminster Standards and the *Three Forms of Unity* rightly summarize Scripture's teaching when they deny that the sacrament of baptism should be understood as the occasion when recipients are customarily regenerated by the Holy Spirit. Denial of baptismal regeneration is an important step towards understanding the place of the children of believers in the church, but more reflection is needed. If our children are members of the church, and if our children have received the sacrament of baptism, then what precisely is their standing before the church and before God? What privileges and responsibilities belong to them that do not belong to children outside the church? How should families, elders, and ministers shepherd the children of the church? What kind of pastoral oversight should the church give them?

We may refine these reflections by asking and answering four specific, practical questions. First, how are we to view the children

---

4. Just as, in many Presbyterian bodies, the church may indefinitely suspend from the sacraments certain adults as an act of discipline. Such persons, while restricted with respect to this privilege of membership, nevertheless remain members of the church.

of the church? Second, how are we to shepherd the children of the church? Third, when and under what circumstances ought a child of the church to approach the Lord's Table? Fourth, how may pastors and elders help God's people understand and receive the Lord's Supper?

How Are We To View The Children of the Church?

What relationship do the children of believers have to the church? In what follows, we will argue that the Scripture understands the children of at least one believer to be members of the church by birthright. We will then consider some implications of their membership. We will conclude by responding to the objection that recognizing children of believers as members of the church corrupts the church.

Members of the Church ... By Birthright

The children of at least one professing Christian parent are members of the church. They are members of the church by birthright. Where do we see this position taught in the Scripture? The answer to this question will not be found in a single verse. We must look at Scripture's teaching and consider some implications that surely follow from that teaching.[5]

We begin with the covenant that God made with Abraham in Genesis 17. God intended this covenant to confirm the promises he had made to Abraham in Genesis 12 (see Genesis 17:5-6). This covenant embraced Abraham and his children so that Abraham and his children were recognized as part of the visible people of God. On this basis, Abraham's male children were to receive the covenant sign of circumcision: 'And I will establish my covenant between me and you and your offspring after you throughout their generations for an everlasting covenant, to be God to you and to your offspring after you' (Gen. 17:7); and, 'This is my covenant, which you shall keep, between me and you and your offspring after you: Every male among you shall be circumcised' (Gen. 17:10).

---

5. What follows is substantially drawn from Chapter 1 of Guy Waters, *How Jesus Runs the Church* (Philippsburg, N. J.: P&R, 2011).

Further, the covenant that God made with Abraham is an evangelical covenant. That is to say, this covenant administers the promises of the gospel. This is Paul's reasoning in Galatians 3:8: 'And the Scripture, foreseeing that God would justify the Gentiles by faith, preached the gospel beforehand to Abraham, saying "In you shall all the nations be blessed."' Paul quotes here the promise that God makes to Abraham in Genesis 12. He further describes God's declaration of this promise to Abraham as 'preaching the gospel beforehand'. It is this promise that God designed the covenant of Genesis 17 to administer.

Not only was the promise evangelical, but the sign of the Abrahamic covenant is evangelical also. This is evident from Paul's description of circumcision at Romans 4:11, 'a seal of the righteousness that Abraham had by faith' (compare Romans 4:1-5). In signifying justification by faith alone, circumcision served to point Abraham and his children to the promise by which he – and believers in every age – were saved.

God has not nullified this covenant. This covenant embraces New Testament believers. This is why Paul calls believers 'Abraham's offspring' and 'sons of Abraham [through faith]' at Galatians 3:29 and Galatians 3:7. Paul calls the blessings of the gospel that New Testament believers presently enjoy the 'blessing of Abraham' (Gal. 3:14). It is as 'Abraham's offspring' that we are 'heirs according to promise' (Gal. 3:29).

But if the Abrahamic covenant continues, what of the covenant sign of circumcision? What has become of circumcision? Under the New Covenant, the Scripture argues, baptism has replaced circumcision as sign and seal of the covenant of grace. This is what Paul argues at Colossians 2:11-12:

> In him you also were circumcised with a circumcision made without hands, by putting off the body of the flesh, by the circumcision of Christ, having been buried with him in baptism, in which you were also raised with him through faith in the powerful working of God, who raised him from the dead.

What is Paul saying here? He is saying that believers have been 'circumcised' by the 'circumcision of Christ'. This is not physical circumcision. It is 'made without hands'. That is to say, it is a work of God. This circumcision Paul describes in terms of the 'putting off the body of flesh'. Here, Paul is saying that each believer has a new relationship with sin ('the body of flesh'). Sin no longer has dominion over a believer. It no longer sits in the driver's seat, determining the believer's thoughts, choices, and actions. Paul can therefore say that the 'body of flesh' has been *put off* (compare Colossians 3:9, 'you have put off the old self with its practices'). This *putting off* or 'circumcision' describes what took place at the believer's regeneration. Recall what Paul says at Romans 2:29: 'but a Jew is one inwardly, and circumcision is a matter of the heart, by the Spirit, not by the letter.' God has made the believer, once alive to sin and dead to righteousness, now, in Christ, dead to sin and alive to righteousness.

But 'circumcision' is not the only way that Paul here describes the decisive change in a believer. He also says that believers have been 'buried with [Christ] in baptism' and 'raised with him'. So fully has God united believers with Jesus in his death that Paul can say that they were 'buried with him'. God has so united believers with Jesus in his resurrection life that Paul can say that they were 'raised with him'.

But Paul says that believers have been 'buried with [Christ] *in baptism*.' Is Paul talking about water baptism here? No. Paul is not primarily thinking of physical baptism any more than he is thinking of physical circumcision in Colossians 2. 'Baptism' is Paul's way of talking about the decisive change that God has wrought in believers so that they have a brand new relationship with sin and with righteousness: 'in which you were also raised with him through faith in the powerful working of God, who raised him from the dead.'

Just as spiritual circumcision once had its counterpart in physical circumcision, so we may infer that spiritual baptism now has its counterpart in water baptism. That is to say, circumcision once served as sign and seal of the regeneration of the Old Testament believer. Now, baptism serves as sign and seal of the regeneration of the New Testament believer. We have the same grace represented under different signs.

This picture is precisely what we see in the New Testament. Christ commissions his disciples to 'baptize' those who respond in faith to the gospel (Matt. 28:18-20). Later in the New Testament, we see that after persons make public profession of faith, they are baptized (Acts 2:38 with Acts 2:41, 8:12, 16:14-15, 16:31-33). Circumcision is no longer required of God's people (see Acts 15). Baptism does the job now that circumcision did prior to the first coming of Christ.

This observation brings us to our final point. The children of believers during the Old Testament were, by divine command, to receive the covenant sign of circumcision. In the same way, the children of believers during the New Testament are, by the same command, to receive the covenant sign of baptism. In both cases, they are entitled to the sign of the covenant because they are by birthright members of the church.

Do we have any indication that the New Testament recognizes the children of believers to be members of the church? We do. Notice what Paul says in Ephesians 6:1-3:

> Children, obey your parents in the Lord, for this is right. 'Honor your father and mother' (this is the first commandment with a promise), 'that it may go well with you and that you may live long on the earth.'

Which children does Paul address? He addresses the children of believers in the church at Ephesus. How does Paul address these children? He addresses them as among 'the saints who are in Ephesus, and are faithful in Christ Jesus' (Eph 1:1). That is to say, he addresses them as members of the congregation. Why does he call the members of the church at Ephesus 'saints' or 'holy ones'? Paul here is not saying that they are all inwardly holy. He is saying that they are, by calling, set apart from the world, and set apart for God.

Children, then, are members of the church and, as such, are called to pursue holiness. In Ephesians 6:1-3, Paul tells the children of the congregation how they ought to live in light of that calling. And in 6:4, Paul tells the fathers of these children to 'bring them up in the discipline and instruction of the Lord'.

These children, in other words, are called to be students in the school of Christ, to be disciples of Jesus.

Consider what Paul argues in 1 Corinthians 7:14: 'the unbelieving husband is made holy because of his wife, and the unbelieving wife is made holy because of her husband. Otherwise your children would be unclean, but as it is, they are holy.' The children of at least one believer are 'holy', not 'unclean'. They are 'holy' in precisely the way that Paul called them holy in Ephesians 1:1. They are, by calling, set apart from the world, and set apart for God.

One might object, 'But Paul says that the unbelieving wife is made holy because of her husband. Are you saying that unbelieving spouses should join the church simply because they are married to a believer?' In reply, observe the concern that Paul addresses in this passage. His main concern is the standing of the child of that believer. Which spouse, the unbelieving or believing, determines that child's standing? Paul replies that the child ought to be recognized as a member of the visible church because of his relationship with his believing parent. In what sense are unbelieving spouses 'holy'? They are 'holy' in the sense that they are the ones through whom these 'holy' children have come into the world.

One final set of passages showing the recognition of the membership of children in the church and their entitlement to the sacrament of baptism is the 'household baptisms' of Acts. We read that Lydia 'was baptized and her household as well' (Acts 16:15). The Philippian jailor 'was baptized at once, he and all his family' (Acts 16:33).

These household baptisms are precisely what we expect to see. In Genesis 17, we saw that professing believers and their households received the covenant sign to indicate their membership in the church. In these New Testament passages, we see professing believers and their households also receiving the covenant sign to indicate their membership in the church.

One might object that there are no children, much less infants, mentioned in either of these baptisms. We may reply that it is not necessary for the Scripture to tell us precisely who was or was not part of that household. The important point for what we are trying to show is that the 'household' was baptized upon the profession of faith of the head of that household.

One might also object that in Acts 18:8 the Scripture says that Crispus' 'entire household' believed. Does that not imply that the members of the jailor's household and Lydia's household believed also? Not necessarily. Whether or not the household believed, they were entitled to the sign of baptism once the head of the household made profession of faith. They were entitled to that sign because they were members of the church by virtue of their relationship with the person professing faith.

In summary, the Scripture recognizes the children of a believing parent to be, by virtue of that relationship, members of the visible church. Negatively, the membership of the children of the church is not grounded upon either the presumption of or the fact of their election. God has not given such knowledge to the church in order to determine her membership (Deut. 29:29). Neither is the membership of the children of the church grounded upon either the presumption of or the fact of their regeneration. The Scripture does not teach that all covenant children are regenerate from the womb. Nor does it assure believers that God will inevitably regenerate every covenant child. Still less does the Scripture ground the membership of the children of the church upon their baptisms. We do not baptize the children of the church so that they might become church members. We baptize them because they are already church members.[6]

What does it mean that the children of at least one professing believer are members of the visible church by birthright? Two observations merit reflection. First, we affirm that such children are members of the church in their minority. Consider citizenship in the state. In the United States, for instance, American citizens must reach a certain age before they are legally permitted to serve in the armed forces, to vote, or to hold public office. There are certain privileges of citizenship, in other words, that Americans

---

6. John Mitchell Mason, *Essays on the Church of God* in *The Complete Works of John M. Mason, D.D.*, ed. Ebenezer Mason (4 vols.; New York: Charles Scribner, 1852), 2.438-9.

may exercise only when they have met certain qualifications and requirements. Even so, there are privileges of citizenship that all Americans enjoy in company with their fellow citizens. If, for instance, a minor citizen is traveling in a foreign country, he is entitled to the services of the American embassy in that country no less than his fellow citizen who has reached his majority.

Membership in the church works in a similar way. As Robert L. Dabney observed, children of the church are 'minor citizens in the ecclesiastical commonwealth, under tutelage, training, and instruction, and government; heirs, if they will exercise the graces obligatory on them, of all the ultimate franchises of the Church, but not allowed to enjoy them until qualified.'[7] Which are the privileges that belong to the children of the church? They are the privileges that belong to every church member by virtue of his membership in the visible church. *The Westminster Larger Catechism* enumerates these privileges. They include 'being under God's special care and government; of being protected and preserved in all ages, notwithstanding the opposition of all enemies; and of enjoying the communion of saints, the ordinary means of salvation, and offers of grace by Christ to all members of it in the ministry of the gospel...'[8] The children of the church, furthermore, are 'heirs' of all the privileges that attend church membership in its fullest sense. These privileges include admission to the Lord's Table and voting in congregational elections. Children of the church may not exercise these privileges until they demonstrate biblically requisite qualifications for such exercise. When they come of age and when they make a credible profession of faith, however, we may borrow the strong words of nineteenth-century Presbyterian John Mitchell Mason in saying that they may '*demand* a seat at [Christ's] table, as their *privilege* which the church cannot deny.'[9]

A second observation helps us understand further how children of the church are to view themselves. Children of the

---

7. Robert L. Dabney, *Syllabus and Notes of the Course of Systematic and Polemic Theology Taught in Union Theological Seminary, Virginia* (5th ed.; Richmond, Va.: Presbyterian Committee of Publication, 1871), 794.

8. Westminster Larger Catechism Q & A 63.

9. Mason, *Essays,* 439. Emphasis Mason's.

church, as members of the church, are called to a life of discipleship. In other words, children are, by calling, learners in the school of Christ. Jesus teaches this point in the Great Commission (Matt. 28:18-20). He commands the eleven apostles to 'go and make disciples of all nations'. Then he explains what this command entails. The apostles are to 'baptize them in the name of the Father and of the Son and of the Holy Spirit', and to 'teach them to observe all that I have commanded you' (Matt. 28:19, 20). When the church administers the sacrament of baptism to a child of a professing believer, the church acknowledges that this child is, by calling, a disciple of Christ. This identity means that the child is called to learn all that Christ has taught in the Scripture.

This reality helps us to understand why the church has consistently valued and applied herself toward the instruction of her young members. We will reflect below on the means by which the church is to obey this command of Christ. For the present, notice that this instruction is a duty of the church, and is the birthright of the children of the church. It is not optional. Nor is it a matter about which the church may be slack or indifferent. In the Presbyterian Church in America and other Presbyterian bodies, the congregation frequently answers in the affirmative the following at the baptism of an infant member: 'Do you as a congregation undertake the responsibility of assisting the parents in the Christian nurture of this child?'[10]

The question may be raised, 'Does this calling of discipleship assume that the children of the church are regenerate members? Might such children not be tempted to see themselves as regenerate when in fact they are not?' In response, we may observe that this calling to discipleship does not mean that the children of the church are either regenerate or will certainly become regenerate. We are speaking, rather, with respect to a particular set of privileges and responsibilities that belong to them as members of the church. Part of that set of privileges and responsibilities is to learn from the Word of God. What should they learn? They should learn that they are sinners in the sight

---

10. *The Book of Church Order* 56-5.

of God, that they justly deserve the punishment of God for their sins, and that they need the cleansing of Christ's blood and the renewing of the Holy Spirit. They should be taught to turn to Christ in faith and repentance, and to live lives pleasing to him. They should be taught the Scripture's pattern of mind and life that is pleasing to the Lord. This pattern of teaching, we hasten to add, should regularly be part of the diet of the instruction of *every* church member, not simply her young church members.

An Objection

Some Christians will object to our argument that children are members of the church: 'Doesn't the recognition of children as members of the church corrupt the church? Doesn't the church membership of children result in "flood[ing] the spirituality of Christ's Church with a multitude of worldly, nominal Christians"?'[11]

We may reply to this objection along two lines. First, the objection misunderstands biblical teaching concerning the church and her membership. The church is not a society of the regenerate. In other words, one is not admitted to the membership of the church because he has provided evidence of his regeneration. The church, rather, is a society of those who profess faith in Christ, and of their children. For this reason, we should not be surprised when some church members make false profession or abandon their profession. Jesus taught that his kingdom is like a field in which both wheat and tares grow. The wheat and tares represent 'the children of the kingdom' and 'the sons of the evil one,' respectively (Matt. 13:38). The wheat and the tares will not be separated until the angels separate them at the Day of Judgment (Matt. 13:41-43).[12] In similar fashion, Jesus compared his kingdom to a dragnet 'that was thrown into

---

11. Dabney, *Syllabus*, 792. Dabney, a Presbyterian, is voicing here the objection of Baptists.

12. It is sometimes objected that Jesus declares the field in this parable to be the 'world' and not the 'kingdom'. By 'world' in Matthew 13:38, however, Jesus must mean 'the kingdom as it expands into the world'. The Parable of the Net (Matt. 13:47-50) confirms this interpretation. Suppose, furthermore, that when Jesus speaks of the 'world' he there has no thought for the kingdom. On that rendering, how are we to explain Satan sowing 'sons of the evil one' in a realm that, in one important sense, is already his own? Would it not make more sense to say that Satan is trying to plant 'double agents' in the Kingdom of Heaven? If so, then by 'world' in this parable, Jesus means 'the worldwide kingdom'.

the sea and gathered fish of every kind' (Matt. 13:47). The 'good' and 'bad' fish, representing the 'righteous' and the 'evil', will not be separated until the Day of Judgment (Matt. 13:48-50).

We are not saying, of course, that the church should be lax in her examination of candidates for membership. Neither should the church tolerate, much less encourage, sinful behavior in her membership. We are saying, however, that Christ has not given the church infallible knowledge of any person's heart. This knowledge cannot therefore be a standard of admission into the membership of the visible church. For this reason, it is impossible that the visible church should be, in this age, entirely composed of regenerate persons.

A second reply to the objection that infant members will corrupt the church concerns the responsibilities that belong to such persons as members of the church. As we have seen, all members of the church are subject to the instruction and discipline of the church. They are called, as disciples, to follow Jesus as their Savior and Lord. These matters are no less true of non-communing church members than of communing church members.[13] Furthermore, 'when we teach that all baptized persons "should perform all the duties of Church-members," it is not meant with unconverted hearts.'[14] The church has a particular and ongoing obligation to lay before her young membership their identity as sinners by nature, and to press upon them the way of salvation in Christ. Since this pattern of instruction, guidance, and restraint is, in kind, precisely that exercised by the church toward her communing membership, we cannot say that the fact of infant membership is inherently corruptive of the church.

In sum, we have seen that the children of at least one professing believer are members of the church by birthright. They are members of the church in their minority and disciples of Christ

---

13. It is for this reason that children of the church, as church members, are subject to the discipline of the church. For children, this discipline consists primarily in two matters, instruction and restraint. Dabney stresses that this ecclesiastical instruction and restraint should assume a form appropriate to the age and station of these young members. Both, he urges, should be undertaken not to 'supersede' but to 'assist and re-inforce' the teaching and discipline of the home. See further, Dabney, *Syllabus,* 795-96; and Mason, *Essays,* 444-49.

14. Dabney, *Syllabus,* 793.

by calling. They are entitled to the sacrament of baptism, and to the instruction and discipline of the church. They have the responsibility of pursuing their call to discipleship and, upon maturity, of entering into the full exercise of privileges to which they are heir.

How Are We To Shepherd the Children of the Church?

This recognition of the membership of the church's children raises a related and practical question, how are we to shepherd the children of the church? At the baptism of a child of the church, the parents of the child vow to raise the child in the nurture and admonition of the Lord, while the congregation vows to assist the parents in that nurture.[15] Precisely how or by what means is this nurture to take place? It is one thing to affirm that the children are owed Christian oversight and direction. It is another to specify how that oversight and direction are to take place. In this section, let us consider what means the Scripture has given the church to shepherd her youth.

The primary instrument of shepherding the youth of the church is the family. The Scripture repeatedly refers the instruction and training of the church's children to the home, particularly to the father of the home (Eph. 6:1-4; Col. 3:20-21; Gen. 18:19; Deut. 6:4-9, 20-24; 11:18-21; Ps. 78:1-4; Prov. 1:8 *et passim*). There are many fine works in print that address this pattern of nurture.[16] We may only offer the briefest of comments

---

15. *Book of Church Order* 56-5.

16. Two helpful studies setting the question in historical context are J. I. Packer, 'Marriage and Family in Puritan Thought,' in *A Quest for Godliness: The Puritan Vision for the Christian Life* (Wheaton, Ill.: Crossway, 1990), 259-73; and Leland Ryken, 'Family,' in *Worldly Saints* (Grand Rapids: Zondervan, 1986), 73-88. Three classic treatments of the family and of family worship in particular are B. M. Palmer, *The Family in Its Civil and Churchly Aspects: An Essay in Two Parts* (Richmond, Va.: Presbyterian Committee for Publication, 1876); J. W. Alexander, *Thoughts on Family Worship* (Philadelphia, Pa.: Presbyterian Board of Publication, 1847); and B. M. Smith, *Family Religion, or The Domestic Relations as Regulated by Christian Principles* (Philadelphia, Pa.: Presbyterian Board of Publication, 1859). Some helpful contemporary treatments include *Book of Church Order*, 'Chapter 63: Christian Life in the Home;' J. Ligon Duncan and Terry Johnson, 'A Biblical Call to Family Worship,' in *Give Praise to God: A Vision for Reforming Worship: Celebrating the Legacy of James Montgomery Boice*, eds. Philip Graham Ryken, Derek W. H. Thomas, and J. Ligon Duncan III (Phillipsburg, N.J.: P&R, 2003), 317-38; Joel Beeke, *Bringing the Gospel to Covenant Children in Dependency on the Spirit* (Grand Rapids, Mich.: Reformation Heritage Books, 2001); and *Family Worship* (Grand Rapids: Mich.: Reformation Heritage Books, 2005).

with respect to what form this pattern should take in the home. First, parents 'should set an example of piety and consistent living before the family'.[17] Children will see the Christian life most powerfully and vividly displayed in the lives of their parents. How do mom and dad handle disappointments, or respond to disagreements? Are mom and dad demonstrating by example the graces of patience, self-control, joy, kindness, and faithfulness? How does the way that they spend their time, their money, and other resources communicate what is important to them? Are mom and dad, for instance, committed to gathering with the people of God for public worship on the Lord's Day? How are they teaching their children to look at themselves, the world, and the church? How are they bringing scriptural principles to bear on the life and circumstances of the family, and of the family members?

Second, parents should set aside stated times for the family to gather for 'prayer, reading the Scriptures, and singing praises; or … some briefer form of outspoken recognition of God.'[18] Reformed writers have often termed such gatherings *family worship*. It is here that children may receive systematic instruction in Scripture and the catechisms of the church, may pray with and for their fellow family members, and may praise God in song. It is here that children learn how to join with the church in public worship and to worship God privately. Family worship is difficult to do, and faces many obstacles in the often over-scheduled lives of modern families. For these reasons and more, family worship does not happen by accident. It happens because the parents recognize its importance for the life of the family, and prioritize it in their schedules. Parents must, furthermore, be flexible, adaptable, and sensitive to the ages and maturity of their children.[19] When they do so, regular family worship, under the blessing of the Spirit, can be a tremendous means of spiritual growth and encouragement to the family.

---

17. *Book of Church Order* 63-5.

18. *Book of Church Order* 63-3.

19. See here the wise counsel of Douglas F. Kelly, 'Family Worship: Biblical, Reformed, and Viable for Today,' in eds. David Lachman and Frank J. Smith, *Worship in the Presence of God* (Greenville, S.C.: Greenville Seminary Press, 1992), 125-7.

If the family has the primary responsibility for the nurture of the children of the church, then the church plays a supporting role in this nurture. What form does this supporting role take? One primary way in which the church may support the nurture of children is through the ministry of the preaching of the word. This may surprise many who are accustomed to think primarily of Sunday School teachers as those who should communicate biblical truth to the youth of the church. This is neither to deny nor to depreciate the invaluable contributions such make to the lives of covenant children. It is to say, however, that the pulpit is a powerful and, by the Spirit's blessing, spiritually effective way of training the youth of the church. Historically, Reformed and Presbyterian ministers took this responsibility very seriously. They not only gathered the children of the church and addressed them independently of the whole congregation, but also addressed them directly from the pulpit during the Lord's Day morning sermon.[20] This part of our heritage should encourage those of us who minister the word to think of ways to address children simply, plainly, vividly, and compassionately. This is not to say that the entirety of our sermons should be set at a first-grade reading level. It is to say that our sermons should have something to say to all the members of the church, even and especially to the young ones. Parents may help here as well. If fathers were to review the sermon with their family during the afternoon hours of the Lord's Day, two things might happen. First, this review might drive home the content of the sermon to the family, and allow for further and particular application to be made specifically to the family. Second, this review might help children in the family learn how to listen to the sermons that they will hear in weeks to come.

A second way that the church may support the nurture of the children is through pastoral visitation. At such times, the elders may speak directly with children about the things of God. They should also make a point of speaking with parents, during visitation, about the instruction and nurture of the children in the home. Elders may then pray with and for the family

---

20. The ministry of Jonathan Edwards is particularly illustrative in this regard.

about any matters that arise during these conversations. Or, if a congregation has a children's Sunday School program, elders might consider regularly teaching children's classes. Such efforts will help them to form relationships with the children and parents of the church, and, by teaching the Scripture directly to those children, assist the parental instruction that should be taking place in the home.

A third way that the church may support the nurture of the children is by encouraging catechesis. Most churches in the Protestant tradition have adopted catechisms – question and answer statements summarizing leading teachings of the Scripture. It has long been a practice within the Reformed church for parents to catechize their children, and for the church to assist parents in that work. What form might this encouragement take? At the very least, elders might encourage and instruct families to undertake the work of catechesis. If there is a children's Sunday School program in place, then is catechetical instruction part of that program? When a child is able to recite the catechism, this is a time for celebration. The church should think of ways that it can honor and encourage the child and the family for this accomplishment.

A fourth way that some churches have found helpful to support the Christian nurture of the children of the church is by offering a communicants' class for children in their early teen years.[21] This option has both benefits and pitfalls. Positively, a communicants' class can help to ensure that every child of the church is given appropriate instruction about what it means to make public profession of faith, and what is involved in receiving the Lord's Supper. Such a class can also help reinforce the pastoral bonds between a child, the pastor, and the elders.

---

21. In this connection, Presbyterian pastors would occasionally prepare manuals or catechisms to assist young persons in their preparations for making public profession of faith and, therefore, approaching the Lord's Table. See, for example, Scottish Presbyterian John Barr, *Plain Catechetical Instructions for Young Communicants, Designed to Assist Them in Forming Scriptural Views of the Lord's Supper, With an Address to Young Persons Not Yet Communicants, and a Few Meditations and Helps for Self-Examination* (1st American ed.; Philadelphia: Presbyterian Board of Publication, 1842), and Southern Presbyterian Robert P. Kerr, *Presbyterian Communion-Class Catechism: A Book of Questions For Use in the Special Instruction of Persons About to Make a Public Confession of Christ* (Richmond, Va.: Presbyterian Committee of Publication, 1896).

The downside of a communicants' class is that it can sometimes pressure children to pursue the exercise of the full privileges of church membership before they are ready. If churches clearly communicate that attendance in such a class does not necessarily mean that one is ready to make public profession of faith, and that mere completion of such a class does not entitle one to the full exercise of the privileges of church membership, then this downside can be minimized.

In summary, the church has many ways in which it is able to assist parents in their commitment to the Christian nurture of their children. It is important to stress that the church's role is a supportive one. One danger is that parents will forfeit their calling to this nurture, and rely on the church to do the work that is properly their own. This state of affairs simply means that churches must be clear and deliberate in communicating the lines of biblical responsibility that belong to both home and church with respect to the Christian nurture of children.

When Ought A Child of the Church to Approach the Lord's Table?
The prayer and desire of both parents and the church is that the children of the church will turn to Jesus Christ, as Savior and Lord, in faith and repentance, and profess the same publicly. This common goal raises two questions. First, what exactly is the young person (not) doing when he steps forward in this fashion? Second, for what should parents look in their children to determine whether they are ready to make such a step? How may pastors and elders equip and prepare parents for such a responsibility?

It is important to stress, first, that when a young person approaches the session, makes public profession of faith, and is admitted to the Lord's Table, he is not 'joining the church'. To think so, John M. Mason argues, 'is a great mistake. The children of Christian parents are *born* members of the church.'[22] The child cannot join the church because he is already a member of the church by birthright. What changes, then, when he makes a credible profession of faith? What changes is that he is admitted

---

22. Mason, *Essays*, 438.

to the full privileges of church membership. These privileges include approach to the Lord's Table, voting in congregational elections, and, if a qualified male, standing for church office.

For what do parents look in the lives of their children? How will they know when their children are ready to approach the session and make profession of faith? How ought pastors and elders to instruct parents in this area? We may first offer three negative answers to this question.

First, parents should not look to the membership of their children *per se*. In other words, the fact that children are already members of the church by birthright does not by itself qualify those children to exercise the full privileges of membership. The contributors to this volume have persuasively argued that children of the church must demonstrate certain biblical qualifications before the session may admit them to the Lord's Supper. As valuable and as important as the membership that children of believers enjoy by birthright is, it is not sufficient for them to come to the Lord's Table.

Second, parents should not look to a set age. The Scripture does not prescribe a set age at which children are entitled to step into the exercise of the full privileges of church membership. Neither does it prescribe a set age before which these children may not exercise these privileges. What counts is whether the young person demonstrates the biblical qualifications necessary for him to approach the Table. For this reason, the PCA's *Book of Church Order* wisely observes that 'the time when young persons come to understand the Gospel cannot be precisely fixed. This must be left to the prudence of the Session, whose office it is to judge, after careful examination, the qualifications of those who apply for admission to sealing ordinances.'[23]

Third, parents should not look for a conversion experience *per se*. We wish to be careful in not being misunderstood at this point. We are not saying that the family and the church should not pray for the conversion of its young people, nor press them to be converted by the means of God's appointment. Nor are we saying that the unconverted can ever profit spiritually from

---

23. *Book of Church Order*, 57-2.

the Lord's Supper. Nor are we saying that the church should be indifferent to the spiritual condition of those who would approach the Lord's Table.

What we are saying is that a conversion *experience* by itself is not a biblical requirement for church membership. If a child were regenerated early, he will likely not have conscious memory of a conversion experience. This state of affairs means neither that he is unconverted nor that he is disqualified from approaching the Lord's Table. It means, rather, that he is unable to recount his experience of conversion. Furthermore, elders of the church are neither competent nor called to assess the authenticity of the experience *per se*. As desirable as conversion is, a narration of a conversion experience *per se* is no requirement for admittance to the Lord's Supper.

For what then are parents to look in the lives of their children in order to counsel with respect to their readiness to approach the session concerning admittance to the Lord's Table? Parents should ascertain whether their children are prepared to make what Presbyterians have called a 'credible profession of faith' before the session.

What do we mean by a credible, or believable, profession of faith? The nineteenth century American Presbyterian theologian, A. A. Hodge, summarizes the difference between an historical Congregationalist and an historical Presbyterian understanding of the phrase.

> The Congregationalists understand by 'credible profession' the positive evidence of a religious experience which satisfies the official judges of the gracious state of the applicant. The Presbyterians understand by that phrase only an intelligent *profession* of true spiritual faith in Christ, which is not contradicted by the life.[24]

At least three elements stand out in Hodge's definition of a credible profession of faith. First, the profession must be intelligent. In other words, it must be made with understanding. The one making profession should have a knowledgeable grasp of the

---

24. A. A. Hodge, *Outlines of Theology* (1879; repr. Edinburgh: Banner of Truth, 1972), 646.

teaching of Scripture, particularly as it bears on God, sin, and salvation. Second, the profession is of 'true spiritual faith in Christ'. The candidate must profess not merely knowledge of and assent to the teaching of Scripture. He must profess a trusting reliance in Christ and in Christ alone as His Savior from sin. Third, the profession must 'not [be] contradicted by the life'. There must be nothing in the candidate's life that counters what he has just publicly professed. A candidate who habitually gives himself over to the service of sin, for instance, would not be deemed one making a 'credible' profession.

With this understanding, we may frame three questions to assist parents and elders in assessing young people with respect to their readiness for making profession of faith. First, 'Does this young person understand the teaching of Scripture?' In Presbyterian churches, the session does not expect of those making profession of faith a full embrace of the Westminster Standards.[25] Nor does the session expect a depth and penetration of the candidate that they might expect of a candidate for church office. They do expect, however, the candidate to voice his understanding and embrace of the leading teachings of the Scripture. The Membership Vows frequently used in the Presbyterian Church in America are a good barometer of the readiness of the candidate's understanding. They are as follows.

1. Do you acknowledge yourselves to be sinners in the sight of God, justly deserving His displeasure, and without hope save in His sovereign mercy?

2. Do you believe in the Lord Jesus Christ as the Son of God, and Savior of sinners, and do you receive and rest upon Him alone for salvation as He is offered in the Gospel?

3. Do you now resolve and promise, in humble reliance upon the grace of the Holy Spirit, that you will endeavor to live as becomes the followers of Christ?

4. Do you promise to support the Church in its worship and work to the best of your ability?

---

25. Though such persons are subject to discipline according to the Word of God as interpreted by those subordinate standards, see *Book of Church Order* 29-1.

5. Do you submit yourselves to the government and discipline of the Church, and promise to study its purity and peace?

If the candidate is prepared willingly and with understanding to assent to these vows, then he may be deemed, in this respect at least, as prepared to make credible profession of faith. We see, once again, the importance of parental instruction, supported by the efforts of the church. It is through these means primarily that the young people of the church will be prepared to make such an intelligent profession.

We may also see that this understanding should be accompanied with faith. It is not simply that the young person assents to the teachings of Scripture as true. It is that he declares that he embraces these teachings from the heart, by faith. One may not properly assent to these vows, in fact, apart from a believing reception of Christ as Savior and Lord. These vows underscore the importance of a lifetime of exhortation from the home and the pulpit to the young people of the church to put their trust in Christ as Savior, and willingly to take up the yoke of his Lordship.

A second question to assist parents and elders in assessing young people with respect to their readiness for making profession of faith is, 'Does the candidate want to make profession of faith?' On the face of it, this question may sound odd. It is in fact an important question. Young people may step forward to make a public profession for any number of reasons. They may do so because their peers have done it or are doing it. They may do so because they are under direct or indirect family pressure. Social and familial encouragement and support are, of course, important to any young person considering making profession of faith. Critical, however, is that the candidate make profession for the right reasons and at the right time. He must make public profession from a willing heart and not under outward constraint.

A third and final question is, 'Does the candidate's life contradict the understanding that he professes?' Here, the parents' wisdom and experience with their child will prove invaluable. If the young person is so prepared to make credible profession of faith, then parents ought to recognize this fact, and to encourage him to step forward before the elders and to make this profession. If he is not ready, then parents may also communicate this fact to him, and encourage him to wait until he is prepared to make credible profession. In both cases, the parents will be invaluable in assisting the elders in their responsibility for evaluating the credibility of the young person's profession.

We may close our discussion of this question by reiterating the counsel of the PCA's *Book of Church Order.*

> The children of believers are, through the covenant and by right of birth, non-communing members of the church. Hence they are entitled to Baptism, and to the pastoral oversight, instruction and government of the church, with a view to their embracing Christ and thus possessing personally all benefits of the covenant.... Those only who have made a profession of faith in Christ, have been baptized, and admitted by the Session to the Lord's Table, are entitled to all the rights and privileges of the church.[26]

> When [believers' children] are able to understand the Gospel, they should be earnestly reminded that they are members of the Church by birthright, and that it is their duty and privilege personally to accept Christ, to confess him before men, and to seek admission to the Lord's Supper.[27]

> When [believers' children] have reached the age of discretion, they become subject to obligations of the covenant: faith, repentance, and obedience. They then make public confession of their faith in Christ, or become covenant breakers, and subject to the discipline of the Church.[28]

These counsels stress that a certain tone should accompany the parental nurture of the child, and the church's assistance of that nurture. Positively, children of the church should be encouraged

---

26. *Book of Church Order,* 6-1, 6-4.

27. *Book of Church Order* 57-1.

28. *Book of Church Order* 56-4j.

to enter into the exercise of the privileges of their membership as soon as they are ready to do so. Neither the parents nor the church should erect unnecessary barriers to such entrance. Nor should the parents and the church treat such a profession as something that is rote or unimportant. From early years, children should be taught both the nature and the importance of a credible profession of faith, and stirred to pursue it with the encouragement of their parents and elders.

At the same time, children should also be warned. Refusal to make credible profession of faith is fraught with significance. As John M. Mason put it,

> The question, then, with them, when they reach that period of maturity which qualifies them to judge for themselves, is, *not* whether they shall contract or avoid an allegiance which has hitherto had no claims upon them: but whether they shall acknowledge or *renounce* an allegiance under which they drew their first breath? ... Not whether they shall be simple *unbelievers*, but whether they shall display their unbelief in the form of *apostasy*?[29]

Christian parents, supported by the church, have a responsibility to let their children know that they are already members of the church, by birthright, and, as such, are disciples of Christ, by calling. Refusal to make profession of faith translates into the renunciation of their membership and discipleship. It is when we, as the church, weigh the significance of such refusal, that we ought to commit our children, once again, to the mercy of God in Christ, and redouble our efforts to encourage them to make credible profession of faith at the appropriate time.

How Do I Help God's People Understand and Appreciate the Lord's Supper?

We may conclude our reflections by asking and answering a broad question, how may pastors and elders help themselves and the people of God better to understand and appreciate the sacrament of the Lord's Supper?

---

29. Mason, *Essays,* 439.

In asking this question, it is important to be aware of some of the fears and concerns that can circulate in the church concerning the Lord's Supper. We may mention at least five such concerns.

First, some see the Lord's Supper as an occasion for division and not edification within the church. They may wonder whether the church giving concerted attention to this sacrament will not be in the end counterproductive.

Second, many are aware that the Lord's Supper has been subject to abuse in the history of the church. The sacrament has been corrupted into a superstitious rite that has diverted the church from the centrality of the Word, the sovereignty of the Spirit, and the importance of personal faith in Christ.

Third, some may regard the Lord's Supper as, in one sense, superfluous. If the Lord's Supper does not make anyone a Christian, and if the Lord's Supper does not give the believer anything that he could not already get from the Scripture, they reason, then how important could it really be?

Fourth, others may point to the difficulties attending understanding the nature and meaning of the Supper. If some of the greatest theologians in the Reformed church have grappled with and wrestled over the meaning of the Supper, then how can non-specialists be expected to have a firm grasp of the meaning of this sacrament?

Fifth, still others might look at the infrequency of the church's observance of the Lord's Supper and wonder whether all the time and effort to understand this sacrament is worth it.

In light of these concerns, how might pastors and elders help the church to understand and value the Lord's Supper for the means of grace that it is? What are some positive and proactive ways in which those who teach and shepherd in the church may both address some of the above-mentioned concerns and instill a proper appreciation for the Supper in the church? At least four thoughts come to mind.

'Accentuate the Positive'

To borrow a line from the old song, ministers and elders need to 'accentuate the positive' when it comes to the Lord's Supper. In the Reformed church, we face a certain liability when it comes to this sacrament in our teaching. Often we address the Lord's Supper in predominantly polemical contexts, to highlight our disagreements with Rome, the Lutherans, or other groups. Addressing these polemical questions in the church is, of course, appropriate and necessary. The elder, after all, is called not only 'to give instruction in sound doctrine', but 'also to rebuke those who contradict it' (Titus 1:9). It is easy to leave the mistaken impression, however, that the importance of the Lord's Supper is as a matter for theological controversy. When we address these differences within the church, it is important to explain, with equal emphasis, why it is that Christ has given sacraments to his people. He has given them to us as a help to their Christian living. Consider the way in which the *Westminster Larger Catechism* summarizes the Scripture's teaching on the definition of a sacrament.

> Q. 162. What is a sacrament?
>
> A. A sacrament is an holy ordinance instituted by Christ in his church, to signify, seal, and exhibit unto those that are within the covenant of grace, the benefits of his mediation; to strengthen and increase their faith, and all other graces; to oblige them to obedience; to testify and cherish their love and communion one with another; and to distinguish them from those that are without.

The sacraments, in other words, are helps to Christians' faith and obedience. They are means by which they may grow in their love for God and for one another. The sacraments are eminently and fundamentally practical. To shy away from a better understanding of the Lord's Supper is to shy away from a God-given opportunity to grow in the Christian life.

Teach the Church What the Lord's Supper Teaches the Church
In a nutshell, the Lord's Supper teaches the church the gospel. Consider the way in which the *Westminster Larger Catechism* offers a biblical definition of the Lord's Supper.

Q. 168. What is the Lord's Supper?

A. The Lord's Supper is a sacrament of the New Testament, wherein, by giving and receiving bread and wine according to the appointment of Jesus Christ, his death is shewed forth; and they that worthily communicate feed upon his body and blood, to their spiritual nourishment and growth in grace; have their union and communion with him confirmed; testify and renew their thankfulness, and engagement to God, and their mutual love and fellowship each with the other, as members of the same mystical body.

What does the Lord's Supper teach us? The Lord's Supper calls our attention to the person of Jesus Christ. We are reminded that he took our nature and, as one who was fully human, tasted death for his people. We are also reminded that he is no mere man. He was, is, and ever shall be the eternal Son of God. Death did not conquer him, but he conquered death. For this reason, his people, united to him by faith, may commune with him in the Lord's Supper.

The Lord's Supper calls our attention to the work of Christ accomplished. The Lord's Supper is preeminently a display of the once-for-all, substitutionary, and atoning death of Christ for sinners. The Lord's Supper reminds us that Christ's sin-bearing death has wiped away the guilt of the sins of God's people, and has turned aside from them the wrath of God for their sins. The Lord's Supper not only points us back to the redemptive death of our Savior, but also points us forward to the glorious return of the risen Jesus at the end of the age. In the administration of this sacrament, we 'proclaim his death until he comes' (1 Cor. 11:26).

The Lord's Supper calls our attention to the fact that the work of Christ must be applied to sinners in order to benefit them. The Lord's Supper shows us that the Christian life is not sinners cooperating with God to save themselves. It reminds us, rather, that Christianity is the work of the Savior, sovereignly and graciously applied in time to the undeserving. The Lord's Supper impresses upon us the fact that the benefits of Christ must be applied to the people of God by the Spirit, through faith.

The Lord's Supper teaches us leading truths about the Christian life. The Lord's Supper reminds us that the believer is united to Christ and, in union with him, shares in all his benefits (1 Cor. 10:16-17). The Lord's Supper impresses upon us the importance of the graces of faith and repentance in communing with the Savior. The Lord's Supper confirms to the believer that he is justified, accepted and accounted righteous, only because of the perfect obedience and full satisfaction of Christ, imputed to him, and received by faith alone. The Lord's Supper reminds the believer that he is part of God's family. In Christ, he calls God 'Father' and calls his fellow believers 'brothers'. The Lord's Supper impresses upon the believer how important it is to pursue a holy life, to put sin to death and to present one's members as instruments for righteousness. After all, how can a Christian believingly consider the death of Christ for the sins of sinners and be callous or indifferent to his own sin? As importantly, the Lord's Supper, in setting forth in visible signs Christ crucified, gives the believer a spiritual sight of the Savior by whose death and life alone he may make any progress in holiness at all.[30]

The Lord's Supper, properly observed, is therefore full of Christ. Consider the Puritan Thomas Watson's meditations on the importance of this sacrament:

> Behold here is the best of dainties, God is in his cheer. Here is the apple of the Tree of Life; here is the 'banqueting house' where the banner of free grace is gloriously displayed, 'He brought me to the banqueting house, and his banner over me was love' (Song of Songs 2:4).
>
> In the sacrament we see Christ broken before us, and his broken body is the only comfort for a broken heart. While we sit at this table, Christ's precious spikenard of merit and grace sends forth its fragrance. The sacrament is both a healing and a sealing ordinance. Here our Savior leads his people up the Mount of Transfiguration, and gives them a glimpse of paradise. How welcome should this jubilee of soul be, wherein

---

30. John M. Mason, 'Letters on Frequent Communion,' in *Works* (1852) 4.281-282.

Christ appears in the splendour of his beauty, and draws the golden lines of love to the centre of a believer's heart. Oh! What flames of devotion should burn in our hearts![31]

In his treatment on the worship of the church, Scottish Presbyterian Archibald Hall comments that, chief among the 'excellent uses and ends' of the Lord's Supper, is that it 'keep[s] up the remembrance of Christ'.[32] Specifically, the Supper keeps Christ before the church 'as an hearty, generous friend,' 'as the propitiation for our sins,' 'as an absent friend of ours,' and 'as our Lord that will come again in the clouds of heaven'.[33]

And if Christ has designed the Supper to represent to his people the sufficiency of his saving work, then how could joy not follow in the lives of Christians who attend to Christ in that sacrament? Consider here the reflections of the Irish Presbyterian Thomas Houston:

> The *Christian's joys* and *blessed hopes* are *largely realized* and expressed in the Lord's Supper. Spiritual joy arises in the soul from the actual possession of loved and desired spiritual objects; and hope pointing to the future, sees good things as attainable, the object of assured expectation. Both these graces are fruits of the Spirit, and the certain effect of a living faith. In the feast of the Supper, believers, receiving the atonement, 'joy in God through our Lord Jesus Christ.' Coming to the altar of God, they 'go to God their exceeding joy' – and they know experimentally the grounds of holy rejoicing. They joy in God as their sure portion; they rejoice in what He has done for them – in the endearing and blessed relations which He sustains toward them – and in the blissful prospects which He sets before them. They are made joyful in His house of prayer … [The Lord's Supper] sets before them in the most affecting aspect Christ Jesus as the grand provision of the covenant – and the blessings of life and salvation through Him…. In partaking

---

31. Thomas Watson, *The Lord's Supper* (1665; repr. Edinburgh: Banner of Truth, 2004), vii-viii.

32. Archibald Hall, *Gospel-Worship, Being An Attempt to Exhibit a Scriptural View of the Nature, Obligations, Manner, and Ordinances, of the Worship of God, in the New Testament, in Two Volumes* (Edinburgh: Gray & Alston, 1770), 1.365.

33. Hall, *Gospel Worship*, 1.365-69.

of this provision, the great doctrines of the Gospel become to us matters of realizing and joyful expectation. They are our life, our joy, and hope and blessedness begun; and as we eat and drink in feasting with the King, we 'grow in grace, and in the knowledge of our Lord and Saviour Jesus Christ.'[34]

One benefit of teaching the Lord's Supper in this fashion is that it complements what we are trying to accomplish in the pulpit. If a leading goal of the sermon is to represent the person and work of Christ to the consciences of the hearers, and to invite them to respond to him in faith and repentance, then the Lord's Supper bolsters such an effort. The Lord's Supper becomes a visible representation and confirmation of what the people hear in the sermon. The Lord's Supper, far from being an appendix to public worship, becomes a way in which the word preached may be freshly applied and pressed home to those in attendance. Even those who are not qualified to partake of the Supper may learn much as they witness its administration. Observance of the Lord's Supper, conversely, helps the minister to ensure that his sermons are properly centered upon Christ, and focused upon bringing the claims of Christ to bear upon the hearers. If the minister knows that his sermon will be followed by the administration of the Supper, then he will be likelier to take care that the Supper not be a visible *non sequitur* to the content and emphases of the sermon. He will make sure that the sermon's emphases align with those of the Lord's Supper.

Teach the Church How to Receive the Lord's Supper
Instructing the church about the nature and significance of the Lord's Supper is part of the battle. It is equally important to help the people of God learn how to receive and to profit from the Lord's Supper. How do we go about such a project? We should certainly draw from and point the church to some rich resources already in our possession. *The Westminster Larger Catechism*, for instance, has a series of questions that are designed to help Christians prepare for the Lord's Supper (Q&A 171-3), receive

---

34. Thomas Houston, *The Lord's Supper: Its Nature, Ends, and Obligation; and Mode of Administration* (Edinburgh: James Gemmell, 1878), 61-2.

the Lord's Supper (Q&A 174), and respond to the Lord's Supper after it has been administered (Q&A 175). These questions and answers can help to furnish the mind with ample material for meditation before, during, and after the sacrament. Simply distributing such material to the congregation, or, even better, commenting on this material in print, from the pulpit, or from the lectern, can go a long way towards equipping the church to partake of the Lord's Supper with understanding.

In reading this catechism's questions and answers, one is struck by the continued emphasis upon the mind in the believer's participation in the Lord's Supper. The Lord's Supper is a means of grace, but it does not profit the believer spiritually apart from the engagement of the mind. Believers are to prepare for the Lord's Supper by '*examining themselves* of their being in Christ, of their sins and wants; of the truth and measure of their knowledge, faith, repentance; love to God and the brethren, charity to all men, forgiving those that have done them wrong; of their desires after Christ, and of their new obedience...'.[35] During the Lord's Supper, believers must '*diligently observe* the sacramental elements and actions, *heedfully discern* the Lord's Body, and *affectionately meditate* on his death and sufferings, and thereby stir themselves up to a vigorous exercise of their graces...'.[36] After the Lord's Supper, believers should '*seriously consider* how they have behaved themselves therein and with what success...'.[37] *The Westminster Standards*, following the Scripture, offer no way to believers to profit from the Lord's Supper apart from the engagement of their minds upon that which the Supper represents.

This point is important for at least a couple of reasons. First, understanding the Lord's Supper in this fashion helps us to avoid the magical or superstitious operations that some in church history have thought to attend the sacrament. The sacrament is spiritual, but it is not superstitious. It is the Holy Spirit who makes the Lord's Supper efficacious, and the Spirit does so in

---

35. Westminster Larger Catechism, Q & A 171. Emphasis ours.

36. Westminster Larger Catechism, Q & A 174. Emphasis ours.

37. Westminster Larger Catechism, Q & A 175. Emphasis ours.

conjunction with, not apart from, the activity of the believer's mind. Stressing this dimension of the Lord's Supper in public teaching may go a long way to dispelling some of the fears and concerns that we above identified.

Second, the Lord's Supper benefits believers in precisely the same way that the preaching of the Word benefits believers. In both instances, Christ is set before the believer. The believer, in the strength of the Spirit, responds to Christ in faith and repentance. The believer is thus further nurtured, equipped, and strengthened to serve Christ in his callings. In this respect, the Lord's Supper and the preached Word are not materially different. They both present Christ to the believer. Preaching does so by the ear. The Lord's Supper does so particularly by sight.

This similarity between the Supper and the Word means that believers can no more expect to profit from the sacrament apart from the activity of their minds than they could expect to profit from a sermon apart from the activity of their minds. Archibald Hall explains this point well in addressing what it means to 'remember Christ' in the Lord's Supper:

> This *remembering of Christ* supposes some *knowledge* of him, and some *acquaintance* with him. We cannot be said to remember one we never knew. – It implies *a fixed contemplation* of him, as the propitiation for our sins. – It produces *a powerful impression* of the truth upon the conscience, and *the joyful experience* of its benign influence upon the whole soul, so as to work it into a fellowship with, and conformity to Christ in his sufferings.[38]

In summary, the mind matters. To profit from the Lord's Supper, believers must 'mind the mind', and be taught to do so. We have the benefit of the Catechisms and excellent literature to assist us in profiting from the Supper.[39] Those of us who are

---

38. Hall, *Gospel Worship*, 1.370.

39. A small sampling of which includes Thomas Watson, *The Lord's Supper*; Wilhelmus à Brakel, *The Christian's Reasonable Service* (trans. Bartel Elshout; 4 vols.; Ligonier, Pa.: Soli Deo Gloria Publications, 1993), 2.569-600; Matthew Henry, *The Communicant's Companion: or, Instructions for the Right Receiving of the Lord's Supper,* in *The Complete Works of the Rev. Matthew Henry* (1855; 2 vols.; repr. Grand Rapids: Baker, 1979), 1.284-412; Thomas Houston, *The Lord's Supper*; J. J. Janeway, *The Communicant's Manual, or a Series of Meditations Designed to Assist Communicants in Making Preparation for the Lord's*

called to preach and to teach in the church have the privilege of distilling biblical wisdom from these sources and dispensing it to the profit and encouragement of God's people.

Encourage the Church to Hunger for the Lord's Supper

Fourth and finally, we should encourage the church to hunger for the Lord's Supper. We have above stressed the important of the engagement of the mind in this sacrament. The mind's meditations, however, are not an end in themselves. As Lewis Bayly observes, knowledge must be part of sincere faith:

> Sincere faith is not a bare knowledge of the Scriptures and first grounds of religion – for that devils and reprobates have in an excellent measure, and do believe it and tremble (James 2:19) – but a true persuasion, as of all those things whatsoever the Lord hath revealed in his word; so also a particular application to a man's own soul, of all the promises of mercy which God hath made in Christ to all believing sinners (Heb. 4:2;) and consequently, that Christ and all his merits do belong to him, as well as to any other; – for first, if we have not the righteousness of faith (Rom 4:11), the sacrament seals nothing to us, and every man in the Lord's Supper receiveth so much as he believeth; secondly, because that without faith we communicating on earth, cannot apprehend Christ in heaven, for as he dwelleth in us by faith (Eph. 3:17), so by faith we must likewise eat him; thirdly, because that without faith we cannot be persuaded in our consciences that our receiving is acceptable unto God (Heb. 11:6; Rom. 14: 23).[40]

Our goal, then, in observing the Lord's Supper is that, by the means of the mind, the whole soul would be stirred. *The Larger Catechism* speaks of the Supper as 'spiritual nourishment to the soul'.[41] As physical bread and wine nourish the body, so the sacrament of the

---

Supper (Philadelphia: Presbyterian Board of Publication, 1848); J. C. Ryle, 'Going to the Table,' in *Practical Religion: Being Plain Papers on the Daily Duties, Experience, Dangers, and Privileges of Professing Christians* (1878; repr. Edinburgh: Banner of Truth, 1998), 140-64; and 'Questions About the Lord's Supper,' in *The Upper Room: Being a Few Truths for the Times* (1888; repr. Edinburgh: Banner of Truth, 1970), 426-55.

40. Lewis Bayly, *The Practice of Piety: Directing a Christian How to Walk, that He May Please God* (1611; repr. of 1842 ed.; Morgan, Penn.: Soli Deo Gloria Publications, n.d.), 244.

41. Westminster Larger Catechism, Q & A 177.

Lord's Supper is designed to nourish the soul. The God who has said to his people, 'open your mouth wide, and I will fill it,' will make good on his promise (Ps. 81:10). The believer hungers for any opportunity to have fellowship with his Savior. In the Lord's Supper, Christ makes provision to satisfy just such a hunger.

Encouraging a proper hunger for the Lord's Supper in the life of the church can only be beneficial. Luther once famously remarked that man is *incurvatus in se* – 'bent in on himself.' Christians too often succumb to the temptation to set their gaze exclusively and unwholesomely inward. We can become despairing as we consider in this way our indwelling sin. The Lord's Supper calls us to set our gaze upon ourselves only as we cast a believing sight upon the Savior. To be sure, the Supper reminds us that we are unworthy sinners, deserving only the wrath and curse of God in this life and in the one to come. The Supper is also the place, however, where the Savior invites as many as have put their trust in Christ alone for salvation to come to the Table that he has spread for them. Consider Bayly's description of this invitation.

> Yet if thou comest humbly, in faith, repentance, and charity, abhorring thy sins past, and purposing unfeignedly to amend thy life henceforth, let not thy former sins affright thee, for they shall never be laid to thy charge: and this sacrament shall seal unto thy soul, that all thy sins and the judgments due to them, are fully pardoned and clean washed away by the blood of Christ. For this sacrament was not ordained for them who are perfect, but to help penitent sinners unto perfection: Christ came not to call the righteous but sinners to repentance; and he saith, that the whole need not the physician, but they that are sick (Matt. 9:12, 13; 11:28). Those hath Christ called, and when they came them hath he ever helped. Witness the whole gospel, which testifieth, that not one sinner who came to Christ for mercy, ever went away without his errand. Bathe thou likewise thy sick soul in this fountain of Christ's blood, and doubtless, according to his promise (Zech. 13:1), thou shalt be healed of all thy sins and uncleanness. Not sinners, therefore, but they who are unwilling to repent of their sins, are debarred this sacrament.[42]

---

42. Bayly, *Practice of Piety*, 248.

It is at this feast, spread by Christ himself, that we make fresh confession of sin, trust once again in the merits of Christ, rejoice in his love, give thanks for new supplies of his grace, and depart with renewed and unreserved dedication to his service. In this way, the Lord's Supper further assures believers that the Christ they now behold and embrace by faith, they shall one day behold by sight. When they do so, Jesus shall seat them at the 'marriage supper of the Lamb' (Rev 19:7).

Perhaps now we can better see why the Lord's Supper is such an important help to the Christian life. The Supper is a means that Christ has given to his church to display his beauty, majesty, glory, and sufficiency for his people. Here the church finds what she needs to live the Christian life in the way that Christ intended it to be lived. In an age where gimmicks and false spiritualities run amok, even within the visible church, the Lord's Supper directs our 'minds' to the 'simplicity and purity of devotion to Christ' (2 Cor 11:3 NASB).

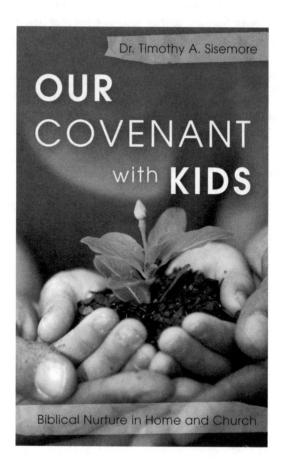

Dr. Timothy A. Sisemore

OUR
COVENANT
with **KIDS**

Biblical Nurture in Home and Church

Our Covenant With Kids

Biblical Nurture in Home and Church

TIMOTHY SISEMORE

Dr. Sisemore teaches you about – Christian parenting in a hostile world, educating children spiritually and academically, cultivating godliness, disciplining and discipling, honoring parents, how are children saved? The church's responsibility towards its children, children's involvement in worship and sacraments.

This is a practical and theological approach to parenting and children's ministry – and shows how to nurture children to be disciples.

Here is a straightforward, readable, challenging and practical manual just what parents are looking for.
Sinclair B. Ferguson ⁓ Senior Minister,
First Presbyterian Church, Columbia, South Carolina

His approach is what the Bible calls wisdom... as rich in Biblical instruction as it is in psychological insight.
Edmund P. Clowney ⁓ Late Professor of Practical Theology,
Westminster Seminary in California, Escondido, California

Anyone who has a true concern for the spiritual welfare of children in this present age must read this book!
Mark Johnston ⁓ Senior Pastor,
Proclamation Presbyterian Church, Bryn Mawr, Pennsylvania

Dr. Timothy Sisemore is one of America's leading child and adolescent Christian psychologists. He is the Clinal Professor of Psychology and Counselling at the Psychological Studies Institute. He maintains a clinical practice at the Chattanooga Bible Institute Counseling Center and has been published in Professional Psychology Research & Practice, The Journal for Christian Educators and the Journal of Psychology & Christianity. Ruth Sisemore is his wife and vitally helps Tim translate theory into practice!

ISBN 978-1-84550-350-5

"These four pieces fit together well. They
show the responsibility that parents have
for bringing up their children."

from the Foreword by Allan Harman

FAMILY RELIGION

Principles for raising a godly family

MATTHEW HENRY

Family Religion
Principles for raising a Godly Family

MATTHEW HENRY

You are a Christian – but how do you look after your family?

Matthew Henry is one of the best known of our spiritual ancestors. His Commentary on the whole Bible is still a staple book for those seeking understanding of God's word to the world. Henry recognised that the future of the church was in the home where the Holy Spirit could direct and mature believers. A spiritual home would help grow the church and enable the community to live peaceably. In this collection of his writings on family life, Henry expounds good sense and gives us better patterns for our devotional, practical and spiritual needs.

Key Sections:

- What, why and how to structure family devotions
- How to catechise children
- Jesus' attitude towards children
- The necessity, nature, efficacy and improvement of baptism.

Matthew Henry (1662-1714) is a beloved commentator, was a pastor of a church in Chester and was a prolific writer.

ISBN 978-1-84550-313-0

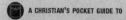
A CHRISTIAN'S POCKET GUIDE TO

JUSTIFI CATION

BEING MADE RIGHT WITH GOD?

GUY WATERS

A Christian's Pocket Guide to Justification

Being made right with God?

GUY WATERS

Could you explain Justification if asked to? For many of us, the whole concept of justification is as mystifying as a foreign language, but yet Christians down the ages have fought to defend it – seeing it quite rightly as a vital element of how we are saved. But justification is not a relic of the past – it has direct relevance to us as Christians today. We often struggle with the thought of justification because of human pride; "I can't be that bad" and so justification is often undermined, wrongly presented or just plain ignored. Scripture though, is brutally clear: we have a real problem – the prospect of our lives marred by wrong-doing being laid out before an almighty God who is pure and will not forever let wrong go unpunished. We can't earn our way out of our predicament – as this is just "rubbish" according to the apostle Paul. We need something else, someone who can take the hit we so richly deserve – leaving us to be declared innocent instead. This little book will help you grasp a truth that when understood correctly is explosive, transformational and utterly liberating.

> *Waters' offers a concise yet extremely helpful treatment of what Scriptural justification is, its practical value in the Christian life and how the doctrine is being challenged in our present day. I won't hestitate to give this little book to the university students under my pastoral care.*
>
> Aaron Messner - College Chaplain,
> Covenant College, Lookout Mountain, Georgia

Dr. Guy Waters is the Associate Professor of New Testament at the Reformed Theological Seminary, Jackson, Mississippi who has a particular interest in the letters and the theology of Paul. He is a teaching elder in the Mississippi presbytery of the Presbyterian Church of America.

ISBN 978-1-84550-615-5

THE
LORD'S
SUPPER

MALCOLM
MACLEAN

The Lord's Supper

MALCOLM MACLEAN

Malcolm Maclean's study of the biblical basis, historical development and practical administration of the Lord's Supper in our churches is a rich blend of scholarly analysis and pastoral insight. The question of what Jesus is doing in the Lord's Supper rather than what we are doing challenges the subjectivism that drives much of our practice, and restores a much needed emphasis on the Supper as a means of grace. This study is highly recommended.

Iain D. Campbell ~ Minister,
Point Free Church of Scotland, Isle of Lewis

...something beautifully positive and full of life for the congregation of believers, as well as seekers.

Douglas F. Kelly ~ Richard Jordan Professor of Theology,
Reformed Theological Seminary, Charlotte, North Carolina

A veritable tour de force ...which will be of interest to the entire church. MacLean's handling of the subject is comprehensive and sure-footed, delving into practical areas of frequency and obser-vance as much as the theological principles that underpin the Com-munion Service. A timely and important book that will aid in the rediscovery of importance and function of the sacrament of the Lord's Supper in the life of the church.

Derek W. H. Thomas ~ Associate Minister,
First Presbyterian Church, Columbia, South Carolina

Malcolm Maclean is Minister of Greyfriars Free Church of Scotland in Inverness, Scotland. Prior to that he pastored the Free Church of Scotland in Island of Scalpay in the Western Isles. Malcolm is also the Editor of the Mentor imprint of Christian Focus Publications.

ISBN 978-1-84550-428-1

Christian Focus Publications

publishes books for all ages

Our mission statement –

STAYING FAITHFUL

In dependence upon God we seek to impact the world through literature faithful to His infallible Word, the Bible. Our aim is to ensure that the LORD Jesus Christ is presented as the only hope to obtain forgiveness of sin, live a useful life and look forward to heaven with Him.

REACHING OUT

Christ's last command requires us to reach out to our world with His gospel. We seek to help fulfil that by publishing books that point people towards Jesus and help them develop a Christ-like maturity. We aim to equip all levels of readers for life, work, ministry and mission.

Books in our adult range are published in three imprints.

Christian Focus contains popular works including biographies, commentaries, basic doctrine and Christian living. Our children's books are also published in this imprint.

Mentor focuses on books written at a level suitable for Bible College and seminary students, pastors, and other serious readers. The imprint includes commentaries, doctrinal studies, examination of current issues and church history.

Christian Heritage contains classic writings from the past.

Christian Focus Publications, Ltd
Geanies House, Fearn, Ross-shire,
IV20 1TW, Scotland, United Kingdom
info@christianfocus.com

www.christianfocus.com